MVS JCL
IN PLAIN ENGLISH

MVS JCL

IN PLAIN ENGLISH

DONNA KELLY & JIM HARDING

To order additional copies of this book, contact:

Xlibris Corporation

1-888-7-XLIBRIS

www.Xlibris.com

Orders@Xlibris.com

12444

CONTENTS

SECTION 1

GETTING STARTED

SECTION 2

THE DATA

SECTION 3

RUNNING THE PROGRAMS

SECTION 4

ADVANCED JCL

APPENDIX

Introduction

This book is here to help you learn how to to tell the IBM MVS mainframe computer how and when to execute your programs. To do this you use a language called JCL, for Job Control Language. You use JCL to tell the mainframe how much memory and other resources your programs will need, how long each program should be allowed to run, what order to run them in, where to get the input data, where to put the output data, and so on. JCL controls almost everything related to running programs on MVS.

If you have a comfortable understanding of ordinary English language and are looking for a quick and easy way to learn JCL, this book is for you.

If you already know a little JCL and what you really want is a handy reference guide to bail you out on commonly occurring problems with JCL, you're in luck again—this book is for you there too.

If you're looking for an introduction to some of the more advanced and obscure tricks you might have seen people use in MVS—you guessed it—this book is for you on that as well.

How can this book do all that at once? Because, contrary to its reputation, JCL is not particularly difficult; it just has esoteric aspects that make it seem difficult if you have nobody to explain things. Once explained, all seems clear—as with most things.

This book can be used as a reference book, like an encyclopedia—there are numerous examples and the index will assist you in finding what you are looking for when you need to find a solution to a problem. You can also read the book as an introductory text, from start to finish. Things are explained in plain ordinary language, so even if you have never before seen one line of JCL, you should have no trouble with the text; and by the time you get halfway through the book people should be starting to see you as an expert—probably to your great surprise. When you read the book straight through in this way, you will come across a lot of obscure but useful information to help you in your routine use of MVS.

JCL is a language like any other. If you travel to an area where you do not speak the language, you get a certain amount of satisfaction when you are able to make yourself understood using that language—be it to make a phone call or ask for directions or just to ask the price of something. The more you use the language the more you feel at ease using it. Having good guidebooks saves you a lot of learning time. And who doesn't love it when other people start mistaking us for locals and asking us the directions? That's the same sort of feeling you'll get the first few times your co-workers ask you to help them with their JCL problems; and that will start happening a lot sooner than you might think—because, contrary to appearances, most of them don't know much more about it than you do now. That's why they have so much trouble explaining it to you. That's why you want a good book on it now.

JCL is not generally taught in schools and Universities, so people who need to use JCL generally have to learn it on the job. For the most part they have a difficult time, largely because the people they learn from don't have a good grounding in JCL either. Those other people only learned enough to get by when doing a few things they needed to do; and those few things may not be the same things you need to do now. So your co-workers can be of only limited help to you with learning JCL.

Whether your job is programming, operations, or anything else, whatever your reason for wanting to learn JCL, this book is designed to help you. It will help you learn JCL in the first place and thereafter it will be a useful reference you can keep coming back to, like an old friend to help you out when you get into trouble.

This book is organized into four main sections.

'Section 1. Getting Started' is made up of Chapters 1 and 2. Chapter One is an introduction to the history of JCL and Chapter Two explains the basic structure of the language. Yes JCL does have a language structure, and when you understand that structure you will learn the language much more quickly and it will start to make sense. You might skip Chapter 1, but read Chapter 2.

'Section 2. The Data' spans Chapters 3 through 10. This section explains how data is organized on MVS and how to define and manipulate collections of data. Many people make their first changes to JCL

because there is a requirement to have a program run with different data than usual. For example, if a program has been using a certain data file for reference purposes, say a list of products and the associated prices, and one day for some reason a different reference file has to be substituted, say a new price list has come out—then a simple change to the JCL can bring the new file into use. You will learn how to make this type of change—and many others—in Section 2.

'*Section 3. Running the programs*' is Chapters 11 through 14. This section will give you information about controlling the conditions of program execution (how much time and memory your program will be allowed to use, dependencies on other programs finishing first, and so on) and about creating your own JCL Procedures. A JCL Procedure (or PROC) is a collection of JCL put together for some repeatedly occurring purpose, like a program written in JCL. This can be a powerful tool for automating processes under MVS.

'*Section 4. Advanced JCL*' is composed of Chapters 15 through 20. This section is particularly useful for those who want to know some of the more advanced (and yes, usually esoteric) aspects of JCL. There is also a Chapter that discusses some common standard programs you will use under MVS—such as the various Utility programs you can use to copy data, sort data, rename files, extend or compress or merge files, and so on.

Keep reading and have fun. You'll be pleasantly surprised how easy JCL actually is to learn.

Notes:

References in this publication to IBM products, programs or services do not imply that IBM intends to make these available in all countries in which IBM operates. Any reference to an IBM product, program or service is not intended to imply that only an IBM product, program or service may be used. Any functionally equivalent product, program or service may be used instead.

IBM is the trademark of International Business Machines Corporation.

Volume Allocation Manager is a product of Sterling Software.

MVS.JCL.MadeEasy@iol.ie is our email address.

SECTION 1.

GETTING STARTED

Chapter 1

JCL: ITS HISTORY AND VARIETIES

WHY JCL? - THEN AGAIN, WHY NOT?
INTRODUCTORY REMARKS

Long ago and far away, before video games but after dinosaurs, computers were new.

The personal computer (PC) existed only in science fiction stories.

Real computers were big, and clumsy to use. There were no video display terminals.

The big clumsy computers were told what to do by switches on their front panels. If a switch was turned on, that stored a 1 in one of the many brain cells in the memory of the computer. If a switch was turned off, that stored a zero.

Computer brains are even simpler than dinosaur brains.

Computer brains understand only zeroes and ones. Truth.

Every brain cell in the computer has either a zero or a one in it, all the time. An unadorned computer is not something you would invite to a party.

Vocabulary note: Computer brain cells are called bits.

Never say "computer brain cells" when you talk to computer people. They can be touchy about that kind of talk.

But back to the story.

Even the engineers and scientists who spent their time hanging around these big clumsy computers got a little bored with all the switches and zeroes and ones after a while.

They got ideas.

For one thing, they invented computer languages.

COBOL (COmmon Business Oriented Language). FORTRAN (FORmula TRANslation language). ALGOL (ALGOrithmic Language). PL/1 (Programming Language 1, although it was far from the first). Golly, this was good. Comparatively.

They invented punched cards.

Each cardboard card had 80 columns, so each card represented one line on a sheet of paper. Each column of a card had room for several holes to be punched in it. When a hole was punched, that represented a 1, the same as if a switch had been turned on. An unpunched punchhole was a zero.

They made up a code so that the combination of holes and non-holes in any particular column of the card represented a letter, or a digit, or a punctuation symbol or a mathematical symbol. A character, as such things are called.

Along with this they built card punch machines with typewriter keyboards. If someone typed the letter W on the keyboard, the machine would punch holes for the code for "W", then move on to the next column. If the person typed an "O", the machine would punch holes in that column for the code for the letter "O". Then the person could, say, type another W, and get the W code again in the third column of the card. Wow.

Each card represented one typed line to a human being.

To the computer, each card represented 80 characters of data. Yum-yum. The scientists and engineers built card reader machines to suck the zeroes and ones off of the cardboard cards and feed them into the computer's brain cells.

Progress was occurring at a dizzying pace.

The scientists and engineers could write programs in their new computer languages, type the programs onto the cards, and read the programs into the computer.

Great.

But wait. WAIT.

How was the computer going to know IN WHICH computer language the program on the cards had been written? And suppose the program needed to use data that was stored on a disk or a tape someplace? How would the computer know which data to use?

This was getting complicated.

But they had more ideas.

They could have one program that would be running all the time for the purpose of reading all the cards and deciding what to do with them. Sort of a master control program. But there would be a lot of work for it to handle, too much for one little program to do by itself. So they made a set of programs, and called it a "System". An Operating System to operate the computer for them. O.S. for short. OS grew up to be MVS, but that was later.

To communicate with OS (known familiarly as "the system"), they would, of course, make ANOTHER language.

It would control how the other cards would be handled. It would tell the computer whether the other cards would represent COBOL programs or FORTRAN programs. Sometimes it would tell the computer to store a program to use again later, or to execute an old program it had already stored. In fact it could tell the computer to store libraries full of programs on disk, just waiting to be executed. Another great leap forward.

Each group of punched cards represented a particular set of things someone wanted the computer to do. That would be called a JOB. The super new language that would control its execution would be called Job Control Language. JCL for short.

The wonders of modern science!

Okay, but now you want to know, why, well, to be straightforward about it, why is JCL so, well, okay, so AWKWARD?

Ah. Awkward.

Remember, JCL (Job Control Language) was not designed by linguists and English professors. JCL was designed by scientists and engineers. And they did not have the benefit of 20 years of experience with interactive video display terminals and PCs, which had yet to be invented. They did the best they could. Their hearts were in the right place.

They never intended for you to find it awkward to have to say

LRECL=80 sometimes. They thought that would be a nice abbreviation for saying, "The Logical RECord Length of the records in this file is 80 characters." Logical as opposed to physical. In other words, read in a big lump of contiguous data (a physical record) and treat the data as if it is composed of separate lines (logical records), each line being 80 characters long.

See all the typing they saved you?

And why should you need to type out anything as cumbersome as "Data Set Name"? DSN would do nicely.

In retrospect, the design may not have been ideal. Live and learn.

By the time people generally came to realize its awkwardness, it was too late to turn back. There are many millions of lines of JCL residing snugly on disks throughout the world, performing useful functions for their owners, most of which are large companies (like the one you work for now, am I right?). This represents a tremendous financial investment on the part of many large companies.

JCL is entrenched.

New computer systems are being designed without JCL.

Good.

More user friendly.

Like the PC.

When, using the PC, you say:

```
CD C:\PCOMMSLL
```

That's user friendliness in action, right? See how modern people have learned from the past? Progress advances.

But you, what have you gotten yourself into? Right. You are working on a system that uses JCL. Am I right? How do I know? You're reading this, aren't you? You must have an awfully good reason. Is it your fault what kind of computer system your company uses?

So there it is.

You want to learn JCL.

Read on.

It will be a lot easier than it appears at first glance.

You may even live happily ever after.

Vocabulary footnote:

A group of several adjacent bits (brain cells) is called a byte. One byte represents one character, such as a letter, a digit, or a punctuation or mathematical symbol. On big IBM mainframe computers there are 8 bits in each byte. Half a byte is a nibble (I'm serious here). A lot of people think that the use of the word nibble in a computer context is just a little too kinky, however, so it is often referred to as "one hexadecimal digit" instead (a byte contains two hexadecimal digits). 4 bytes are a word. Half a word is a halfword (2 bytes). 8 bytes is a double-word. The part of the computer's brain that actually does the computing is called the Central Processing Unit, or CPU for short. The rest of the computer's brain is called its memory, but the official non-anthropomorphic term for memory is real storage, or main storage. As opposed to auxiliary storage, which means the disks and other physically external storage devices attached to the computer by cables. Opposed also to "virtual storage", a strange mix of real and auxiliary storage which will be covered soon, under paging and swapping. Real physical computer equipment is called hardware, and programs are called software. The intermediate area between hardware and software is called firmware (or microcode).

FROM MVS/370 THROUGH MVS/SP, MVS/XA, AND MVS/ESA

This section is a historical footnote, introduced mainly to clarify the various names by which MVS goes.

If you are not curious you may skip this section, or skim it. Know, though, that it does contain some vocabulary you might want.

O.S., the Operating System, grew up, you recall, to be MVS. During the transition it was briefly known as VS/2 and the term is occasionally still used, even though MVS is the correct name.

MVS: MULTIPLE VIRTUAL SYSTEM.

By juggling allocations of memory, the operating system could do more things simultaneously, and let individual programs pretend to have more room in memory than was really available.

Real storage, you remember, means the same as memory. Virtual storage is pretend memory. The pretence is accomplished through paging and swapping (about to be explained).

Areas on magnetic disk are used to accomplish this magic. A program pretends to refer to memory it does not actually have. Since the program does not actually refer to all of its memory all of the time, a trick is pulled. The unused part of the memory is copied out to disk and the actual memory is given to someone else to use for a while. When the first program actually refers to the memory again, it is quickly brought back into real storage from disk (auxiliary storage). The program continues as if nothing had happened. This is called paging. The chunks of memory involved in this operation are called pages.

Sometimes the actual processing of a program is suspended and all or most of its memory is placed out on disk. This is called swapping.

Swapping and paging, though quick relative to human perception, are quite slow relative to operations that take place in real storage. Access to a disk requires physical mechanical movement, whereas operations in real storage take place at the speed of light. Quite a difference.

So swapping and paging slow things down a bit.

To run MVS, one needed to buy additional hardware, of course; a DAT box (Dynamic Address Translation box) at a minimum. There were new faster disks that the older versions of the system had not been written to use. If one wanted to use the new faster disks, one needed to convert to MVS. IBM made money in those days by selling hardware.

One of the earliest computers to run MVS was the IBM model 370. Hence early MVS is sometimes known as MVS/370. The computer just prior to the 370 was the 360, reported to have been so named because there are 360 degrees in a circle. But the more likely reason is that it was a third generation of computer hardware and it arrived in the 1960s.

MVS/SP: MVS System Product.

An enhanced version of MVS that cost money rather than being thrown in for free along with the computer. "Product" means "costs money". SP2 means MVS/SP Version 2, and so on.

MVS/XA: MVS with eXtended Architecture.

A structural change that allowed the system to pretend to have up to 32 billion bytes of storage, rather than the mere 16 million allowable to traditional MVS.

The structural change in question was this: Computer memory could optionally be addressed by means of a 4 byte address rather than the old 3 byte address.

You remember that a byte is 8 bits, and that a word is 4 bytes. In other words (feel free to skip ahead), a word is 32 bits. Also known as a full word, as opposed to half words and double words.

The way the thing is structured, an address is used to identify every location in memory. The computer instructions that refer to addresses in memory use one word (4 bytes) for the reference.

In the original (3 byte) addressing scheme, the leftmost byte in the 4-byte word was unused, except sometimes its leftmost bit (high order bit). This is called 24 bit addressing. (3 bytes, times 8 bits, = 24 bits.)

In XA, IBM introduced 31 bit addressing, using all the previously unused bits in the word as part of the address. Hence bigger addresses could be used. (4 bytes, times 8 bits, = 32 bits, minus 1 leaves 31 bits.)

Of course, most of the old, existing programs still used 24 bit addressing. That was the way they had been written. Some of them even depended on it. For example, a program might have been designed with a table of addresses it saved and used, and the frugal programmer might have allowed only 3 bytes for saving each address. Another example: an imaginative programmer used the otherwise unused bits for some other purpose in his program. We speak here of programs written in Assembler language or machine language, of course, such as those within the operating system itself.

But, with XA, large parts of the operating system were rewritten to take advantage of 31 bit addressing.

One did, of course, need to purchase a computer capable of running XA. The old ones could not. By this time, however, IBM had serious competition in the market for hardware sales. The price of the software rose accordingly.

IBM at this time also made moves to reduce the probability of its software being pirated. Some parts of the system and other program products were distributed in executable form only, that is, without the source, thus making them unreadable to any but the most dedicated humans. (Software distributed in executable form only is also known as Object Code Only, or O.C.O., software.) Customers were made to sign non-disclosure agreements unlike anything that had been demanded of them before. It isn't as Draconian as at first it sounds: their competitors were naturally among their customers, as near the head of the queue as possible.

MVS/ESA: MVS WITH ENTERPRISE SYSTEM ARCHITECTURE.

This allowed the computers really to have up to 2 billion bytes of memory, rather than just pretending.

One could, of course, buy expanded storage for the new computer one bought to run ESA.

Expanded storage (expanded memory) is add-on real memory that is used differently than ordinary real memory.

Ordinary real memory goes up to 24 Megabytes. From there up to 2 Gigabytes one has, or can have, expanded memory: Real enough physically, but used differently.

The expanded memory can only be used for data buffers. Programs sitting in ordinary real memory can refer to data that is sitting in expanded memory. And swapped-out programs can be put into expanded memory while they are suspended. But a program that is executing must have its program code in ordinary real memory while it executes.

The virtual form of expanded memory is called hiperspace (high performance space) or dataspace, depending on how it is used exactly. MVS was enhanced to use the expanded memory.

IBM was holding steady against its hardware competitors, and had struck a deal with INTEL, the main independent supplier of add-on memory.

Nevertheless, software had grown into a big business, and the price of developing a tremendously complicated operating system had to be recouped by charging a high price for it.

One got more than expanded memory for one's money.

The software continued to be enhanced. The IF-THEN-ELSE-ENDIF construct was made available in JCL at this point, for example. But read on. We come to that in due course.

Chapter 2

THE GRAMMAR AND STRUCTURE OF JCL

GRAMMAR, SYNTAX, SPELLING, AND PUNCTUATION CONVENTIONS

The NOUN=ADJECTIVE construction and the use of parentheses and commas.

Suppose for a moment that you wanted to make a statement such as this:

The dog is black.

If it were possible to make such a statement in JCL, it would be phrased like this:

DOG=BLACK

Of course it is not possible to talk about dogs in JCL. The vocabulary of JCL is concerned with things like magnetic tapes and disks and what kind of paper you want for your printouts. But we are going to use dogs to discuss the basic structure, because dogs are easier to understand intuitively. After, and as, you understand the construction, we will proceed to the vocabulary.

A painless method.

The odd use of the equals sign seems to be based on the presumption that the whole is equal to the sum of its attributes.

Vocabulary note: The NOUN=ADJECTIVE construction is referred to as the use of keyword parameters. A limited number of nouns is valid. These nouns are referred to as keywords. The adjectives are referred to as values.

Not all JCL parameters are keyword parameters. The other possibility is referred to as positional parameters, which we will explain shortly.

Back to the keyword parameters.

Suppose you wanted to say something a bit more complicated about your dog, something like this:

The dog has a waggly tail.

You can probably guess that in JCL the construction would be:

DOG=TAIL=WAGGLY

Sorry, but its true.

Suppose you wanted to say that the dog has both a waggly tail and floppy ears? Parentheses are used to group the phrases that together define the dog:

DOG=(TAIL=WAGGLY,EARS=FLOPPY)

Let's bump up the complexity again, for example:

The dog is black, with floppy ears and a waggly tail.

For the above sentence you might say something like:

DOG=(BLACK,EARS=FLOPPY,TAIL=WAGGLY)

This is where it gets a little worse.

In the above example, the color of the dog - BLACK - is a positional parameter.

You remember we warned you we would come to this shortly.

You know that in English the subject of a sentence has generally to precede the verb; and the direct object, if there is one, comes after. That is to say, "Joe kicked the horse" means something quite different from "The horse kicked Joe".

So you are already familiar with the concept that meaning can depend on order.

The JCL equivalent of this is the use of positional parameters.

To continue.

Assume that your dog's tail can be either waggly or still, but not both, and that it can also be either short, medium, or long, but not all three.

These attributes of the tail might be called waggliness and length.

But WAGGLINESS is a relatively long word, so the designers of JCL would have tended to avoid a construction such as this, which we already recognize:

TAIL=(WAGGLINESS=WAGGLY,LENGTH=SHORT)

Instead they would have preferred this sort of thing:

TAIL=(WAGGLY,SHORT)

In this case waggliness and length would be made to follow the rules of positional parameters. Waggliness has arbitrarily been made the first positional parameter and length the second. Once this rule is established, it has permanence, it is a rule of grammar. Always and for all time waggliness must precede length if length is mentioned. It will be correct to say TAIL=WAGGLY or to say TAIL=(WAGGLY,SHORT) or to say TAIL=(STILL,LONG) but not to say simply tail=short, bypassing mention of waggliness.

So how do you express the idea that the dog has a short tail, when you prefer to avoid mentioning its waggliness? You denote the missing item by leaving in place the comma and the parentheses, like a placecard at an empty seat at dinner. It looks like this:

TAIL=(,SHORT)

In this case the listeners or readers make their own assumptions about the state of the tail's waggliness. The assumption the computer software makes is called the default (another vocabulary item: Defaults).

Sometimes there are several positional parameters. A dog's tail, for example, might have the attributes of waggliness, length, furriness, and color.

If these were positional, in that order, and you wanted to say only that the dog had a white tail, you would end up saying:

TAIL=(,,,WHITE)

Awkward to say the least. But now you know the worst of it.

If you have mastered the syntactical concepts necessary to say that your dog has floppy ears and a waggly white tail, you ought to take it in stride if you see that you need to say:

UNIT=(TAPE,,DEFER)

or even:

UNIT=(3480,,DEFER)

When you want to indicate that your program will require the use of a tape drive unit, model number 3480, but you want the actual mounting of the tape onto the tape drive machine to be deferred until such time as the program is ready to use the tape.

(Think of DEFER as an abbreviation for DEFERRED. What kind of UNIT do you want? A deferred tape unit, or a deferred 3480.)

This use of DEFER shows consideration for the computer operators, in the event that your facility does not have an automated tape library with robots to mount the tapes. It means that they will not be put to the trouble of placing the tape onto a tape drive unit if your program happens to stop before it gets to the part where it uses the tape. You see that your lazier and less knowledgeable neighbors are being much less well-mannered than you are when they say only UNIT=TAPE or UNIT=3480 and then run a program that fails before the tape is actually used. Imagine how embarrassed someone would be when he ran a program that failed ten times with ten different problems, if he realized that a computer operator

31

had been called on to mount his tape on a tape drive machine ten separate times in succession. And yes, the computer operators do notice these things, and who is doing them. Keep that in mind next time you have to go to the computer room to pick up some printed output. On the other hand, the opposite consideration could apply at your own particular facility: If your facility uses tape cartridge units that allow the operators to put a stack of tapes into a hopper to be mounted automatically in order, then the operators may want to mount all the tapes your job will use into the hopper at once, and may be annoyed if they are prevented from doing so because you have specified DEFER in your JCL. You have to find out how things stand before you can decide which is better for you to specify.

Another similar parameter related to tapes and commas is the VOL or VOLUME parameter. VOL is an abbreviation for VOLUME. An individual magnetic tape is referred to as a tape volume, and it is identified by its serial number, abbreviated SER. Tape volume serial numbers are 6 characters in length. Even though they are called numbers they may contain letters as well as numbers. You describe your tape volume in JCL naturally enough as:

VOL=SER=123456

If 123456 happens to be the serial number of your particular tape, that is.

When you use the same tape in several consecutive programs within the same job, you can use the RETAIN positional subparameter in your description of the VOL each time, as follows:

VOL=(,RETAIN,SER=123456)

This means you want the tape volume to be retained on the tape drive unit from one program to the next within your JOB. If you leave out the RETAIN subparameter, the computer operator may be asked to take the tape off the tape drive after each program and then to mount it again for the next program that uses it each time.

A subparameter is, of course, just a parameter within a parameter. Like a subset is a set within a set. And a subcategory is a category within a category. You get the idea. The word parameter is often used interchangeably with the word subparameter, which fact should surprise no one.

Obviously it is more polite for you to use the RETAIN subparameter than not. On the other hand, if you have a limited number of tape drive machines available and a lot of tapes to use, then maybe not.

But I've digressed.

Back to the dog for a minute yet.

Positional parameters can occur together with keyword parameters in the same list. For example— Okay, the VOL parameter above was an example. But let's get back to the dog, that is, to the generalized case.

Suppose that the JCL designers, after having established the foregoing rules for describing a dog's tail, suddenly came to the realization that a dog's tail can be simultaneously black and white if the dog is a spotted dog.

Oops.

Upon realizing this, they might change the rules so that all of the other parameters remained positional, but COLOR reverted to the more traditional keyword parameter form.

With positional subparameters perhaps, or else with keyword subparameters maybe.

Say they decided on positional subparameters, with the first being the primary color and the second being the color of the spots, or the secondary color. Third and fourth colors could be allowed for lesser spots.

Now you could express the following English sentence:

The dog has a long waggly tail that is black with white spots.

In JCL as follows:

```
DOG=TAIL=(WAGGLY,LONG,COLOR=(BLACK,WHITE))
```

When keyword parameters or subparameters, such as COLOR in the above example, are intermixed with positional parameters or subparameters, such as WAGGLY and LONG in the above example, the rule (which should be obvious) is that the positional kind have to come before the keyword kind when both are used.

If only keyword parameters are used, that is, if positional parameters exist but you don't mention any of them, then you need not indicate their invisible existence by commas.

Hence, in our example, it is acceptable to say:

DOG=TAIL=COLOR=(BLACK,WHITE)

In this case you are accepting the defaults for waggliness and length, whatever the defaults may happen to be.

The worst of it is over now. Was that easy? (You clear your throat at this point.)

You have a certain latitude in the use of parentheses. The following two statements are equivalent:

DOG=BLACK
DOG=(BLACK)

This is something like the use of commas with dependent clauses in English. They are sometimes but not always optional.

In general, parentheses are required in JCL only when a noun has more than one attribute associated with it. You have to enclose the list of attributes in parentheses.

But sometimes people add parentheses where they are not strictly required, that is, when there is only one item in the list.

This is analogous to the custom some people practice of interspersing decorative commas between every clause and phrase of an English-language sentence.

Take our recent example:

DOG=TAIL=COLOR=(BLACK,WHITE)

Only one attribute of the dog has been mentioned, its tail. Only one attribute of the tail has been mentioned, its color. Hence the descriptions of these need not be enclosed in parentheses. But they could be if you felt like it, or if you thought people looking at your JCL might find it easier to understand that way.

The following three phrases, then, are each completely equivalent to each other and to the one above:

DOG=TAIL=(COLOR=(BLACK,WHITE))
DOG=(TAIL=COLOR=(BLACK,WHITE))
DOG=(TAIL=(COLOR=(BLACK,WHITE)))

It looks awful, but now that you understand it you can handle it without resorting to tranquilizers.

Let us make a final definitive statement about our dog. You know that the overall color of the dog is a positional parameter. (Only the color of the tail was made into a keyword parameter, with positional subparameters.) Let us say now that there are second, third, fourth, and fifth positional parameters available for fidelity, spottedness, warmth, smell, and friendliness. Suppose we have a keyword parameter for SPOTS with keyword subparameters of SIZE and COLOR. Suppose we also have the keyword parameter SIZE for overall size if the dog, and the keyword parameter NAME for the name of the dog. Now we can tell all we want to tell about the dog:

DOG=(BLACK,SPOTTED,FAITHFUL,WARM,,FRIENDLY,
EARS=FLOPPY,SPOTS=(SIZE=LARGE,COLOR=WHITE),
TAIL=(WAGGLY,COLOR=(BLACK,WHITE)),
SIZE=MEDIUM,NAME=PAL)

See how easy it is? You're almost an expert already. Now that you have mastered the basic structure, let us proceed to concrete examples of real JCL.

Review questions:
1. What is the difference between Keyword parameters and Positional parameters?
2. When are parentheses required?
3. Does order matter when several keyword parameters are specified?
4. When both positional parameters and keyword parameters are specified, which come first?
5. In the final example, what do the two consecutive commas signify between WARM and FRIENDLY?

THE PARTS OF SPEECH OF A JCL STATEMENT

There are parts of a JCL statement just as there are parts of an English sentence.

The five basic parts of a JCL statement are the ID (identification) field, the name field, the operation field, the operands field, and the comments field.

It looks like this:

//NAME OPERATION OPERANDS COMMENT

A statement in JCL begins with the ID field. This is somewhat like the English language idea of starting a sentence with a capital letter, or starting a quotation or a parenthetical expression with an opening quote mark or an open parenthesis, or starting a paragraph with an indentation.

The ID field consists of two characters in columns one and two of a line of JCL.

Normally this will consist two slashes (//).

This convention originates from the use of punched cards. where the identifier in columns one and two was designed to make the computer aware that this particular card was to be interpreted as JCL, and was not part of the program itself.

Following the identifier field, starting in column 3, is the name field. This will sometimes be blank and will sometimes contain a useful name. Its role in JCL most nearly resembles the role played in English by the subject of a sentence.

We will come back to the name field in a moment.

There is a small exception for JCL comment lines, which are identified with //* in columns one through three, and there is no name field then - just //* and the comments. For other types of JCL statement the name field exists and begins in column 3.

The next field after the name field is the operation field It is separated from the preceding field by one or more blank spaces. It need not start in any particular column. It plays a role similar to that of the verb in a sentence.

Common examples of the operation field are:

DD for Data Definition —This tells MVS where to find the data that your program will use, or where to put its output data.

EXEC for execute—This tells MVS to execute a particular program (or a particular procedure).

JOB for job— This identifies your set of JCL statements as a unique entity separate from other people's sets of JCL, that is, other jobs.

PROC for procedure—This is a group of JCL statements which in turn contains one or more EXEC statements that execute programs. It usually also contains some associated DD statements.

PEND for procedure end.

Following the operation field, separated by one or more intervening blank spaces, is the operands field. This is the complicated part where all those parameters like UNIT and VOL will be found. It must end before column 72 and is terminated by any blank space. So remember, no embedded blank spaces.

After the operands field is the comments field. This is distinguished from the operands field by the presence of one or more intervening blanks.

The operands field, you notice, ends as soon as any blank space occurs.

The comments field comes next.

Quick, what does that imply?

Right. It implies that if you mistakenly put a blank space in with your operands, the rest of the operands on that line will be interpreted as comments rather than as operands. This is an important point, and a very common source of JCL-related problems. This is especially so if the operands being ignored as comments happen to be of the optional kind, as many important operands are. The system assumes the defaults in this case. No warning or error message is given to you about this. After all, you are allowed to have comments that look a lot like operands if you want.

Now that you know what the operation field is, you will want to be aware of the relationship between the operation field and the name field.

Vocabulary:

The name field on a DD statement is called the DDNAME. The name field on an EXEC statement is called the STEPNAME. On a JOB statement it is referred to as the JOBNAME. On a PROC statement it is the procedure name.

A name on an EXEC statement within a procedure is sometimes called a procedure step name, or PROC STEP NAME or procstepname.

DD statements define the data that will be used by a program.

You specify that you want a program executed by the use of an EXEC statement; you follow the EXEC statement by all of the DD statements that describe the data the program will use.

You will have one DD statement for each file the program uses. The ddname will be the same name that the program uses to refer to the file.

For example, suppose the program you are going to execute is a PL/I program, and the PL/I program contains the following statements:

```
DECLARE OUTLIST FILE RECORD OUTPUT;
DECLARE OUTREC CHARACTER(80);
OUTREC = 'GOOD DAY TO YOU';
WRITE FILE(OUTLIST) FROM(OUTREC);
```

Then you will need an OUTLIST DD statement in your JCL:

```
//OUTLIST DD ... etc ...
```

The ... etc ... in the above example will form the subject matter of Section 2.

For another example, if the program you are going to run is written in COBOL, your program associates a file, say OUTLIST, with the above DD statement by using a set of statements something like this:

```
ENVIRONMENT DIVISION.
INPUT-OUTPUT SECTION.
FILE-CONTROL.
    SELECT OUTLIST ASSIGN TO UT-S-OUTLIST
```

```
       DATA DIVISION.
       FILE SECTION.
       FD OUTLIST LABEL RECORDS ARE OMITTED.
       01 OUT-RECORD.
          05 CARRIAGE-CONTROL  PIC X.
          05 PRINT-LINE     PIC X(79).
```

You will open the OUTLIST file and write to OUTLIST in your COBOL program using statements such as this:

```
       OPEN OUTPUT OUTLIST.
```

```
       WRITE OUT-RECORD.
```

Then you will need the same OUTLIST DD statement in your JCL:

```
       //OUTLIST DD ... etc ...
```

Again, you will find out what to use for the ... etc ... in Section 2.

Beyond the fields just discussed, we have the following.

Columns 73 through 80 are sometimes used for line numbers. In the days of punched cards this was very useful, since a dropped deck of cards could be put back in order easily enough if the cards were numbered. These days you will often see the line number area blank, or used as part of the comments.

You need to be aware of it because of this: your operands may not extend into the line number area. Your comments may, of course. But not your operands. In fact your operands must end by column 72.

Column 72 is very special.

Column 72, you realize, is the last column just before the optional line numbers.

In the early days of JCL, column 72 was the continuation column. If you wanted to continue a JCL statement onto more than one card, that is, onto more than one line, you needed to place a non-blank character in column 72 to indicate that the next card would be a continuation.

This is no longer necessary.

Today it is recognized that if a line of JCL ends with a comma, well then, there must be more operands yet to follow, and so the next line must be a continuation.

Nevertheless, column 72 is still special.

Its specialness has been preserved for compatibility with old sets of JCL that people are still using. Some of these old sets of JCL rely on column 72 as a continuation column.

You yourself need never place anything in column 72.

However, if you do, it will be interpreted as meaning that a continuation follows. If no continuation presents itself on the next line, an error results.

The error message will say simply, "expected continuation not received".

When does this happen?

When you have comments that happen to extend through the end of the line, and something happens to fall into column 72 by chance, and the next line is not a continuation.

Or, when you have no line numbers and no comments, and you happen unwittingly to extend your operands across column 72.

It happens occasionally. Now you know.

On this matter of continuations and special columns, You should know that column 16 also is special for continuations.

It happens like this.

To continue your operands onto another line, you first end your then current line with a comma.

On the following line you begin amicably enough with slashes in columns one and two, to identify this as a JCL statement. You follow this with one or more blank spaces, because you know that the operands must be preceded by one or more blank spaces, and anyway column three is the place for the name field and that would appear ridiculous on a continuation. So you space over to the right a little, leaving a few blanks, maybe lining up neatly with the start of the operands on the line above, just for appearances.

Be careful not to go beyond column 16 before starting to enter the operands.

The computer software that looks for continuations gives up looking if it has not found anything by the time it comes to column 16.

The error message you will receive in such a case will be the same as mentioned above: "expected continuation not received". Your operands on the continuation line will be considered as comments.

Just another little feature to carry with you in your already cluttered brain. It gives character to JCL, do you not think so? Well, maybe not.

Let us end this section with a very simple example, just so you have the overall picture clear in your mind.

Suppose you are running a program that normally writes a great lot of printed output to a file that the program calls TRACE. Suppose further that you want to stop this rubbish from appearing. You look in the JCL that you have been using, and you find a line with DD in the operation field and TRACE in the name field. Good. You've identified the responsible DD statement. Now you check to verify that the line does not end in a comma, and does not contain the DCB parameter. (The DCB parameter will be covered in Chapter 6). Replace the offending DD statement with this:

//TRACE DD DUMMY

Here // is the ID field, TRACE is the name field, DD is the operation field, and the operands field is composed entirely of the word DUMMY. You have, in computerese, "dummied out the TRACE DD statement". Good work. The comments field is blank - but use your imagination.

If the original had included the DCB parameter, you would have been required to include the same DCB following the word DUMMY, with an intervening comma of course. (This will be explained at length soon.)

Optional homework assignment: Find a PLIDUMP DD statement and dummy it out. Or A SYSABEND, or SYSUDUMP. Or as many of these as you wish.

Review questions:
1. What columns contain the ID field on a JCL statement?

2. What field starts in column 3?
3. What is the operation field?
4. How is a JCL statement continued?
5. What happens if you have a blank space anyplace within your operands?

//*, //, and /*   STATEMENT TYPES

The title is not a printing error, if that's what you're thinking. Those are three types of JCL statement.

```
//*
//
/*
```

You see that the three are quite different.

But, can you believe it? People get them confused.

A line beginning with //* in columns 1 through 3 is a JCL comment.

You can have other stuff on the same line with the //* if you wish. Comments, for example. MVS will ignore any line that begins with //* in the first three columns.

You can have otherwise blank comment cards containing only the //* and no actual comments. Placed correctly these can make the JCL deck easier for human beings to read. They are the JCL equivalent of blank lines.

Quite separate and distinct from the otherwise blank comment card is the job terminator card.

A line containing only // in columns 1 and 2, and nothing else, terminates a job. This is called the null statement.

If any JCL happens to occur following the lone // it will be ignored. If you happen to be watching the MVS operator console at the time, you might be treated to the message "skipping for JOB card" as your JCL is ignored. The // statement is not required. Without it, the JCL for your JOB will be considered complete as of the last line.

Separate and distinct again from either of the above is a line which contains /* in columns one and two, rather than //. Such a card signals the end of an instream input data file and is called a delimiter statement.

An instream input data file is a group of lines that are not JCL, that is, they do not begin with // in columns 1 and 2.

Such an instream file might be preceded by a statement that says // SYSIN DD * or something similar. This is optional. If your job contains a group of non-JCL lines and they are not preceded by some such statement, the system assumes you must want those lines to be used as SYSIN.

In olden days you signaled the end of such a group of lines by terminating the group with a card containing only the /* ID field.

Eventually someone realized that it would be just as easy to assume that the group of non-JCL lines ended as soon as any line beginning with // occurred.

So the /* line is optional now, in most cases.

The one exception occurs with the //filename DD DATA statement. In this case DATA signifies that the following lines are to be treated as input data, even if they look exactly like JCL. This allows your program to read JCL cards as input.

Obviously in this case you need some way to tell the system that the DATA is ended. A /* statement does this nicely.

What if the input data contains not only JCL but even contains embedded /* statements?

No problem. The DLM parameter on the DD DATA statement allows you to specify a different delimiter. (DLM for delimiter, another abbreviation.)

Simple example:

```
//MYJOB JOB 0
//STEP1 EXEC PGM=MYPGM
//INPUT DD DATA,DLM=@@
//*
//* jcl-like statements for use
//* as input data for the file
//* named INPUT within program;
//* including even /* lines
```

```
/*
//* continuing until the
@@
//* NOW WE ARE BACK INTO
//* THE REAL JCL, AND THESE
//* LINES ARE COMMENTS, BECAUSE
//* EACH STARTS WITH //*
```

Another case where lines begin with /* or //* is when they are JES2 or JES3 control statements, rather than actual MVS JCL. JES2 uses /* and JES3 uses //*. JES2 and JES3 are job scheduling (and output scheduling) subsystems (new word: subsystem. A subsystem is a major set of programs that stand between ordinary programs and the operating system).

JES2 and JES3 control statements are called JECL, as opposed to actual JCL. They occur interspersed with JCL and look very like it. JECL means Job Entry Control Language.

Your own MVS system almost certainly has either JES2 or JES3 but not both. What you probably have is JES2. Since most places run JES2 rather than JES3, we will assume in this book that you have JES2. If that is the case, then any JES3 statements you see in JCL decks will probably be there because the JCL was copied from another system where they were running JES3. MVS systems with JES2 treat the JES3 cards as comments, which is to say that the cards are ignored. Consequently you will occasionally see JES3 cards simply because nobody bothers to remove them.

JES2 control statements will be covered in Chapter 18, on the assumption that you have JES2.

Review questions:
1. How do you specify a comment statement in JCL?
2. What happens when MVS sees a line with // in columns 1 and 2 and nothing else on the line?
3. What signifies the end of a set of instream input data if DLM is not specified?
4. What happens if a JCL deck contains JES3 control statements but you don't have JES3 on your system?

5. If you only want to execute the first half of your JCL deck, what line
can you insert to make sure the rest of the JCL is ignored?

The Widespread Use of Abbreviations and the Importance of Correct Spelling

As you now realize, computers are not very clever.

They have good memories and they can add and subtract quickly,
but they are very narrow minded. They adhere to strict rules and they
expect you to do the same.

Take the matter of spelling.

If someone writes you a check, and your name is misspelled slightly,
your bank may very well accept the check all the same. Some banks will
not. If a computer were a bank it would be of the latter sort.

The basic rule is that your spelling must be perfect. If you make a
mistake, you may as well be writing in Swahili. The computer makes no
intuitive assumption about what you probably meant.

Some JCL words have synonyms and abbreviations that may be used
interchangeably, but whichever version you choose, it must be spelled
flawlessly. For example, DSN is a synonym and an abbreviation for
DSNAME, meaning data set name. SHR can be used in place of SHARE,
and it usually is, which shows that the people who use JCL today are not
entirely different in nature from its designers.

Which brings us to the next point: abbreviations, acronyms, and
other shorthand forms.

Knowing that brevity is the soul of wit, and being witty folk, the
designers of JCL were into brevity in a big way.

They preferred to avoid excessive typing.

Be honest, so do you. So do I.

Maybe they were a bit more serious about this aversion than you or
I would have been. Okay.

As it happened, they settled on many abbreviations and shorthand
forms of expression that seem imposing at first glance, but are quite
acceptable once you understand them.

Some examples.

SHR for SHARE or shareable, meaning that a data set your program is using is shareable with other programs. This ought to be the case if your program is reading it, but not writing anything into it.

Of course if you were writing into the data set, you would not want to share it with other programs, especially not other programs that also wanted to write into it. If two programs both write into the same data set at the same time, without co-ordinating in any way with each other, the data in the data set ends up as an unpredictable mixture.

Another example.

DISP for disposition.

The disposition of a data set means more than one thing.

First of all it means that either the data set already exists, in which case it is an OLD data set, or else the data set does not already exist, in which case it is NEW, that is, the system is to create the data set for your program there and then, according to the specifications you describe on the DD statement.

But then there were problems with OLD.

For example, if two programs wanted to use the same old data set at the same time, should they be allowed? This is where SHARE comes in. SHARE (or SHR) would be used to mean they were allowed, and OLD would mean only one program could use it at a time.

Still not good enough of course. Suppose you want to write into an old existing data set? Do you overwrite the existing data set, replacing everything, or do you add new records at the end of it, extending it?

This is where MOD comes in. MOD would mean modify it, and OLD would mean overwrite it. You see the haphazard way these things grow.

MOD for MODIFY, meaning that a data set your program is using already exists and will be modified by your program.

Actually MOD means the data set will be modified in a special way, by adding records onto the end of it.

The meaning of MOD was later expanded, so that, if you say MOD for the disposition of a data set, and the data set does not in fact already exist, the system will create a new data set for you using your specified data set name, and let you add records onto it, just as if it had already existed and had been empty. So the meaning of MOD has become warped by growth. But basically it is an abbreviation for MODIFY. Simple enough.

DISP, by the way, has positional subparameters.

You guessed that. When we said that the disposition of a data set means more than one thing.

You might at some time have seen the DISP parameter coded something like this:

DISP=(NEW,CATLG,DELETE)

The NEW/OLD/SHR/MOD group we just discussed constitute the first positional subparameter. That is to say, you get your choice as to whether to say that the data set is to be treated as NEW, OLD, SHR, or MOD.

The second subparameter is something like KEEP or DELETE. Self explanatory, right? If you say DISP=(NEW,DELETE) then MVS will create a new data set for you and delete it when the program ends.

If you say DISP=(NEW,PASS) that will create a new data set for you and pass the data set on to the next program in your job (the next STEP, as we say) to use also.

If you say DISP=(NEW,CATLG) it will create a new data set for you, and not only will it KEEP the data set, it will also create a catalog entry to enable you to find it again if you ever want to use it in the future.

What if you say DISP=(OLD,DELETE)? You guessed it, your data set is history.

What if you say DISP=(NEW,CATLG,DELETE)? Now you're really learning JCL. The third subparameter tells the software what to do with the data set if the program abends. (You know what abend means, right? ABnormal END. Also said to blow up, bomb out, etc.)

So if you say DISP=(NEW,CATLG,DELETE) this will cause the MVS operating system software to create a new data set for you, and, if your program ends normally, to keep the data set and create a catalog entry to enable you to find it again; however, if the program bombs, the new data set will be deleted. The point of such a contrivance is this: you, or someone acting on your behalf, can then run the same set of JCL again after it has once abended, without first changing the DISP or manually deleting the redundant data set.

If you do not specify any DISP at all for a data set, the default is DISP=(NEW,DELETE,DELETE). Like most defaults in JCL, this is rarely what you want.

Those were examples of abbreviations.

There are other abbreviations that make little enough sense even when you know what they represent. DCB springs to mind. It stands for Data Control Block, which doesn't seem to mean anything either. In fact it refers to a description of the structure of the data set, for example, the length of the records, whether the data set is a library or a flat file... this will be covered in Chapter 6, because there are quite a lot of subparameter values possible for DCB. The point at the moment is that these seemingly nonsensical acronyms and abbreviations are all short for something sensible, and they were put forward by perfectly well-meaning folk who felt better about thinking and remembering acronyms than about typing, folk who naturally assumed you would feel the same.

Whether you feel the same or not, you will probably find the things easier to understand and remember if you think of them as abbreviations for sensible words.

Another point here: In their concern for succinctness, the designers of JCL placed a length limit of 8 characters on most names.

There are some exceptions. We will mention the main ones now, even though we have not yet explained these parameters. Trust us that they will be explained as we go along in the book.

Exceptional lengths of things:

> Data set names may be up to 44 characters in length, but if they are to be cataloged so that you can find them again the excess over 8 characters must be divided up into sections, called levels, of 8 or fewer characters each, separated by a period between each (a period is also called a dot, a point, or a full stop). Names of data sets on tapes are truncated to 17 characters. There are additional rules for naming data sets, and some tricks and hazards. We'll get to that in Chapter 4.

The programmer name field on the JOB statement can be up to 20 bytes long.

The value assigned in the PARM on the EXEC statement may be up to 100 characters in length, an unparalleled magnanimity.

The names of disk and tape volumes can only be six characters long.

The form-names of special paper and the character set names of special typestyles can only be 4 characters long.

Just about every JCL entity other than the ones just mentioned is limited to a length of 8 characters.

The bottom line: Brevity of form and flawless spelling are important concerns in JCL.

Let us proceed.

WHAT'S A COMPILER? WHAT'S A LOAD MODULE?

What's a Compiler? What's a Load Module? What's the Linkage Editor? What's object code? What's a computer program, for that matter? Look at all these strange words and concepts and things ... how are you supposed to understand all this?

Some of you reading this are not actually computer programmers. Strange, but true.

Therefore it would be appropriate to clear up a few more basic terms before proceeding, so we can start on a level playing field here.

If you are a programmer yourself, please skip this part while we talk about you behind your back. Yes, this means you. Go on. Skip this if you're a programmer.

A computer program is a set of instructions you want the computer to perform. Things like add and subtract. There are only about three hundred basic operations that the computer can perform. It can add the contents of one word in memory to the contents of another word in memory to come up with a sum, which it places in some third word in memory. It can do the same for halfwords and double words. It can subtract full words and halfwords and double words, and multiply them. It can divide full words and double words. You've got eleven basic operations, called basic instructions, right there. But wait, it can do more. It can move a byte of data from one place in memory to another. It can move up to 256 bytes of data at a time from one place in memory to another. And it can move more than 256 bytes. Those are three more separate operations it can perform for you if told to do so. Now you have, what, fourteen things you can tell it to do. Forget it. You'd rather write in a regular computer language like PL/I or COBOL, where you say vaguely English-like things such as this:

> MOVE 'SMITH' TO NAME.
> ADD 1 TO NUMBER-OF-NAMES.

or:

> NAME = 'SMITH';
> NUMBER_OF_NAMES = NUMBER_OF_NAMES + 1;

The first example is COBOL. The second example is PL/I. You see that there are minor differences of syntax. In COBOL a statement ends with a period, for example, whereas in PL/I each statement ends with a semicolon. Things like that.

But wait you say—perhaps the computer programs you have seen have looked more like this:

> MOVE 'SMITH' TO NCUS-GOBBLEDYGOOK.
> ADD 1 TO I.

or:

> NCUS_GOBBLEDYGOOK = 'SMITH';
> I = I + 1;

What is the difference between our first pair of examples and our second? Right, the names have been changed.

The names in these examples are called variable names. The things which they name are variables. When one sets up a variable in a computer program, one is in effect setting aside a little area of memory to be called by the name one assigns. The contents of this little area of memory can be changed, that is, the contents vary; hence the name variable. The name is based on the idea of a variable in an equation in algebra.

The programmers choose the variable names. They are not deliberately obfuscating in most such cases.

The worst you can say about them realistically is that they sometimes lack both imagination and consideration, or at least they don't take the trouble to bring such powers to bear on the task of making up the names they use in writing computer programs. They tend to choose short names, in the grand tradition, to avoid lengthy typing. The letter I is a favorite for numbers, not out of egocentricity but because it is a traditional abbreviation for the word integer. Integer as opposed to a number that has decimal places. You see how it is.

And far worse: many companies actually have standards for made-up names, standards that compel the programmers to use incomprehensible rubbish for the names. This is true.

At any rate, a computer program is written in a language such as PL/I or COBOL. These are called high level languages. As opposed to a low-level language, called Assembler language, wherein one statement in the language corresponds directly to one basic computer operation.

A fourth generation language (4GL), you may as well know, is the next step ahead after the high level languages. It is supposed to be even easier to use. Like LOTUS 1-2-3 or Easytrieve or whatever.

The computer, of course, understands only the basic computer instructions, so the English-like high level computer languages have to be translated into basic computer instructions. Enter the compiler.

A compiler is a program that takes statements written in PL/I or COBOL and translates them into basic computer instructions, expressed in nice zeroes and ones.

The zeroes and ones are called object code.

The compiler writes the object code out to whatever data set you tell it to use (you tell it this in JCL).

It is then called an object deck or an object module. There isn't much difference. At one time you could have the object code punched out onto punch cards rather than being saved on disk, and the punch cards containing object code were called an object deck. Actually, you can still do this, if your company has a card punch machine available, but it probably doesn't. Cards have rather fallen out of fashion. Still the phrase object deck persists, but it is no longer very distinct from object module.

Now, the computer cannot execute the object code exactly as it stands. Some further manipulations are required.

Consider.

A program does not do everything on its own. It asks other programs to do part of its work. The other programs that do this sort of subcontracting are called routines or subroutines.

So, when, in a COBOL or PL/I program, you say that you want to print a line of printed output, the compiler does not, then and there, insert a large body of object code designed to accomplish this. It inserts a note to the effect that some standard printing routine is to be called at this point. (When a program asks another program to do something, this is referred to as CALLing the second program.)

This note it inserts is called an external reference. Because the main program refers (makes a reference) to some other program outside itself (external).

Along comes another program after the compiler finishes. This program is called the Linkage Editor. It reads the notes and, if it has been told to do so, it inserts the object code for the subroutines in the appropriate places. Alternatively, it can be told not to insert them, but rather to insert appropriate code to provide for them to be brought in when the program actually runs. Also it may fail to insert some of them because of being unable to find them. In this case they are known as unresolved external references. Similar to unresolved problems.

The Linkage Editor produces as output a seemingly amorphous blob of code called a load module.

The load module is what is actually used when you tell MVS to execute a program.

Note that a load module is required to be a member of a library. MVS will not execute it if it is a flat file. This is because part of the information about the load module is stored in the directory portion of the library. (We will talk more about libraries shortly, under DSORG in Chapter 6.) What kind of information is stored in the directory? We'll talk about that in the section on the Linkage Editor in Chapter 17.

But now you at least understand the basic process. Your computer program in PL/I or COBOL (source code) is translated into basic computer instructions (object code) by a compiler: a PL/I compiler for PL/I, a COBOL compiler for COBOL, a COBOL2 compiler for COBOL2, and so on. The object code is then further digested by the Linkage Editor and a load module is produced. A load module is a program in executable form (also called executable code or, occasionally, relocatable code).

Now, if you are not a computer programmer, but you want to sing along, you may want a little sample program to use.

Most of the examples we give in this book use IBM-supplied programs that require no programming knowledge on your part. Still, some of our examples involve little sample programs in PL/I and COBOL, and you may want to understand a little about programming and have a simple program of your own to play around with.

We'll give you one just below, in both COBOL and PL/I. If you have both COBOL and PL/I on your system and you are free to choose between them, here's the difference: programming in PL/I is more like driving a Ferrari, and programming in COBOL is more like driving a Ford. Take your pick.

In order to use the sample program of your choice, you will need some JCL to compile and link edit it. The JOB statement you will have to get from somebody at your company. JOB statements differ a lot from one place to another. They contain things like accounting information and JOB class that are very site-specific. You have to ask someone to help you, or else you have to copy a JOB statement surreptitiously from someone somehow. It is a better idea to ask someone. When they realize you are learning JCL, they will hopefully help you when you need to ask about other site-specific items later in the book. Site-specific means that something differs a lot from one place to another. Like local customs.

Following the JOB statement you need an EXEC statement. Probably you can use one EXEC statement to bring in a whole set of JCL (called a procedure, covered in Chapter 12) that will run the compiler of your choice and then the Linkage Editor right after it, producing a load module at the other end.

In the examples below we give a JOB statement that you will almost certainly have to change, followed by an EXEC statement that you can probably use as it is but that you might possibly have to change. Ask the same person that gives you the JOB statement, if they seem reasonably friendly. (If not, find somebody else. Life is difficult, not hopeless.)

You will need to be able to LOGON to TSO to run your JOBs, or else you will need to be able to LOGON to some other alternative thing that allows you to type in JCL and programs and run JOBs. Ask somebody, if you don't have such a thing. In this book we assume you have TSO, but it isn't a requirement. Actually, you are not required to run any JOBs or really DO anything, you can just read the book if you want. However, if you have a system you can use, and you intend to use it for something practical, then you will probably want to try at least some of the things in the book on your real system. What's the use of learning to drive a car if you never really drive it?

In the examples, we assume that you have your own library for keeping your load modules. We call it SMITH.LOAD because we pretend your name is Smith and your TSO userid is therefore also SMITH. An unlikely occurrence in reality. Ask your adoptive programmer (the one who gave you the JOB statement) to help you set up a load library. Then use the name of that rather than SMITH.LOAD whenever we use a name such as SMITH.LOAD in the examples.

Okay, the examples.

What should we have the program do? Something simple. Something inutterably simple. Okay, it will read some data from INFILE and write that data to OUTFILE. Okay.

Let's call the program COPYCAT.

If you want detailed explanations of the following two sample programs, look in Appendix 1 at the back of the book. It explains the programs almost line by line.

Example 1, in PL/I, follows.

Notice that each complete PL/I statement ends with a semicolon.

Notice that in PL/I comments are identified by being framed with a slash-asterisk /* on the left and an asterisk-slash */ on the right. Comments can continue onto many lines until the asterisk-slash ending marks the end of the comment.

The ending */ is required. If you leave it out, all of the following program statements are treated as part of the comments.

This has nothing to do with the /* or the //* statements in JCL.

Notice also that PL/I program statements start in column 2 rather than column 1, and they end by column 72. Within that range the statements are free format, that is, they can be anyplace on the line and they can continue onto multiple lines. A PL/I statement ends when there is a semicolon.

```
//SMITH1 JOB 1,CLASS=I,
//      MSGCLASS=X
//PLIXCL  EXEC PLIXCL
//SYSPRINT DD  SYSOUT=*
    /* COPYCAT
ULTRA-SIMPLE PL/I PROGRAM
READS DATA FROM WHEREVER IT SAYS
ON THE INFILE DD STATEMENT IN
THE JCL WHEN THE PROGRAM RUNS,
AND WRITES THAT DATA OUT TO
WHEREVER IT SAYS ON THE OUTFILE
DD STATEMENT IN THE JCL */
```

```
COPYCAT: PROC OPTIONS(MAIN);

DECLARE INFILE INPUT FILE;
DECLARE OUTFILE OUTPUT FILE;

DCL LINE CHAR(80) INITIAL(' ');

DCL END_OF_INPUT CHAR(3) INIT('NO');

ON ENDFILE(INFILE)
  END_OF_INPUT = 'YES';

READ FILE(INFILE) INTO(LINE);

DO WHILE(END_OF_INPUT = 'NO');

WRITE FILE(OUTFILE) FROM(LINE);
READ FILE(INFILE) INTO(LINE);

END; /* END OF DO-WHILE */

CALL PLIRETC(0);
/* SET RETURN CODE TO ZERO */

 END COPYCAT;
 /* END OF PROGRAM */
//LKED.SYSLMOD DD DISP=SHR,
//   DSN=SMITH.LOAD(COPYCAT)
//*
//COPYCAT EXEC PGM=COPYCAT
//STEPLIB DD DISP=SHR,
//   DSN=SMITH.LOAD
//SYSPRINT DD SYSOUT=*
//INFILE  DD *
THIS IS THE FIRST LINE OF DATA
```

```
          THIS IS THE SECOND
          THAT'S ENOUGH
          //OUTFILE DD SYSOUT=*,
          //    DCB=(LRECL=80,
          //    RECFM=FB,
          //    BLKSIZE=800)
```

Example 2 is the same as example 1, but using COBOL rather than PL/I.

If you use the COBOL version, take warning that everything needs to be in the right columns.

Within the COBOL program, columns 1 through 6 contain optional line numbers. You can leave columns 1 through 6 blank if you'd rather.

Also within the COBOL program note that an asterisk in column 7 means that the asterisked line is to be ignored as a comment line. Actual program statements must not start before column 8, and some types of COBOL statements must not start before column 12. This is explained in the Appendix 1.

```
          //SMITH2 JOB 2,CLASS=I,
          //    MSGCLASS=X
          //COMPILE  EXEC COBUCL
          000001 IDENTIFICATION DIVISION.
          000002   PROGRAM-ID. COPYCAT.
          000003 ENVIRONMENT DIVISION.
          000004*  INFILE AND OUTFILE ARE
          000005*  OUR DDNAMES.
          000006 INPUT-OUTPUT SECTION.
          000007 FILE-CONTROL.
          000008   SELECT INFILE ASSIGN
          000009   TO UT-S-INFILE.
          000010   SELECT OUTFILE   ASSIGN
          000012   TO UT-S-OUTFILE.
          000013 DATA DIVISION.
          000014 FILE SECTION.
```

```
000015 FD  INFILE LABEL RECORDS
000016    ARE OMITTED.
000017 01  INPUT-RECORD.
000018    05 INPUT-LINE
000019       PICTURE X(80).
000020 FD  OUTFILE LABEL RECORDS
000021       ARE OMITTED.
000022 01  OUTPUT-RECORD.
000023    05 OUTPUT-LINE
000024       PICTURE X(80).
000025 WORKING-STORAGE SECTION.
000025  01 WORKING-RECORD.
000026    05 WORKING-LINE
000028       PICTURE X(80).
000029 PROCEDURE DIVISION.
000030 OPEN-FILES.
000031    OPEN INPUT INFILE.
000032    OPEN OUTPUT OUTFILE.
000033 READ-A-LINE.
000034    READ INFILE AT END
000035    GO TO END-OF-PROGRAM.
000036    MOVE INPUT-RECORD
000037    TO OUTPUT-RECORD.
000038    WRITE OUTPUT-RECORD.
000039    GO TO READ-A-LINE.
000040 END-OF-PROGRAM.
000041    CLOSE INFILE.
000042    CLOSE OUTFILE.
000043    STOP RUN.
//LKED.SYSLMOD DD DISP=SHR,
// DSN=SMITH.LOAD(COPYCAT)
//COPYCAT EXEC PGM=COPYCAT,
//    COND=(8,LT)
//STEPLIB DD DISP=SHR,
//    DSN=SMITH.LOAD
```

```
//       DD DISP=SHR,
//       DSN=SYS1.VSCLLIB
//       DD DISP=SHR,
//       DSN=SYS1.VSCOLIB
//SYSPRINT DD SYSOUT=*
//SYSOUT  DD SYSOUT=*
//INFILE  DD *
 THIS IS THE FIRST LINE OF DATA
 THIS IS THE SECOND
 THAT'S ENOUGH
//OUTFILE DD SYSOUT=*,
//       DCB=(LRECL=80,
//       RECFM=FB,
//       BLKSIZE=800)
```

If you don't want to use either of these programs, that makes perfect sense to me. But at least you have programs you could use if you wanted to do so. Now let's go on and learn some JCL.

SECTION 2.

THE DATA

Chapter 3

DD - THE DATA DEFINITION STATEMENT

BASICS OF THE DD STATEMENT - OVERVIEW

The DD statement, as you recall, is used to describe a file that your program will use.

Actually MVS does not notice whether your program uses the file or not. You can put in extra DD statements if you want.

On the other hand, you are not permitted to omit DD statements. Each file that your program actually attempts to use must have a corresponding DD statement in the JCL, to enable MVS to identify and allocate the proper data for that file.

Fine.

Files, of course, are of three types:

Input files, which your program reads. A mailing list might be used as an input file.

Output files, which your program writes. A printed report is a fine example of an output file.

Update files, which your program both reads and writes. A payroll database might be an example of this, if employees receive both pay checks and pay increases.

Very good.

And files may reside in various sorts of places.

Paper, for example.

An output file can reside on paper.

Magnetic tape, for another example. Either input or output files can reside on tape. A tape file cannot ordinarily be updated in the sense of replacing individual records within the file, but it can be updated in the sense of appending records onto the end of the file.

Disk, for a versatile example. Very popular for update files. Also for input and output.

Cards. Not used for output much anymore. Not used at all much anymore really, but for one curious exception: simulated cards. This is so common, in fact, that the word "card" is used in ordinary conversation as a synonym both for "line" and for "statement". Since a JCL statement can continue onto more than one line, you might think this could lead to ambiguities, but in practice the meaning is generally clear enough. More about cards in the following pages.

You will want to let MVS know where to find or put your file. Disk or tape or paper or cards, for example. And if disk or tape, which disk? Which tape? What kind of paper, for that matter?

How big is it going to be, if it's new?

Is it new?

What is it named, or what ought its name to be?

These and similar questions will be covered in the remainder of Section 2.

Perhaps you're wondering why you want to learn about DD statements prior to learning about JOB statements and EXEC statements. After all, JOB statements and EXEC statements both occur prior to DD statements in the JCL "deck".

Right. But once you've actually run a few jobs under MVS, you're bound to realize that:

(a) You rarely change your JOB card very much at all. You get one that works and you more or less stick with it.

(b) You use different EXEC statements, but they don't differ all that much. More than JOB cards but still not much.

(c) DD statements vary tremendously and have all those complicated parameters and things. They're confusing. And you have to change them constantly.

(d) Consequently, if you don't quite finish reading this book, the stuff you learn about the DD statement before you quit reading is going to be the most useful stuff for you in practical reality. And you ought to get something practical back in return for whatever time you're putting into reading this, right?

So, in what order are we going to approach these JCL statements? Right. Most useful first.

Before we proceed, a note about SMS (System Managed Storage, an optional part of MVS), and a simple example you might find useful. If you have SMS, as you probably do, you can in many cases avoid a lot of the DD statement parameters and let the system decide for you. This only works for disk data sets, though. With SMS, to create a new disk data set exactly like an existing disk data set you use the LIKE parameter. The system will copy the DCB, VOLUME, UNIT, and SPACE parameters from the existing data set. For tapes and printed reports you will still need JCL though.

However, you might be interested in an example of an easy way to create a new disk data set exactly like an existing disk data set (assuming you have SMS, and TSO). And this works for all kinds of disk data sets, including VSAM KSDS files. Under TSO/SPF, go to option 6 (command). In the entry field, enter the following :

```
ALLOCATE     DSN('SMITH.NEW.DATASET')
LIKE('SOME.OTHER.DISK.DATASET')
```

and press enter. That's all there is to it. This is the TSO command equivalent of using the JCL parameter LIKE. If you are planning to run a batch job to use your new data set immediately after, you should also free the new data set from your TSO session by entering the additional command:
FREE DSN('SMITH.NEW.DATASET')

Logical records, Physical records, and their sizes

Before we go any further, we need to understand the word "record". "Record" is used to mean two different but related things.

When your program reads a record, writes a record, or updates a record, your program is processing a logical record.

A logical record is, in other words, a record in the ordinary sense of the word. A record as we conceive it to be.

The qualification "logical" is used to distinguish this from a physical record.

A physical record is a block. A physical record is composed of any number of logical records grouped together. Sort of a handful of logical records. A bunch.

An example.

Consider your terminal screen.

Let's assume you have the most common type of terminal screen. Each line on the display is 80 bytes long, and there are 24 of these lines on the screen.

Each line of the display can be considered to be a logical record. It might show one line of JCL, for example. One "card" of a "deck".

The screen in its entirety can be thought of as a block. In the simple model we are using, it would be a block of 1920 bytes, and the system would write an entire screenful of data to the terminal in one write operation. (24 lines, multiplied by 80 characters per line, equals 1920 characters per screen.)

Suppose that the object of your attention on the terminal screen happens to be the source for a computer program you have written. Each logical record then - each line - would probably be 80 bytes long. Suppose you have this program stored in a data set on disk. How big is each physical record in this data set of yours? It could be 80 bytes. It could be 1920 bytes. It could be 23440. Any multiple of the logical record length would do. You get to decide. (Up to the maximum, usually 32767, the biggest number MVS can fit into 2 bytes of storage.) ·

But how can you decide? What does it all mean?

It means that one read of a record from the disk or one write of a record to the disk will occur for each physical record (each block).

(Read and write operations are called I/O's, an abbreviation for Input/Output, by the way. I/O is pronounced Eye Oh, like Hi-ho without the aitches.)

There are, really, three considerations in regard to the size you should choose for a block. These are briefly as follows:

1) SPEED

The larger the size of each block, the fewer I/O operations will be required to fetch your data set from disk for you, or to write it back onto the disk. Bigger block size = faster speed.

This is usually the decisive consideration.

I/O operations are desperately slow compared to anything else the computer normally does for you.

Since it is impossible for me to convey properly to you in words the magnitude of this consideration, I want you to do an experiment, if you have TSO/ISPF available, which you probably do. Often called just SPF. Almost every MVS system has this, and you are probably passably familiar with it already. In some places, people use alternate, non-IBM text editors, so there is a chance you do not use SPF. If you do not have it, you may skip this experiment. But do the experiment if you can. It has the emotional force of seeing a magic trick.

Find the source for a very large program, the larger the better.

Allocate for yourself, using ISPF option 3.2 under TSO, two new empty data sets, as follows:

Select any appropriate name for the first one. Fill in this name on the option 3.2 screen, specify A for allocate, and hit enter.

For example, suppose your TSO userid is SMITH and you have chosen the name SMITH.BAD.DATASET for your first data set. You fill in the relevant information on the 3.2 screen something like this:

OPTION ===> A

ISPF LIBRARY:
  PROJECT ===> SMITH
  GROUP ===> BAD
  TYPE   ===> DATASET

After you hit enter, the allocation screen will be displayed. Fill in the blanks on the SPF 3.2 allocation screen for this first data set by requesting a RECORD LENGTH of 80, a BLOCK SIZE of 80, a RECORD FORMAT of FB, 0 DIRECTORY BLOCKS, and 5 each for PRIMARY QUANTITY and SECONDARY QUANTITY, with SPACE UNITS specified as TRACK. If GENERIC UNIT is blank, try SYSDA or 3380; if it is not blank, leave it as it is. Leave VOLUME SERIAL as it is or blank. Leave expiration date blank. Hit the enter key.

For example, fill in the blanks on the allocation screen something like this before hitting enter:

DATA SET NAME: SMITH.BAD.DATASET

SPACE UNITS   ===> TRACK
PRIMARY QUANTITY ===> 5
SECONDARY QUANTITY ===> 5
RECORD FORMAT   ===> FB
RECORD LENGTH   ===> 80
BLOCK SIZE   ===> 80

Now select a second name for your second data set and allocate it in exactly the same way as the first, except that BLOCK SIZE is to be 23440. (23440 amounts to half a track). Example, starting from SPF option 3.2:

OPTION ===> A

ISPF LIBRARY:
  PROJECT ===> SMITH
  GROUP ===> GOOD

TYPE   ===> DATASET
(hit enter key)

DATA SET NAME: SMITH.GOOD.DATASET

SPACE UNITS   ===> TRACK
PRIMARY QUANTITY ===> 5
SECONDARY QUANTITY ===> 5
RECORD FORMAT   ===> FB
RECORD LENGTH   ===> 80
BLOCK SIZE   ===> 23440
(hit enter key)

When this is done, copy your very large program into each of your new data sets, using ISPF option 3.3 if you have it.

The set up is complete. You have two data sets that are identical except for the block size. One has a block size almost as small as possible, the other has a block size almost as large as possible. Now the actual experiment commences.

Go to option 2 of ISPF, the EDIT option. Give the name of the data set having the block size of 80. Hit enter. You will not require a stop watch to observe and lament the slowness of this experience.

When that has finished, leave your block size 80 data set, and go into EDIT on the block size 23440 version.

This should make up your mind forever on the question of block size.

In case were not able to perform this experiment, let me tell you the ending: The bigger block size makes things go a lot faster. Very nearly 293 times faster. (293 x 80 = 23440).

2) ECONOMY

Any additional considerations will seem anticlimactic if you have once performed the experiment described in (1) above, but for completeness let us proceed.

Economy is the second consideration. Basically you get more data on the same amount of disk space if you have a larger block size. This is because a small gap is left on the disk between each block, and this gap (called an inter-record gap) is wasted.

For example, if your logical records are 80 bytes in length, and you write a thousand of them using a physical record size of 80, you will use 13 tracks on a 3380 disk. If you used a physical record size—a block size—of 23440 instead of 80, you would use only 2 tracks on the same disk.

If you used 24000 rather than 23440 you would only get one block per track rather than two, so you would be wasting space. (Your data set would take up 4 tracks rather than 2.)

Fortunately this consideration points in the same direction as the consideration of speed: When it comes to block sizes, bigger is better (up to half a track on disk or up to 32760 on tape. The actual maximum on tape is 32767, but a lot of programs cannot handle more than 32760, and you never know what program might end up reading the tape; so stick with 32760 as the maximum.)

3) REGION

REGION will be explained in Chapter 11. It basically means how much memory your program is allowed to use.

This is the only factor that weighs against a large block size. The larger the block size, the more memory is required for buffers.

The word "buffer" is used as the name for an area of memory where the system puts your data when the system reads your data for you.

Buffers are subtracted from the memory region allocated to your program when it executes.

Since data is obtained as one physical block for each read operation, the size of a buffer in memory is equal to the size of a block.

This means that a situation could occur where you might not have enough room in your memory for large blocks. When would this happen? Either:

A. if your program uses a very large number of files which are all open at the same time, implying that a large number of buffers would be allocated at the same time;

B. if, due to some limitation on your own particular system, only a small region of memory is available for your program.

If neither of these considerations applies—and usually they will not—then you should use the largest reasonable block size possible. Remember to make the block size an integral multiple of the logical record size. (23440, for example, is 293 x 80, and is half a track on a 3380) (27920 uses half a track on a 3390).

(Exception: In the case of varying length records, that is, RECFM=VB, you add 4 to this. The extra 4 bytes per block are used to store an indicator of the actual length value for that particular block. This will be explained again in the section on RECFM under DCB in Chapter 6.)

BLKSIZE AND UTILITY PROGRAMS

If the program being executed is a utility such as SORT or IEBGENER, and the output LRECL is different from the input LRECL, then the program may copy the output BLKSIZE from the input BLKSIZE, rather than allowing the system to compute the BLKSIZE. In this case the, the copied BLKSIZE may not be may not be a multiple of the LRECL, causing the program to fail.

SYSTEM DETERMINED BLKSIZE

You will hear the claim that the newer versions of MVS/ESA will figure out the optimum BLKSIZE for your data sets if you either leave off the BLKSIZE parameter or specify BLKSIZE=0. Optimal is supposed to mean the largest BLKSIZE appropriate to the particular type of disk being used. When it works correctly, this gives you a BLKSIZE of about half a track.

However, you should know that this doesn't always work as you might like. If you read the IBM manual (SC26-4749-00) you can figure out that, in order to take advantage of this offer, you should also specify the following:

1) DSORG=PS or DSORG=PO
2) LRECL=the logical record length
3) RECFM=any record format starting with F or V, that is RECFM=VB, or RECFM=FB, or RECFM=VBA, and so on.

What happens if, forgetting the above in a moment of madness, you omit DSORG from the DD statement? any of the following things:

1) Sometimes it works correctly, giving you a good BLKSIZE and defaulting the DSORG to either PS or PO as appropriate.
   This is good.
2) Sometimes it might give you BLKSIZE equal to LRECL.
   This is bad.
3) It might give you blanks rather than a proper DSORG.
   This is not too great either.

So, if you rely on the system to decide your BLKSIZE, make sure you specify DSORG of PS or PO, LRECL and RECFM of F.... or V.... Check on it afterwards to be sure you got good results.

That about concludes our brief introductory discussion of the meaning of the word "record".

Chapter 4

DSN or DSNAME

Every data set has a name of its own, as people have. Data Set Name is abbreviated DSNAME or DSN. The names must follow rather strict rules. As follows.

First there is the matter of syntax.

A data set name may be no longer than 44 characters.

If the data set is to reside on tape, the name is truncated to 17 characters.

If the data set is not to be cataloged, the name may consist of almost any string you like, provided you enclose the string in single quotes (apostrophes) and adhere to the length limit. The quote marks do not count towards the total.

If the data set name is not enclosed within apostrophes; or if the data set is to be cataloged, that is, if you want MVS to keep track of it for you; then the name must adhere to the following additional restrictions.

The permissible characters are limited to the uppercase alphabet, the digits, the at sign (@), the cross-hatch sign (#), the character known variously as the full stop, period, dot, or decimal point (.), and, additionally, depending on where you are, either the American dollar sign or the British Isles pound sign. The at sign, cross-hatch sign, and dollar or pound are referred to as national symbols or national characters. Recent releases of MVS have added two more characters to this set. One of these is the hyphen or minus sign. The other is a sort of left-hand curly bracket, represented internally as hexadecimal C0, which makes it the character just before the letter A in the collating sequence. This means that data set names with C0 will appear above names with a letter A in the same position. Visually the hex 'C0' looks like the opening bracket in the pair of brackets used in set theory to enclose a list of the members of a set. Too bad they didn't add x'D0' as well, the close bracket equivalent.

Notice that the full stops are included when counting the length limit of 44 characters.

A data set name is divided into sections. Each section is eight characters or less and is separated from the other sections by a full stop. Such a section must not begin with a digit. It must begin with a letter or a national character, not a digit.

Each of these sections is called a qualifier, and it is also called an index. The first section of a data set name, preceding the first full stop, is the high level part. Thus this is either called the high level index or the high level qualifier. Sometimes it is called the prefix. The second such part is called the second level qualifier or the second level index, and so on.

The high level qualifier is important because it is used to group together sets of data sets. All of the data sets belonging to one person or to one project will typically start with the same prefix. Thus the prefix of a data set name performs a function similar to that of a person's family name.

You will usually want to use your TSO userid as the high level qualifier for your own data sets. In most cases, when you refer to a data set under TSO, your userid will be assumed as the prefix if you do not enclose the data set name in single quotes (apostrophes).

Thus, if your userid is SUZUKI, the data set that you know in TSO as TIME.FLIES.LIKE.ARROWS will be called SUZUKI.TIME.FLIES.LIKE.ARROWS when you refer to it in JCL.

Also keep in mind that in JCL you must always type the name in upper-case (capital) letters, even though TSO lets you type the name in lower case. (TSO translates your lower-case letters to upper-case before using the name).

In SPF you might refer to the data set either like this:

OTHER PARTITIONED OR SEQUENTIAL DATA SET:
DATA SET NAME ===> Time.flies.like.arrows

or like this:

>OTHER PARTITIONED OR SEQUENTIAL DATA SET:
>DATA SET NAME ===>'SUZUKI.TIME.FLIES.LIKE.ARROWS'

If you have a data set with a shorter name, something like DAISETZ.TEITARO, you might refer to it in SPF like this:

>ISPF LIBRARY:
>   PROJECT ===> SUZUKI
>   GROUP ===> DAISETZ
>   TYPE   ===> TEITARO

or this:

>OTHER PARTITIONED OR SEQUENTIAL DATA SET:
>DATA SET NAME ===> DAISETZ.TEITARO

or this:

>OTHER PARTITIONED OR SEQUENTIAL DATA SET:
>DATA SET NAME ===> 'suzuki.daisetz.teitaro'

But in JCL they look like this:

```
//A DD DISP=SHR,
// DSN=SUZUKI.TIME.FLIES.LIKE.ARROWS
//B DD DISP=OLD,
// DSN=SUZUKI.DAISETZ.TEITARO
```

If you are working on a project together with other members of a team, you may all be sharing data sets that begin with the name of your mutual project, rather than with your individual userids. In this case you may need to enclose the data set names in single quotes (apostrophes) when you use them in TSO. If so, remember that you will usually need to omit the quotes when you refer to the data sets in JCL.

Another little point about sharing data sets.

At most big companies MVS will use some security system such as RACF.

The main point of the security system is to prevent people from using data sets that belong to other projects.

For example, you might not be allowed to look at the payroll database if you are not working with the payroll team.

The ordinary way of arranging the necessary restrictions is to make the access permission automatic in a way that is based on the high level index of the data set name.

For example, you might be automatically allowed to read and write any data sets that begin with the prefix SUZUKI, VANDAMME, MOZART, or CURIE, if those are the userids of the people in your group. You would also be allowed to read and write data sets beginning with the word XRAY (the name of your mutual project).

You would be automatically prevented from reading and writing data sets beginning with other people's userids or with the words FINANCE, PAYROLL, SECURITY, TANGO, or TWADDLE (some other projects at your company).

Also you would automatically be allowed read-only access to a large set of data sets belonging to the system itself, IMS and CICS data sets and so on. These would have names beginning with SYS1, IMS, IMST, IMSV1R3, and/or other such official sounding prefixes.

Sounds simple enough in concept.

Besides being controlled automatically in the way just described, it is possible to give (or withhold) access to particular individual data sets explicitly. That takes more work, of course.

You might, for example, be allowed to write into IMS.TFORMAT, the data set where you put new IMS screens, but only be allowed to read from IMS.RESLIB, a library containing the IMS program load modules distributed by IBM.

So, if you have a security system on your MVS system, you cannot just pick any old name for your data set. It has to start with some prefix you are authorized to use. Your TSO userid, for example. Or the name of your project.

The following are examples of valid catalogable data set names:

SMITH.DATASET1
SMITH.SECOND.DATASET
SMITH.DATA.FOR.FLIGHT.#123.@4.OCLOCK
AUGUSTO.CESAR.SANDINO
MY.COUSIN.VINNIE
EDWARD.VIII
MARIE.CURIE
MARGARET.MEAD
NOAM.CHOMSKY
WOLFGANG.AMADEUS.MOZART
JULIA.ROBERTS
TOM.CRUISE
EDDIE.MURPHY
DOWN.WITH.SNOW
UP.WITH.BALLOONS
THE.LONGEST.JOURNEY.BEGINS.WITH.A.SINGLE.STE
NEW.SHOW-OFF.TYPE.NAME
ANOTHER.{NEW.SHOW-OFF.TYPE.NAME
The last example of { in the DSName is hex 'C0'.

The following examples are wrong:

SMITH.7TH.DATASET
FLIGHT.401
EDWARD.8TH

Why wrong? the second-level qualifier begins with a digit. You may not begin any level of the name with a digit.

HENRY.THE.8TH

Why wrong? 3rd level starts with digit.

BEDTIME.IS.10.P.M.

You know you can't do that.

SMITH.DATA.FOR.FLIGHT.#123.@4.O'CLOCK
JEANNE.D'ARC
EDNA.O'BRIEN
THERESA.O'NEILL

Why wrong? An apostrophe is not a legal character in a data set name.

DENZEL.WASHINGTON
WILLIAM.SHAKESPEARE
BRUCE.SPRINGSTEEN
LUDWIG.BEETHOVEN

Why wrong? The second level exceeds the maximum allowable length. Eight characters is the maximum per level.

MY.100%.STUPID.DATASET

Why wrong? Because the second-level qualifier contains %, which is not an allowable character. It also begins with a digit, which is not allowed.

DON.McCULLIN

Why wrong? Lower case letters are not allowed.

ALMOST...BUT.NOT.QUITE

Why wrong? You cannot have morethan one consecutive full stop (...).

THE.LONGEST.JOURNEY.BEGINS.WITH.A.SINGLE.STEP

Why wrong? too long.

THIS.IS.THE.END.

Wrong again. A data set name must not begin or end with a full stop. The full stop is used only as a separator between levels of the name.

NEXT THERE IS THE MATTER OF UNIQUENESS.

If data sets are not cataloged and reside on different disk volumes, they may have the same name.

On tape, you may have as many data sets of the same name as you want on the same tape, or on different tapes, provided they are not cataloged.

For example, if you have a cataloged disk data set named SAMPLE.JCL you may simultaneously have any number of uncataloged tape data sets of the same name, should you ever happen to wish to do so. Perhaps you might want to produce five hundred identical tapes to distribute to customers, for example.

If, however, you have a cataloged disk data set named SAMPLE.JCL and you try to create another cataloged disk data set with the same name, one of the following error situations will result.

ERROR SITUATION (A):

If you specify the same disk volume for the new data set as that used by the data set that already exists, or if the system happens to select for you that same disk volume, then you will be given the error message "DUPLICATE DATA SET NAME ON DIRECT ACCESS VOLUME", or something similar. This means that you cannot have two data sets with the same name on the same disk volume. The catalog is not involved. The data set is not created and your job fails.

Notice it would be okay to have two (uncataloged) identically named data sets on the same tape volume. Just not on the same disk volume.

Error situation (b):

If, on the other hand, you try to put the new data set on a different disk volume than the one used by the data set you already have, then the new data set will be created correctly enough, but will not be cataloged. You will receive the message "NOT CATALOGED 2", or words to that effect. The use of the 2 is coincidental; there are various reasons the system might refuse to catalog a data set for you, and error code 2 happens to be assigned to the situation where two data sets of the same name exist. So in this case you end up with an uncataloged disk data set that you will not be able to access again unless you specify the volume name explicitly when doing so.

For a further illustration of this situation, consider what happens on a PC, if you are familiar with the PC.

If you try to create a file on your PC, and a file with that name already exists, the existing file will be overwritten. That is the equivalent of specifying DISP=OLD in MVS.

Now what if, on your PC, you create a second file having the same name as one that already exists, but you put it on a different diskette, or in a different directory? Works great. This is like creating the same data set on two separate disk volumes in MVS.

How do you access the second copy on your PC? You explicitly specify the directory or the drive.

How do you access the second copy under MVS? You explicitly specify the volume. VOL=SER=DISK02 or whatever it may be. Not as handy as going through the catalog.

Error situation (c):

The third awkward possibility arises only when two or more catalogs are involved.

Suppose you have two computers at your site, say a test system and a production system. Each has its own main catalog, called a "master catalog".

At most sites, in addition to these "master catalogs", there exist "User catalogs".

The ordinary way of setting up systems like this is to have ordinary users of the system use the user catalogs. Each master catalog is told that, if a data set starts with a certain prefix (such as the word SAMPLE in the example SAMPLE.JCL) then such a data set is to be cataloged in some specific user catalog. TSO userids and names of projects would be set up this way.

If both master catalogs are given this same instruction, pointing to the same user catalog, then a person such as you or I may happily catalog a unique data set name on one system and subsequently access it on the other with no complexities.

If, however, the two master catalogs do not point in this way, then it is possible to have two data sets of the same name cataloged in two different places, one on each system.

In fact you can have any number of user catalogs, and you can imagine the complications this can produce for the unwary. Beware of STEPCAT and JOBCAT DD statements in this context. If a data set that you think has been cataloged in fact goes missing, examine the JCL that created it, and look for JOBCAT or STEPCAT statements. The data set will have been cataloged in one of the catalogs named there. More about STEPCAT and JOBCAT in Chapter 7.

FINALLY THERE IS THE MATTER OF ENQUEUE CONFLICTS, which is really a tangent, being a cross between the DSN topic and the DISP topic. But it becomes relevant when you try to create a second data set with the same name as another.

What does enqueue mean? Waiting. As when you queue for the bus or the films. Or have your name put on a waiting list.

Enqueue is an English word. The MVS spelling of it is, not surprisingly, ENQ; but this is not a JCL word. In JCL enqueue is handled through the DISP parameter. When you say DISP=OLD in your JCL, you are telling MVS to put your name on a waiting list for exclusive use of the data set name specified in the DSN parameter on that DD statement. Notice that you wait for a data set name, not a data set.

It will often happen that a person will attempt to create a data set on tape, or on some alternate disk volume, as a copy of some existing data set. It is best to give such a copy a different name, maybe a variation on the name of the original. But it often happens that people try to use the same name. They use a DISP in such cases of (NEW,KEEP) and this will work if the original data set is not already in use by some other job or task or user.

The point to realize is that DISP creates an enqueue on a NAME, not on a data set. If I have a data set allocated to my job with DISP=OLD, and you try to allocate to your own job a completely separate data set with the same name, your job will go into allocation problems, claiming to be waiting for data sets. It is really waiting for data set names, not the data sets themselves.

For the purposes of enqueue, a DISP of NEW creates an exclusive enqueue exactly as a DISP of OLD does.

Therefore you cannot create a data set of the same name as an existing data set as long as anyone else in the system has that existing data set allocated, even though they may have it allocated DISP=SHR.

This prevents you from creating on tape a backup copy of a library that is always in use, such as a procedure library or an online library, if you try to use the same data set name for the backup copy as for the original.

Of course, now that you realize that an enqueue is on a NAME and not on a data set, you will probably decide to use a different name for the backup. No problem.

Other data set name considerations:

TEMPORARY DATA SETS

If you are creating a temporary data set that will be used only for the duration of the one job, being deleted at the end of the job, then you can omit the DSN parameter. If you do not specify the DSN parameter for a new data set the system will make one up for you, based on things like the time, the date, the jobname and the job number. Something like SYS01064.T135044.RA000.JOBNAME.R0015270, that sort of thing.

Such data sets are usually deleted automatically at the end of the job. Occasionally they are not deleted in this way. The systems or operations staff will generally run a job every night to delete leftover data sets of this sort. By the way, if you need to find out today's date in YYDDD format (called the Julian date), you can find it out easily by looking at a JCL listing with a temporary data set name in it anyplace. In the above example, the 01064 in SYS01064 is the current date in YYDDD format, that is, the 64th day of year 01. Which just goes to show that everything in the universe has a useful purpose if you can only find it.

Also, if you are creating a temporary data set that will be used only for the duration of the one job, being deleted at the end of the job, then you can specify a special sort of temporary name preceded by two ampersands (&&). The system will make up a name for the data set as it did if you omitted the DSN parameter altogether. The merit of specifying a temporary name preceded by two ampersands (&&) is that you can then refer to the same data set again later in the job, using that short name.

For example, the first time you use it you might say:

```
//OUTFILE DD DISP=(NEW,PASS),
//    DSN=&&FILE1
```

and then later it might be:

```
//INFILE DD DISP=(OLD,PASS),
//    DSN=&&FILE1
```

and the last time you use it, it could be:

```
//INFILE DD DISP=(OLD,DELETE),
//    DSN=&&FILE1
```

If a procedure is not involved, you can get away with using just one ampersand here, that is, DSN=&FILE1 rather than &&FILE1. However, this leads to confusion, because, within JCL procedures, a single & denotes a symbolic parameter. So it is best to use the double ampersand for temporary data set names at all times, even when, strictly speaking, one ampersand would be enough.

If you are specifying the name of a member of a library, then you specify it in parentheses immediately following the data set name. For example, to specify the member VITAMINA in the data set U.N.MEDICAL.SUPPLIES you might use a DD statement like this:

```
//SYSUT1 DD DISP=SHR,
// DSN=UN.MEDICAL.SUPPLIES(VITAMINA)
```

The name of the member does not count towards the 44 character maximum name length, and neither do the parentheses.

The rules for a valid member name are the same as the rules for a single level within a data set name. The maximum length is 8 characters. The first character must be a letter (uppercase of course) or a national character. The rest of the name is composed of any arrangement you like of uppercase letters, digits, and national characters.

This is probably the place to tell you that a member of a library can have an alias name.

For example, suppose you have a library containing reports on the sales of AK47 assault rifles in Nigeria in the first three months of the current year. Someone reprints these reports to distribute to new salesmen and saleswomen when they join your company. This happens fairly often because these salespeople never stay long. In fact nobody stays long. You're looking for something else yourself. Meanwhile your data set is SMITH.NIGERIAN.SALES.DATA and it has three members, named JANU-ARY, FEBRUARY, and MARCH. The printing of the reports is usually handled by someone whose native language is Spanish, so you think it would be a thoughtful gesture to have the members be known also by the Spanish equivalents of their names, that is, ENERO, FEBRERO, and MARZO. And of course you might add the aliases JANVIER, FEVRIER, and MARS. And so on.

This is fine as long as the members are not rewritten.

When a member is rewritten, the alias will still point to the old version.

You have to delete and re-assign the alias name to get it to point to the new version correctly.

Similarly, if a member is deleted, the alias names have to be deleted separately.

SPF does not provide you with an easy way to assign alias names, so this idea of alias names may be new to you. It is generally more trouble than it is worth, because of the difficulty that the alias does not follow the member when it is replaced. Nonetheless, I know you well enough by now to know that you want to know how to do it.

Sure, why not.

One way is with IEHPROGM, but don't bother.

Go to SPF option 6 and type the following commands:

```
RENAME 'SMITH.NIGERIAN.SALES.DATA
(JANUARY)' (ENERO) ALIAS

RENAME 'SMITH.NIGERIAN.SALES.DATA
(FEBRUARY)' (FEBRERO) ALIAS

RENAME 'SMITH.NIGERIAN.SALES.DATA
(MARCH)' (MARZO) ALIAS

RENAME 'SMITH.NIGERIAN.SALES.DATA
(JANUARY)' (JANVIER) ALIAS

RENAME 'SMITH.NIGERIAN.SALES.DATA
(FEBRUARY)' (FEVRIER) ALIAS

RENAME 'SMITH.NIGERIAN.SALES.DATA
(MARCH)' (MARS) ALIAS
```

After you do that, your members will have the alias names you gave them, at least for a while.

If you later replace a member, the alias will still point to the old version.

If you see a name that looks as if it specified a member of a library, but there is a number in place of the member name, the entity being referenced is a generation data group.

Right, what does that mean? And what does it look like?

It looks like this:

```
//SYSUT2 DD DISP=(NEW,CATLG),
//    DSN=MY.GDG(+1)
```

or:

```
//SYSUT1 DD DISP=SHR,
//    DSN=MY.GDG(-1)
```

So, what does that mean?

A generation data group is a group of flat files, usually used for something like backups. For example, if you wanted to create a backup copy of a database every night, and you wanted to keep the most recent 7 copies, you could define a GDG of seven generations. You would create a new generation by saying (+1) in the JCL. You would refer to an existing generation by saying (0) for the current generation, (-1) for the one just before that, and (-6) for the oldest one.

This means that the data set you refer to today as MY.BACKUP(0) will probably be referred to tomorrow as MY.BACKUP(-1) and the next day as MY.BACKUP(-2). Unless of course someone makes a mistake and runs, seven times in the same day, the job that creates MY.BACKUP(+1). This sort of mistake happens surprisingly often, in which case you have nothing left but seven copies of today's data.

The oldest version may or may not actually be deleted from the system when a new generation is created. The oldest one might just be uncataloged but not really deleted. It depends on what was specified when the GDG was defined. The most common practice is to delete the thing if it resides on disk. After all, why keep it if it isn't cataloged? If, however, it resides on tape, the tape might be kept, or it might be returned to a pool of available tapes, waiting for someone at random to ask to write onto some unused tape (a scratch tape).

But about the name. All six remaining data sets don't change their real names every time you run your job, right? Right. The real names are of the form MY.BACKUP.G0099V00 or MY.BACKUP.G0012V00, affectionately referred to by systems programmers as Goo-voo names, though I wouldn't advise using that sort of language in more general company.

If you should ever want to do such a thing as define a GDG for yourself, you do it using the program IDCAMS, a program which IBM supplies along with MVS; provided your catalogs are either ICF (Integrated Catalog Facility) or VSAM catalogs, which, in this day and age, they probably are. The older method is to use IEHPROGM, another program which IBM supplies along with MVS; but you will do it with IEHPROGM only if you are using a type of catalog called a CVOL (pronounced See-vahl), which you probably aren't.

That's enough for GDG for now. Chapter 20 will cover it in more detail with examples.

DSN=NULLFILE

This has exactly the same effect as coding DD DUMMY. Which is described in more detail in Chapter 8. In other words, the following two statements are equivalent:

```
//SYSPRINT DD DUMMY
```

is the same as

```
//SYSPRINT DD DISP=OLD,
//    DSN=NULLFILE
```

Keep in mind that with DSN=NULLFILE, as with DUMMY, you need to supply DCB information if the program does not contain it. Most common programs contain DCB information for output files (such as SYSPRINT) but not for input files.

DSN=*.STEPNAME.DDNAME

This is called a referback.

Let's take an example.

```
//JOB3D1 JOB etc
//STEP1 EXEC PGM=IEFBR14
//OKAY DD  DISP=OLD,
//      DSN=MY.AULD.DATASET
//STEP2 EXEC PGM=IEFBR14
//FINE DD  DISP=OLD,
//      DSN=*.STEP1.OKAY
```

What happens here? In STEP2, for the ddname FINE, the system goes back and looks in STEP1 (refers back to STEP1) for the ddname OKAY. It then uses the same data set for FINE in STEP2 as it used for OKAY in STEP1, that is, in this case, MY.AULD.DATASET.

There is a more complicated version of this:

DSN=*.stepname.procstepname.ddname

This can be used when you execute a procedure, which we haven't explained yet. A procedure is a collection of JCL that is stored as a member of a procedure library. A procedure contains one or more EXEC statements, specifying programs to be executed; each such EXEC statement within the procedure is followed by its associated DD statements. This will be shown in more detail in the Chapter 12.

You execute a procedure by specifying the name of the procedure on your EXEC statement.

Based on that sketchy definition of a procedure, let us proceed to an example of using the complicated form of referback to refer to a data set that was named on a DD statement within a procedure.

The procedure named PLIXCL is supplied by IBM. It contains JCL statements that allow you to compile and link edit a program written in the PL/I programming language. Within the procedure named PLIXCL there is a step name LKED. The LKED step link-edits your program. It produces, as output, a load module, that is, an executable machine-language version of your program, all translated into nice zeroes and ones that the computer can understand. This load module is written out as a member of whatever library is specified on the SYSLMOD DD statement for that step.

The step within the procedure itself is named LKED. That is the procedure step name, sometimes written procstepname. The ddname of interest within that step is named SYSLMOD. That DD statement is later referred to as LKED.SYSLMOD for purposes of referring back to it. Referring back to it is called "referback". LKED.SYSLMOD is a "qualified ddname".

Now, for the sake of the example, you want to use that same library for STEPLIB (Step library) in the next step of your job. You could just refer to it by specifying the DSN in a straightforward way, but here is how you would do it using a referback, should you wish to use one. Or, more likely, should you happen to see it in some existing JCL and wonder what in the world it means.

If the first step of your job is named, as in the following example, STEP1, then you refer to the data set of interest as *.STEP1.LKED.SYSLMOD, like this:

```
//JOB3D2 JOB etc
//STEP1 EXEC PLIXCL
//* compile and link-edit your program
//SYSIN  DD DISP=SHR,
// DSN=YOUR.PLI.LIBRARY(GO)
//SYSLMOD DD DISP=SHR,
// DSN=YOUR.LOAD.LIBRARY(GO)
//STEP2  EXEC PGM=GO
//STEPLIB DD DISP=SHR,
// DSN=*.STEP1.LKED.SYSLMOD
```

89

There is also a simple version of the referback:

>   DSN=*.ddname

Example: Use the same data set for CLAUDE as for JEAN:

```
//JOB3D3 JOB etc
//STEP1 EXEC PGM=IEFBR14
//JEAN DD DISP=SHR,
//    DSN=AMIABLE.DATASET
//CLAUDE DD DISP=SHR,
//    DSN=*.JEAN
```

Some hints about data set names on tape

When you create a data set on a Standard Label tape, the name of the data set is stored in the tape header label that precedes the actual data. The header label has room for only 17 characters. This leads to a complication.

If the name is longer than 17 characters, the first part of the name is truncated and only the last 17 characters are stored in the label (called a HDR1 label, pronounced header 1).

If the data set is cataloged, then the entire long name is cataloged. You use that name when you refer to the data set.

For example, suppose you create a data set on tape using a DD statement something like this:

```
//UH DD DISP=(,CATLG),
//  UNIT=(TAPE,,DEFER),
//  LABEL=(1,SL),
//  VOL=(,RETAIN,SER=WANDA),
//  DSN=AINT.GONNA.WORRY.NO.MORE
```

In this case, what is stored in the label will be:

NNA.WORRY.NO.MORE

You can refer to it in the future as:

```
//OKAY DD DISP=OLD,
// DSN=AINT.GONNA.WORRY.NO.MORE
```

Fine with you, right? Sure. But now suppose you unexpectedly receive a tape in the post from someone in Persia and you find yourself unable to read the accompanying letter, which is written in Farsi. You're curious what's on the tape. You hope it might contain military secrets that have been misdirected in the post. At your company you have a program that dumps tape labels and tells you something about what is on the tape. You run that program, pointing it at your mystery tape, and you find that it has labels that look like this:

```
VOL1PERSIA
HDR1.MILITARY.SECRETS
```

which is to say that the VOL1 label contains the volume serial number PERSIA, and the HDR1 label contains the following data set name:

```
.MILITARY.SECRETS
```

Now you want to know how best to refer to this in JCL. Answer: make up any prefix you like to complete the name. For example, you could use a DD statement such as this:

```
//SYSUT1 DD DISP=OLD,
// UNIT=(TAPE,,DEFER),
// LABEL=(1,SL),
// VOL=(,RETAIN,SER=PERSIA),
// DSN=SMITH.MILITARY.SECRETS
```

MORE HINTS ABOUT DSN AND SECURITY SYSTEMS, SUCH AS RACF

At almost any big company, the security system is set up in such a way that it will slow down your work tremendously. You will frequently find that you are not allowed to use some data set you require. This you will recognize by a 913 abend code.

Usually it is just a matter of someone having forgotten to give you the necessary authorization. All that is necessary is to make your request to the appropriate authority and wait a day or so.

If you have gotten one 913, though, you will usually get another. They seem to travel in groups. This is because few activities require the use of just one data set. Several are usually involved. And whoever forgot to allow you to use one of them forgot to allow you to use the whole set.

You will be well off if you can identify the entire set of related data sets at the first sign of the first 913.

Typically, though, you get one 913, request access, wait a day for access to be given to you, re-run your job, get your next 913 on the next data set you need to use, request access, wait a day for access to be given you, re-run your job, get another 913 on the next data set, and so on.

When this happens to you, keep an accurate list of the data sets that together make up the set. This way, the next time it happens with a similar set, you may be able to identify the entire set at the beginning and request all of your access permissions in one fell swoop. (Typical example: a new release of IMS or CICS is installed, and the systems programmers forgot that you would need to use the data sets.)

When you request access, request it for everyone in your group, not just for yourself. Argue the point if need be. Make sure everyone else in your group follows the same policy.

As an additional nuance, some security systems allow those who control access to a data set to specify a time limit on how long you will be allowed to use it.

Consider an example.

You are assigned to work on a project that is expected to take six months to complete. Within less than a month everyone in your group has been granted access to all of the data sets you need to use. Those responsible have specified that your authorization is to be valid for three months.

All three months eventually pass. The project has not in fact been completed (what an unusual example this is!) and everyone is under pressure now.

What happens?

Your authorization to use the data sets begins to expire. First one, then another. In exactly the same order as the order in which access was originally permitted.

This improves the mood of no one.

But you have kept your list.

After the second or third data set (sooner if you're alert) you realize what is happening.

You present your complete list to the Security Officer, or to whomever is appropriate, with an accompanying request that the time limit be extended appropriately for all data sets on the list, both for yourself personally and for everyone else in your group as well.

Golly, you're a hero now. You've saved loads of time for your project at a tense moment. Lucky thing you kept that list.

Chapter 5

DISP - TELLING MVS WHAT TO DO WITH THE DATA SET

DISP means disposition, which is to say, how you want MVS to dispose of the data set when your program finishes with it. Keep it or delete it, for example.

DISP also means the existing disposition of the data set at the time your program starts to run, which, admittedly, stretches the ordinary English meaning of the word disposition. This loose interpretation allows us to use DISP to create new data sets as well as just using old existing data sets.

You should probably know right at the start that when DISP is used to request exclusive use of a data set MVS really reserves only the data set name, not the actual data set. For ordinary processing this is good enough, but there are some programs that are not barred from using your data set at the same time; for example, system backups. More details of this later.

DISP in general applies to entire data sets, not to the members of library data sets. So, since DISP applies to entire data sets, remember to use extra caution with DISP when you are also specifying a member name. In particular, never try to delete a member by the use of DELETE in the DISP field - you will delete the entire data set.

There is one relatively new feature of DISP with libraries, relating only to PDSE libraries (PDSE stands for PDS-Extended, a new type of SMS-managed PDS). When more than one job is using an ordinary PDS, with DISP=SHARE or SHR, the MVS system does not prevent the jobs from updating the same member at the same time, which results in loss of data. With a PDSE, the MVS system does prevent multiple jobs from updating the same member at the same time.

And an aside about the use of DISP with VSAM files. Until fairly recently, you could not use the DISP parameter to create and delete VSAM files from JCL. However, now you can. Most people still create and delete VSAM files using the program IDCAMS, which will be discussed in Chapter 17. Many parameters are available in IDCAMS that are not available in JCL. If you are dealing with IMS or DB2 databases, note that these databases are usually set up as VSAM files and then formatted into IMS or DB2 format with utility programs specific to the type of database. Although you can set up and delete the VSAM files themselves using JCL, you generally still need to use the database utility programs to format the VSAM files for use as databases. This is also true for many other types of databases. The main advantage of allocating and deleting a VSAM file with the DISP parameter is the fact that you do not need to see the IDCAMS control statements to know what is happening with the VSAM file.

Now, DISP.

There are three subparameters for DISP.

The first describes the situation when your program starts.

You can specify the first subparameter of DISP as OLD, if you are using a data set that already exists and you want to lay claim to exclusive use of it for a while.

This claim to exclusive use is also known as "exclusive enqueue".

If you specify OLD and your program opens the data set for output, the existing data that was already there in the data set will be lost. Any records your program writes to the data set will replace whatever was there before. Whatever was there before will be gone.

If you have a gigantic data set for which you specify DISP=OLD on the DD statement, and your program opens the gigantic data set for output, writes nothing, and then closes it, the data set will be empty.

Oh, come on, you say?

When you close a data set, MVS writes an end of file marker where it considers the end to be.

Not all of the old data has really disappeared, but it would be difficult to recover.

So that is what DISP=OLD will do for you.

Rather than being OLD, you can specify that the data set is NEW. You do this if you want MVS to create it for you then and there. NEW, like OLD, implies an exclusive enqueue on the name of the data set.

Similar to specifying OLD is specifying SHR (or SHARE). This means that the data set already exists, but you are willing to let other programs use it at the same time as you are using it. In other words, SHR is the same as OLD except that you do not have an exclusive enqueue. Generally you will want to specify DISP=SHR if your program is reading from a data set but will not update the data set.

In most cases you should specify OLD rather than SHR or SHARE on the DD statement for a data set that your program uses for output. This is because, if two programs both have the data set open for output at the same time, the resulting output can be badly mangled. It might end up as an interleaved mishmash of data created by each of the two programs, particularly if it is a large data set or member; or the data from one of the programs may completely overwrite the data from the other program.

An amusing anecdote as illustration.

A programmer (similar to yourself, but less knowledgeable) has a library which contains several members, one of which is the JCL he is EDITing under SPF option 2.

This programmer (not you) is editing a member named JCLDECK in a data set named USER.ALLIN.CNTL

The member JCLDECK contains some JCL that will write some output someplace. This silly programmer decides to write the output as a new member of the same library. He specifies DISP=SHR, using a DD statement something like one of these:

```
//SYSUT2 DD DISP=SHR,
// DSN=USER.ALLIN.CNTL(OUTDATA)
```

Or maybe:

```
//SYSLIN DD DISP=SHR,
// DSN=USER.ALLIN.CNTL(OBJMOD)
```

Or maybe:

```
//SYSPUNCH DD DISP=SHR,
// DSN=USER.ALLIN.CNTL(OBJDECK)
```

This programmer submits this JCL, and then hits the PF3 key, which tells SPF to save the member JCLDECK and end the EDIT session.

Meanwhile the job that was submitted has begun to execute, and is quickly adding the new member to the data set.

What happens to this programmer? If the timing is right - or rather, wrong - then the directory of the library is doubly updated to point to the same location for both the member JCLDECK and the new member; That location thereafter contains the data for the new member, and the JCL that used to be in member JCLDECK is lost. Happens surprisingly often.

Such are the dangers of DISP=SHR, or DISP=SHARE.

People are often prone to overlook, to their risk, the fact that DISP applies to an entire data set. Why is this so easy to overlook? Consider.

When you edit a member of a library with SPF under TSO, the SPF editor issues two separate enqueue requests. One is for the data set itself, requested as DISP=SHR. The other is a special enqueue request completely unrelated to JCL, a request for an additional enqueue on a special SPF name which includes the member name. This way SPF knows if another SPF session is using that member name. But a non-SPF task relying on JCL does not respect the special SPF enqueue on the member name, and is in fact not aware of it.

The linkage editor does something similar to lock out other link-edit tasks that may be trying to update the same member at the same time. Again, you cannot expect this to be known to any other programs.

People become accustomed to the SPF and linkage editor lockouts, and sometimes forget that they do not necessarily lock out all other programs, only their own kind. But now you know.

With the exception of PDSE data sets, DISP=SHR means the entire data set is available for any other task to use at the same time; DISP only applies to the name of the data set as a whole, and does not control individual member names within libraries.

When your data set is a PDSE, you can specify DISP=SHR and code a member name within the DSN, and you will reserve only that member name. Other jobs and TSO users can use other members at the same time. We still don't recommend this practice if it can be avoided, because people copy JCL, and someone else copying your JCL might not be aware of the subtle difference; or you yourself might be in a hurry someday and copy your own old JCL, not stopping to think that on this new occasion you are using a PDS rather than a PDSE.

As a final possibility for the value assigned to the first subparameter of DISP, the value can be specified as MOD, meaning modify, which is a bit complicated. In the case of MOD, the data set may or may not exist already.

If it does not already exist, specifying MOD has the same effect as specifying NEW.

If, however, it does exist, then specifying MOD is similar to specifying OLD except that it means something more like APPEND. But there is no parameter called APPEND. That meaning is conveyed by DISP=MOD, where MOD means MODify. If your program writes to an existing data set with DISP=MOD, then the records your program writes will be appended to the end of the data set, rather than overwriting the existing data.

Do not use DISP=MOD with a library, that is, a partitioned data set, or PDS. If you do specify DISP=MOD with such a data set, one of two things will happen: either (1) the job will be terminated (if you specify a member name and the member already exists), or (2) the data will be written at the end of the data portion of the library, but the directory will not be updated to point to it, so the data will be lost, having been written to an unretrievable location; but you won't get any messages to tell you about the problem; and you'll find yourself some time in the future wondering where your data disappeared to.

Those are the possibilities: NEW, OLD, MOD, SHR or SHARE.

Now a few words about MVS's enforcement methods.

The intent of the first subparameter of DISP is to control the allocation of a particular data set as just described. It is rather imperfectly implemented, however, so that what it actually controls is mainly the use of a particular data set name.

Just the name.

MVS keeps a big look-up table of names that are currently in use. Data set names that are controlled by DISP are entered in the table with a "major name" of SYSDSN and a "minor name" of the actual DSN. By looking up the name in this table, MVS is able to control other tasks attempting to use the same data set name through the DISP parameter.

There are three problems with this.

The first problem occurs when you have or want two or more data sets with the same name, perhaps one on disk and the other(s) on tape, for backup.

Since specifying NEW creates an exclusive enqueue, this means that you cannot create a backup copy on tape having the same name as an existing disk data set as long as anyone else is using the existing data set. This is a problem for libraries that are shared by a number of users. The answer, obviously, is to name the copy something different.

The second problem is that saying DISP=SHR for a VSAM file does not make a VSAM file shareable. The shareability of a VSAM file is determined by the SHAREOPTIONS keyword when the VSAM file is created (discussed under IDCAMS in Chapter 17). However, the names of VSAM files are kept in the table of names when one specifies VSAM files in the JCL, that is, they are made subject to the enqueue mechanism, so if you say DISP=OLD it prevents other jobs from accessing it at the same time through JCL.

Nevertheless, you should say DISP=SHR in the JCL for a shareable VSAM file. This is because if you say DISP=OLD you will prevent it from being shared, and if you leave off the DISP, MVS will try to create a new, non-VSAM file of the same name (and in most cases will fail miserably, because you haven't given it a UNIT, SPACE, or any of that; but if you happen to specify a data set name in a format that is defined to SMS with default UNIT, SPACE, etc., then you may get a new data set if you leave off DISP; or your job might be terminated due to a duplicate data set name). Recall also that the default DISP of NEW causes an exclusive enqueue on the name, which can cause additional problems if the VSAM file is already allocated to another JOB.

An example to illustrate the "additional problems". Let's say that you have a shareable database, created with appropriate VSAM SHAREOPTIONS, and it is used by an IMS or CICS online system that is running all the time, but a number of batch jobs also read it. Now suppose that you forget to code DISP on your DD statement for this file, so that DISP=NEW is assumed, creating an exclusive enqueue; or suppose you inadvertently code DISP=OLD, which also creates an exclusive enqueue. Your job will appear to be hung, and you should get a message at your TSO terminal saying that your job is "waiting for data sets". You should then cancel the job. If, however, you have walked away from your terminal before the job begins to execute, so you don't see the message and hence don't cancel the job, then your job will remain hung indefinitely. The complication arises for all the other jobs that come along after your job hangs and try to read the database with DISP=SHR, which would ordinarily work for them. However, because your job is ahead of theirs in the enqueue service queue, and you have requested exclusive enqueue, they all have to wait, in other words, those jobs also hang. And this situation continues until someone notices it and cancels your job. It can be embarrassing.

The same thing happens with non-VSAM data sets. It is fairly common with load libraries, for example, which are used as STEPLIB by some jobs while other jobs write into them (adding and replacing programs). So you have to be cautious about requesting exclusive use of these data sets. But, on to the third problem.

The third problem occurs when you rely on MVS to control access to data, not realizing that in general MVS really uses the first subparameter of DISP to control access only to the NAME. Someone can, using various methods, access your data set even while you are using it, even if you have asked for DISP=OLD (e.g., system backups). But problems occur even when the DISP is SHR.

Consider an example. (This example will not work for SMS-controlled data sets.)

The scene is this:

Various people, using SPF option 2 under TSO, are EDITing various members of some communal data set (some shared library). Someone tries to SAVE a member, only to find that the data set is full; the member cannot be SAVEd into the data set. This frustrated but determined person places the modified member into some other library for the time being, using the CREATE subcommand of the SPF editor.

In case you don't know how to use CREATE to do this, but you would like to, here it is. You go to the top line of the member you are editing, put CC over the line number at the left of the top line; then you go down all the way to the bottom line of the member and put CC over the line number at the left of the last line; then you press the HOME key (or use the cursor keys) to return the cursor to the Command ==> line; and there you type the word CREATE and press the Enter key. A new screen will then appear, on which you can enter another library name and member name, and your data will be saved there; unless that data set is also full, in which case you will have to keep trying again until you succeed with some other library.

So, back to the person in our story. Having saved his modified data, the person decides to re-allocate the offending library with a larger SPACE allocation.

Notice that the data set is allocated DISP=SHR to several users at this point, so you would probably think, offhand, that the frustrated but enterprising person would not be allowed to proceed with such an intention.

Supposing that it is you yourself who wish to implement this plan, however, and assuming of course as always that you are exercising the best possible judgment under the circumstances, the scene proceeds as follows (if the data set in question is not SMS-controlled. For SMS-controlled data sets and VSAM data sets the UnCatalog request, upon which this example relies, is not valid. Anyway, if the data set is not SMS-controlled, you proceed):

1) Find out the name of the volume where the ill-fated data set currently resides. Write this down. This step can be done using SPF option 3.2 under TSO.

2) Allocate a new data set on a different volume with all of the same attributes as the first data set, but with a different name and a bigger SPACE allocation. This step can be done using SPF option 3.2 under TSO.

3) Copy all of the members of the old data set into the new data set. This step can be done using SPF option 3.3 under TSO.

4) UnCatalog the original data set. This step can be done using SPF option 3.2 under TSO as long as the data set is not SMS-controlled.

5) Rename the new data set to have the same name as the original data set had. This step can be done using SPF option 3.2 under TSO.

The new data set now has the name of the original data set, and is in every way a replacement of the original, except that it has the larger SPACE allocation you gave it and it resides on a different volume, and except for matters relating to the (unfortunate and probably unsuspecting) users who happen to be running with the old copy allocated.

The sort of behavior outlined above can be an annoyance if someone does it to a data set you thought you were using.

On the other hand, the above described keyboard acrobatics can be a useful trick on the rare occasions when you are certain that whoever or whatever has the data set allocated is definitely not updating it and probably not even using it at all. (For example, it is late at night, you know they've gone home, but they left their TSO session logged on and the data set is still allocated to the TSO session.)

However, the trick is mentioned here not to suggest that you use it, but to warn you about the sort of thing that can happen, so you know not to expect more from DISP than DISP can provide.

Variations on the theme proliferate.

Which variation you use depends on which programs you have available to do the renaming, and what they will allow you to do. Currently SPF will not allow you to rename a data set if anyone else has the name allocated with DISP=OLD, which is quite reasonable. Other programs exist which have no such qualms. Backup and restore programs, for example, are often set up to ignore the enqueue protocol.

Another way you can run into problems occurs when you have shared DASD, that is, disks that are physically cabled up to more than one computer. This is okay as long as the computers talk to each other, that is, as long as each of the computers has been told that the other computers need to be considered in resolving enqueue allocations (using GRS, Global Resource Serialization). But sometimes the systems aren't set up this way. Somebody might have a little small test system off in a corner someplace that is not. Occasionally problems occur this way.

A much more common source of problems involves the SPF RECOV-ERY facility. You know, when your SPF EDIT profile specifies RECOV-ERY ON.

In case you don't know but would like to: when you are editing a data set under SPF, type PROFILE on the Command===> line. You will be shown several lines of data concerning parameters that control your edit-ing, such as NUMBER ON or NUMBER OFF. One of these parameters is RECOVERY. You can turn this on by typing RECOVERY ON on the command line. That done, SPF will save a copy of all your changes into a temporary data set while you are editing, so that, if your session is dropped or cancelled, you will be able to get right back to where you were (more or less) when next you Logon, and you don't lose all your editing work. The periodic copies are not saved into the data set you are editing. They are saved into system-allocated Temporary disk data sets. This allows you to get a second advantage from setting Recovery On. When you have Recovery On, you can use the UNDO command to undo changes you make that you decide you don't like. And you can type UNDO several times to retract several changes. The old versions are re-constructed from the temporary data sets. Incidentally, you have a differ-ent copy of your Edit Profile for each data set Type. In this sense a data set Type is determined by the rightmost qualifier of the name, typically something like .CNTL, or .COBOL, or .PLI; and you can set the PROFILE parameters, including RECOVERY, to different values for different Data set types. When you exit from your EDIT session, SPF remembers the settings, and will use the same PROFILE every time you edit any data set of that type, that is, any data set with the same low-level (rightmost) qualifier. If the SPF PROFILE is news to you, then you should also know about the HILITE parameter. When you are editing your JCL, type HILITE ON JCL on the Command===> line to turn on a highlighting facility that will put different syntactical parts of the JCL in different colors, making it easy to spot errors. There are also HILITE ON PLI and HILITE ON COBOL versions available to you, among others.

The example goes like this.

You and Joe are working on the same data.

You are EDITing the data in SPF while Joe is at lunch.

You have made numerous changes, but have not SAVEd the member. A power failure transpires. This leads you to decide it is time to go to lunch.

The electricity comes back.

Joe comes back.

Joe EDITs the data. He makes numerous changes and SAVEs the member, then goes to a meeting.

You come back.

SPF, going through its recovery routine (because you had RECOVERY ON in your EDIT profile), pops you right back where You were when the power failure occurred, oblivious to Joe's changes that have taken place in the meantime. Great, you say, also oblivious to Joe's changes. You SAVE the member, unwittingly overwriting Joe's changes. You go on to other things and give it no further thought.

Eventually, perhaps days or weeks later, Joe looks at the data, and his changes have disappeared. Why? Because you wrote over them when you SAVEd. Of course you didn't know about Joe's changes, and have since forgotten that you even edited the data that day.

All concerned conclude that Joe's word is unreliable, or the computer is haunted by a poltergeist, or perhaps some evil or careless systems programmer or computer operator has replaced the data set with an old backup copy and not told anyone about it.

But now you know the sad truth.

And it doesn't require a power failure for this sort of thing to transpire. More commonly, you will be editing the data when someone walks up and asks you a question, or the telephone rings. You become distracted on some tangent. Your TSO session times out, that is, it is automatically cancelled after being idle for some amount of time (abend code 522).

The next time you use the SPF editor, the recovery scene is played out. If anyone else has changed the data in the meantime, you will wipe out their changes if you SAVE. You are not given any warning that any-one has been changing the data in the interim. If the data set is a library, one thing you can do is to go into SPF split screen before you save, select SPF option 1 View or Browse, specify the data set name, and check the SPF statistics to see the date and time of the last update. If the statistics are missing or the data set is a flat file, you really have no way of know-ing. And most of the time most people do not think to check anyway, even if it is a library data set with statistics available.

It's just one of those facts of life.

Some people don't believe this example. If that is the case with you, find a cooperative friend and try the experiment.

So don't expect too much from DISP as far as reserving the use of your data set for you. It has limitations.

To conclude the discussion of the first subparameter of DISP: If you do not specify DISP, the default of NEW is assumed.

Incidentally, depending on the language and the level of the com-piler you are using, data sets will sometimes be allocated dynamically. What this means is that if you do not include a DD statement for a file, one will be generated as if by magic, using the default DISP of NEW to create a new temporary data set which will go away after the program ends. This is okay for a print file. Otherwise it is often not okay, and is just one more thing to watch out for. Oh well. The name for this is dynamic allocation, the same thing SPF uses, except that SPF doesn't rely on the default DISP.

So much for the first subparameter of DISP, which we now know can take on the value of NEW, OLD, MOD, and SHR (which can also be spelled SHARE); and the default is NEW.

No doubt your curiosity has been overwhelming you regarding the matter of the second subparameter. You need wait no longer.

The second subparameter takes on such values as KEEP or DELETE. This value establishes what will happen to the data set after your program completes, provided your program ends normally.

MVS varies the default for the second subparameter depending mainly on the first subparameter. DISP=NEW implies DISP=(NEW,DELETE) whereas DISP=OLD implies DISP=(OLD,KEEP). The default for the second subparameter is generally the state of existence of the file before the program was run. That is, if the file did not exist before then it will not exist after. If it did exist before then it will continue to exist after.

In addition to KEEP and DELETE, the second subparameter can have the values PASS, CATLG and UNCATLG.

CATLG is similar to KEEP except that it means that not only is the data set to be kept, but also a Catalog Entry for it is to be created so that the system - and you - can find it again using just the data set name and not specifying where the data set is (for example, which disk). In general, if you are creating a new disk data set, the parameter you want is CATLG, not KEEP.

You want KEEP for existing data sets. Conveniently, KEEP is the default second subparameter for existing data sets, so all the DISP you really need to specify with these is DISP=OLD or DISP=SHR.

When you create a new data set on tape you might or might not want to create a catalog entry. If you are planning to send or give the tape to somebody on another system, then you probably don't want it cataloged on your own system. If you have several tapes with several copies of the same data set, and you keep them in a drawer or cabinet in your office, you probably do not want to catalog the newest version.

If you do want to catalog the newest version of the data set on tape, and it has the same name as the previous version, and the previous version was cataloged, then you will first need to erase the catalog entry for the old copy of the data set. You do this by using a DD statement specifying DISP=(OLD,UNCATLG) together with DSN=the-dataset-name-to-be-uncataloged. This DD statement must be included in a Job Step previous to the one where you will catalog the new version. Each EXEC statement for a program creates a new Job Step. To create an extra step for the purpose of uncataloging your data set, you can use the convenient do-nothing program name IEFBR14. There will be examples later.

This is the use of UNCATLG. Another use of UNCATLG is to erase the catalog entry for a data set when the data set has been removed from the system but left its catalog entry behind. This happens, for example, when a disk data set is automatically archived to tape because it hasn't been used in a long time, and then, after even more time passes, the tape itself is recycled to hold newer archives. The data set has then vanished, but its catalog entry lives on.

UNCATLG is ignored for VSAM data sets and all SMS-managed data sets, including all PDSE data sets. In fact these days on most systems this includes almost all disk data sets. This means that the usefulness of UNCATLG is generally limited to tape data sets

There is another way to get rid of unwanted catalog entries when the data sets themselves have disappeared. You can use the TSO command DELETE with the NOSCRATCH option (from the READY prompt or from SPF option 6). At least, as of this writing you can still use it.

The final value to be discussed for the second subparameter is PASS. This is similar to KEEP, but the data set remains allocated to your job and is passed along to a later step in that job.

The third subparameter is like the second, except that it determines what will happen to the data set if your program ABENDs (ABnormal END).

Notice that a bad condition code is not an ABEND.

In the case of a bad condition code, the second subparameter still applies. The third one is only for actual ABENDs.

Condition codes will be explained in Chapter 11, the EXEC statement, under the COND parameter (COND is short for CONDition code).

Example: DISP=(OLD,DELETE,KEEP)

This means that the data set in question already exists, and you want exclusive enqueue on its name. If your program ends normally, no matter how miserable the condition code, then the data set will be deleted. If, however, your program ABENDS (as, for example, a 322 ABEND caused by running out of time) then the data set will be kept. So you might say this is generally a bad choice of setting for DISP, since you probably would not really want to delete the data set if the program ended with a bad condition code - you would probably want to keep the data set so you could rerun the program.

Possible values for the second and third subparameters of DISP are:

KEEP Means the data set is to be kept after the program finishes. Just the thing to go with OLD, or SHR. It happens to be the default second subparameter and also the default third subparameter whenever OLD or SHR is specified in first position. So if you say DISP=SHR it works the same as if you had said DISP=(SHR,KEEP,KEEP)

PASS Valid only as the second subparameter. Similar to KEEP, except it means that a later step in your job will also use the same data set, so it is to be passed along.

DELETE Means the data set is to be deleted after the program finishes. This is the default second subparameter for NEW data sets. Please remember that DELETE will delete the entire data set, not just a member.

CATLG Not only is the data set kept, as with KEEP, but a catalog entry is created for it. Just the thing for a NEW data set, but pointless if the data set is already cataloged. Since the default for the first subparameter is NEW, and the default second subparameter for NEW data sets is DELETE, you will often see this: DISP=(,CATLG) which has exactly the same effect as: DISP=(NEW,CATLG)

UNCATLG The data set itself is not affected by this, but the catalog entry that points to it is deleted. Note that this parameter is ignored for SMS-managed data sets and VSAM files, so catalog entries for those are not deleted by UNCATLG.

A few more examples.

DISP=(NEW,DELETE,KEEP)

The above phrase means that the data set is to be created when your program executes. If your program ends normally, no matter how miserable the condition code, then the data set will be deleted. If, however, your program ABENDS, the data set will be kept.

Example: Uncatalog an old version of a tape data set and then create and catalog the new version.

```
//MYJOB JOB (ETC)
//*
//STEP1 EXEC PGM=IEFBR14
//OLDSTUFF DD DISP=(OLD,UNCATLG),
//    DSN=SMITH.BACKUP.FLATFILE.DATA
//*
//STEP2 EXEC PGM=IEBGENER
//SYSUT1 DD DISP=OLD,
//    DSN=SMITH.FLATFILE.DATA
//SYSPRINT DD SYSOUT=*
//SYSIN  DD DUMMY
//SYSUT2  DD DISP=(NEW,CATLG),
//    DSN=SMITH.BACKUP.FLATFILE.DATA
//    UNIT=TAPE,DCB=*.SYSUT1
```

DISP=OLD

The above phrase means that the data set in question already exists, and you want exclusive enqueue on its name. It will be kept, that is, it will continue to exist after your program ends, no matter whether your program ABENDs or not.

DISP=SHR

The above phrase means that the data set in question already exists, and you are willing to share its name (and, by implication, the data set itself) with other simultaneous users. The data set itself will be kept, that is, it will continue to exist after your program ends, no matter whether your program ABENDs or not.

DISP=SHARE

Same as DISP=SHR before.

Following is a *TRICK QUESTION* example:

```
//ETC DD DSN=BIG.OUTPUT.DATASET,
//  SPACE=(CYL,(50),RLSE),
```

```
// UNIT=SYSDA, DISP=(NEW,CATLG),
// DCB=LAST.MONTHS.DATASET
```

Data set is created and deleted. No error message. Notice the blank space after the comma before the word DISP. That means that the rest of the line is treated as comments. Remember the comments field? So, in the above example, DISP=(NEW,CATLG) is a comment. The default value for DISP is assumed. The default is DISP=(NEW,DELETE).

Example to avoid (another *TRICK QUESTION* example):

```
//BADMOVE DD DISP=(OLD,DELETE),
// DSN=SYS1.PROCLIB(USELESS)
```

The above DD statement means that the entire data set SYS1.PROCLIB will be deleted.

No kidding.

Absolutely never attempt to delete a member using DISP. If you want to delete a member from a library, use some tool such as SPF option 3.1 or the TSO command DELETE. If it must be done as part of a batch job, use the IBM utility program IEHPROGM in Chapter 17, or the TSO command DELETE as part of a batch TSO session. So much for DISP. Now you know.

Chapter 6

The DCB parameter - What does it look like? with Basics of SMS

All of the DCB subparameters we are about to discuss are no longer limited, as they once were, to being just subparameters. All DCB subparameters are now also available as full-fledged parameters in their own right. This means that instead of coding //X DD DCB=(LRECL=80,BLKSIZE=23440,RECFM=FB),etc... you can now code simply //X DD LRECL=80,BLKSIZE=23440,RECFM=FB,etc... However, you will usually see this coded the old way, because there is a lot of existing JCL out there from before the subparameters were promoted to their new elevated status. Our examples mostly use the traditional subparameter style. But now you know you can do it the new way if you so choose.

LIKE

LIKE is not really a DCB parameter. It is actually a substitute for using the DCB parameter, and it also dispenses with other nuisances like SPACE and UNIT. When you use LIKE, you tell MVS to copy as much information as possible from some other data set.

The catch is that this only works with data sets on disk. For tapes and print files you still need DCB and other parameters. The other catch is that it only works if you are using SMS (System Managed Storage); but almost everybody is using SMS now. Possibly some disks on your system might not be under the control of SMS, but all the ones you are ever likely to use probably will be.

So, to use LIKE to create a new data set on disk, the only parameters you have to specify on the DD statement are DISP, DSN, and LIKE. Example:

```
//XXX DD DISP=(NEW,CATLG),
//    DSN=SMITH.NEW.DATASET,
//    LIKE=JONES.ANY.DATASET
```

There is a related parameter on the ALLOCATE command under TSO. This is probably the fastest easiest way possible to create a new data set with the same attributes as an existing data set. And this works for VSAM files as well as other types of data set. Just go into SPF option 6 and, on the command line, type the following and press enter:

```
ALLOCATE    DSN('SMITH.NEW.DATASET')
LIKE('JONES.ANY.DATASET')
```

Remember that in TSO, if you enclose a data set name in quotes (single quotes, also known as apostrophes) then you type the entire name including the userid. If you omit the quotes, then TSO appends your own userid as a prefix to whatever name you type.

In fact to accomplish the above example, you probably don't even have to go into SPF option 6. If you prefix the ALLOCATE command with the word TSO, you should be able to enter it from any SPF command line that is long enough to accommodate your chosen names. Example:

```
Command ===> TSO ALLOCATE DSN(new.dataset)
LIKE('JONES.ANY.DATASET')
```

There is also, you may as well know since we're on this tangent, a TSO command called DELETE which deletes data sets. Oh, and there are many parameters available on the ALLOCATE statement that are similar to those on DD statements. An example of the DELETE command in TSO:

Command ===> TSO DELETE 'SMITH.ANY.DATASET'

Now back to the DCB parameter LIKE.
Example of allocating a new data set and copying data into it:

```
//COPY EXEC PGM=IEBGENER
//SYSPRINT DD SYSOUT=*
//SYSIN DD DUMMY
//SYSUT1 DD DISP=SHR,
// DSN=JONES.ANY.DATASET
//SYSUT2 DD DISP=(NEW,CATLG),
// DSN=SMITH.NEW.DATASET,
// LIKE=JONES.ANY.DATASET
```

Add a JOB statement at the top of the above example and submit it, and it will create a new data set named SMITH.NEW.DATASET, and copy all of the necessary attributes from the cataloged disk data set JONES.ANY.DATASET, and since it executes IEBGENER it will copy the data as well, provided it is a flat file. (and provided you change the data set names to names that are valid and authorized for you to use on your own system). If you want to copy a PDS (library), use IEBCOPY for the program name instead of IEBGENER. The LIKE parameter will work with VSAM files as well, but IEBGENER and IEBCOPY won't. See the section on IDCAMS to copy VSAM files. Using LIKE is also a good way to allocate a PDSE.

If the data set you are copying from is similar to what you want to allocate, but not quite identical, you can still use LIKE, and in addition specify whatever parameters you want to change. Your added parameters should override those being copied.

Now, for situations where LIKE alone will not carry you through, we have the rest of the parameters.

DATACLAS

The Data Classes are set up by the people responsible for installing and maintaining MVS at your site.

DATACLAS is obviously an abbreviation for Data Class.

When they set up the Data Classes, they can include in the definition of each class all of the DCB information you will need as well as UNIT and SPACE information. They also have the option of specifying that if your data set name matches a certain naming pattern they specify then it will default to some Data Class they choose for that name. For example, they could decide that all data sets with names ending in CNTL would have default attributes the same as you would expect for a CNTL data set under TSO, that is, records 80 bytes long and so forth.

If they happen to have set up a Data Class that matches your requirements, then using DATACLAS is another easy way for you to allocate a new (disk) data set (provided you are using SMS). Of course, the first catch is that a DATACLAS meeting your requirements has to exist, and the second catch is that you have to know what the Data Classes are, or else what the data set naming conventions are.

If the DATACLAS you decide to use is similar to what you want to allocate, but not quite identical, then, as with the LIKE parameter, you can add onto your DD statement whatever parameters you want to change. Your added parameters should override those being copied from the Data Class specifications. Also, as with the LIKE parameter, DATACLAS is a good way of allocating a PDSE data set.

Example 1: You found out that Data Class PDSE is exactly what you want:

```
//XXX DD DISP=(NEW,CATLG),
//   DSN=SMITH.NEW.CNTL,
//   DATACLAS=PDSE
```

Example 2: You found out that a data set naming structure starting with your userid and ending with .CNTL will default to a Data Class designed to give you exactly what you want. (You can always rename it later):

```
//XXX DD DISP=(NEW,CATLG),
// DSN=SMITH.NEW.CNTL
```

Example 3: You found out that Data Class PDSE is almost what you want, except you want more SPACE:

```
//XXX DD DISP=(NEW,CATLG),
// DSN=SMITH.NEW.CNTL,
// DATACLAS=PDSE,
// SPACE=(CYL,300)
```

There is, of course, an analogous DATACLAS parameter on the AL-LOCATE command in TSO.

DSORG

Pronounced D. S. Org. Or sometimes Dee-Sorg.

DSORG is, obviously, an abbreviation for Data Set ORGanization.

Not that data sets belong to clubs or political organizations. In DSORG, the organization referred to is internal organization. How are your records organized with respect to one another within the data set?

Perhaps you never gave it much thought.

You do deal with different sorts of data sets from time to time, of course. In what are they different?

Some of your data sets are very simple. Like decks of cards. The first record comes first and the second record comes right after it. Nothing fancy. A flat file. Data coming in off a tape. A print report being written.

This sort of organization is called physical sequential, abbreviated PS. It means that the records occur sequentially one after the next physically, as would the cards in a deck.

This situation is specified in JCL as DSORG=PS, a subparameter of DCB on the DD statement.

Not all of your data sets are flat files.

Some are libraries.

Libraries are the data sets that have members.

A library is also called a partitioned data set or PDS because the data set is partitioned into little separate chunks for the various members. This is also referred to as partitioned organization, specified as DSORG=PO in JCL.

A brief digression. There is also a newer type of library available with SMS, which does not have DSORG=PO. It is called a PDSE data set. PDSE stands for Partitioned Data Set Extended. A PDSE is somewhat similar to a PDS, with two main differences. It cannot have Load Modules as members, and you do not have to compress a PDSE. You do not use the DSORG parameter at all for a PDSE. For a PDSE, you use the DSNTYPE parameter instead of DSORG. To create a PDSE using JCL, you select a data set prefix that is defined to SMS at your site as a PDSE data set prefix, and then you specify DSNTYPE=LIBRARY along with DISP=(NEW,CATLG) and DSN= the data set name. That's all. You do not need to specify any DCB parameters, UNIT, or SPACE. These will be copied from whatever was defined in SMS as the default for data sets with the prefix you have used. However, if default DCB or SPACE information was not set up in SMS for the prefix, or if you want different DCB attributes than the defaults, then you will still need to code the parameters in your JCL. You can also create a PDSE by using the LIKE parameter to model your new PDSE after an existing PDSE, and in that case the prefix you use does not need to be defined as a PDSE prefix, and you do not need to code DSNTYPE. You just code something like

```
//NEW DD DISP=(NEW,CATLG),
//    DSN=new.name,
//    LIKE=other.dataset
```

and that's all there is to it. Of course, that last example will work with all the other types of data set too, not just PDSEs.

But, to get back to the main train of thought, there are also VSAM files, and databases based on VSAM files.

Those are the main types of data sets.

We won't be talking about databases much in this book, because there are many types of databases, and the use of databases is an extensive subject in its own right.

Most databases are really VSAM files, and the DSORG parameter is not applicable to VSAM files, so we won't talk much about them in this section either, except to make another digression to point out that you can create a new VSAM file in JCL by using the LIKE parameter in the same way that was shown for a PDSE:

```
//NEW DD DSN=new.vsam.file,
// DISP=(NEW,CATLG),
// LIKE=some.existing.vsam.file
```

As the final examples of types of data set, we want to point out two notable data base types that are really thinly disguised flat files.

The first of these is known as DSORG=DA and also called BDAM (pronounced bee dam). On input, you can read a BDAM file sequentially (like a flat file) as long as you specify DSORG=PS in the DCB on the DD statement that points to the file. On output the records in a BDAM file are arranged rather at random, according to whatever order the program determines. A record on a BDAM file is replaced on the disk, usually after it is read. It is not possible to add a new record to a BDAM file, just to replace one. This file organization is usually used because it is extremely fast.

The other notable exception is the type of file that is known to IMS as GSAM (pronounced jee sam). A GSAM file is just a flat file. You can create a flat file in one job step, DSORG=PS, and read it as an IMS GSAM file in the next step, no intervening magic required. Most IMS databases, however, are not GSAM files, they are really VSAM files.

Now you understand DSORG. Basically.

A little more about using DSORG=PO, the library type.

Each library has an area at the beginning reserved for the purpose of storing the names of the members and telling where each member begins within the data set.

This area at the beginning of the data set is called the directory. It is set aside in units of directory blocks. Each directory block is 256 bytes long. The first member starts right after the end of the directory.

The next member starts right after the end of the first member, and so on.

When a member is replaced, the replacement version is placed right after the end of the last member, and the directory is rewritten to tell the new location of the member.

The old version of that member remains where it was, but unused.

Consequently you can fill up your data set by replacing the same member over and over again. When that happens you can compress your data set to recover all the wasted space. Examples of how to compress a data set will be given in Chapter 17.

How many members can you have in your library? It depends on how many directory blocks you have. Each directory block can point to about five or ten members, depending on what other information you store in the directory besides the names and relative addresses of the members. Request the number of directory blocks you expect to need by specifying directory blocks as a subparameter of SPACE, as discussed in the section on SPACE.

Normally, you never to need to specify DSORG in your JCL. If you create a new data set and you give your data set directory blocks in the SPACE parameter, MVS will assume that you want it to be DSORG=PO, that is, a PDS, a library. If you do not give it any directory blocks, MVS will assume you want DSORG=PS, a flat file. One of the few assumptions MVS makes intelligently.

If, however, you are working on an MVS system onto which has been installed some product such as the non-IBM software product named Volume Allocation Manager (VAM) (a product of Sterling Software), then you may be required to specify DSORG in your DCB. The improper assumption that will be made in such a case is a DSORG of blank, which is, of course, neither PS nor PO. Moreover, it makes the error message look funny. Example:

VAM001 DSORG OF NOT ALLOWED

If you look carefully at such an error message, you will observe that there is more than one blank space between the word "OF" and the word "NOT". The implication is:

DSORG OF blank space NOT ALLOWED

Which is, of course, the same thing as saying that you are required to specify DSORG, and you failed to do so. So much for DSORG.

RECORG

RECORG is the VSAM equivalent of DSORG. It can take the values KS, ES, RR, and LS, meaning, respectively, a Key Sequenced Data Set (KSDS), an Entry Sequenced Data Set (ESDS), a Relative Record Data Set (RRDS), or a Linear Space Data Set (LSDS). If you use RECORG when creating a new VSAM data set in JCL, the value you assign with RECORG overrides the value that was set up in SMS for the data set prefix or data class you are using. However, if you use this parameter to override the default RECORG, then you may find that some of the other parameters do not suit you. For example, if the default is RECORG=ES and you specify RECORG=KS, then you will be creating both an INDEX and a DATA component rather than just a DATA component - and you won't have any default information specific to your INDEX.

There is not always a JCL parameter that is directly analogous to every VSAM parameter available in IDCAMS. See the section on IDCAMS for more information about VSAM parameters. If you use JCL for allocating new VSAM data sets, you will generally need to rely on the LIKE and REFDD parameters, or sometimes DATACLAS.

RECFM

Pronounced as one word, just as spelled. Or sometimes ReckForm. Clearly an abbreviation for RECord ForMat.

If all of the records in your data set are the same length, they are fixed length records. The abbreviation for fixed length records is F. If your fixed length records are grouped together in blocks, they are called fixed blocked records, and the abbreviation for that is FB. Your common garden variety JCL deck or PL/I or COBOL program is this sort, RECFM=FB. Some data sets will contain records that vary in size.

One record might be 133 bytes long, another might be only one byte in length. Print files are often written this way.

You could, of course, pad out the records with blanks to make them all the same length as the longest record, and if you did that you could make your data set have a record format of FB. This is considered to be wasteful of disk space, however, in the event that your file might be saved on disk. Hence there are alternatives: V, for varying, and U, for unformatted. When V type records are grouped together into blocks, they are referred to as VB.

A varying length (V or VB) data set contains a 4-byte prefix on each record (called the RDW, Record Descriptor Word). The system puts this in for you; you do not need to be concerned about it except to account for it in your record length. A data set of record length 80, for example, would need to have its record length specified as 84 if the record format were to be made V or VB. The four byte prefix is used to contain the length of the record (although only two of the bytes are actually used for this purpose, the other two being wasted). In the case of a VB data set, an additional 4-byte prefix occurs at the beginning of each block, telling—you guessed it—the length of that block (called the BDW, Block Descriptor Word).

RECFM=U data sets contain no such prefix. Load modules are RECFM=U. This is not a great choice for data that you will be reading into programs, however, because there is no way for the program to know the actual length of the data in any particular record.

Note, however, that RECFM=U in MVS describes records that, coming from other types of computers, are usually called varying length records. In other words, other types of computers do not generally have a prefix on varying length records.

Now you understand the basic record formats, F and FB, V and VB, and U.

Appended to the F, the FB, the V, the VB, or the U, you sometimes see the letter S or the letter A or the letter M.

The A indicates ASA carriage control. A carriage control character occurs in the first byte in each record (after the 4-byte prefix in the case of VA or VBA). If you write this sort of data set, you need to supply the carriage control byte yourself.

The main carriage control characters are these:

      a blank for ordinary single spacing;

1   the digit one to start a new page;

0   the digit zero for double spacing;

-   hyphen or minus sign to skip 2 spaces (triple spacing);

+   a plus sign to overstrike (as for underlining).

The carriage control character causes its action to take place before the printing of the line on which it occurs.

The letter M indicates machine carriage control characters. These are similar to ASA carriage control characters in spirit, but the codes vary from one type of device to another.

The letter S is equally infrequent in occurrence. It means Spanned in the case of varying length records, and it means Standard in the case of fixed length records, and there is no similarity between these things.

A varying length spanned record (RECFM=VBS) can span a physical boundary, which is to say, the first part of the record can occur at the end of one block while the rest of the record occurs at the beginning of the next block. The records can therefore span blocks. Part of a record can be at the end of a block at the end of a track, and the rest of the record can be at the start of the next block on the next track. Worse than that, the beginning of a record (say, to make it interesting, the record containing some data of financial interest to a close relative of your current sweetheart or spouse), the beginning of such a record can occur at the end of the last block on a tape, say tape VOL=SER=TAPE01, and the rest of the record can occur at the beginning of the first block on the next tape, say tape VOL=SER=TAPE02. Luckily you know enough to say VOL=SER=(TAPE01,TAPE02) and the second tape is neither lost nor damaged. Anyway now you know about VBS records.

Now for FBS.

In a fixed blocked standard (RECFM=FBS) data set, all of the blocks must be of the same length except for the last block, which is permitted to be short.

Ordinarily the size of a block that you specify is really interpreted as a maximum, not an absolute. If, for example, you had a data set specified with a block size of 23440 but you only had five of your 80 byte records in it, the real length of the block would be 400, and that would be okay. If you later wrote another ten records onto the end of it with a program that specified DISP=MOD in the JCL, you would have two blocks, the first one 400 bytes long and the second one 800 bytes long. This would still be okay. Provided that the record format was FB. If the format was FBS, this would not be okay, and would cause various errors when you tried to use it again. The best thing to do, if you run into any FBS data sets, is to change them to FB.

LRECL

Pronounced Ell-Rek-ell. Or El Rec'l. Logical RECord Length. The length of a logical record. You read the section "Logical Records, Physical Records", did you not? So specify LRECL=80 in your DCB if your records are 80 bytes long.

(80 byte records are sometimes referred to as card image data. By far the most popular record length.) However long each record in your data set is, that is the number you specify for LRECL. If your records are of varying length (RECFM=V or VB or VBA or VBM or VBS) then you specify the maximum length + 4. The extra 4 bytes are set aside for each record to hold the length of the particular individual record.

BLKSIZE

Block size. The size of a block, or physical record. For example, if your records are 80 bytes long and are grouped together into blocks of 23440, that is, 293 records per block, then specify LRECL=80,BLKSIZE=23440 in your DCB. Remember that BLKSIZE is, in general, a maximum block size. Your blocks may be shorter than the number you specify. The system uses the number you specify for BLKSIZE to reserve buffers in main storage (memory) for reading and writing your data set. For varying length records, add an extra 4 bytes. This 4 bytes is used to hold the length of each particular specific block. BLKSIZE is explained at length in the earlier section, "Logical Records, Physical Records," in Chapter 3 On most MVS systems, if you do not specify a BLKSIZE for a new data set on disk, or if you specify BLKSIZE=0, the system should compute the optimum block size for you, usually equal to about half a track on whatever type of disk you are using. Also note that if you are using SMS and you are satisfied with the DCB defaults for the data set prefix or data class you are using, you do not need to code any DCB parameters, including BLKSIZE.

DCB=DATASETNAME

Suppose that you want to create a new data set, and you want to make it look just like some other data set whose name you know. Example: the other data set is named OLD.DATA.SET so you code DCB=OLD.DATA.SET in your JCL for your new data set. This causes MVS to copy all of the DCB parameters from the data set you name. Cheap and easy.

You can combine the DCB=datasetname form with the other DCB parameters. Suppose, for example, that there is a data set named YOUR.JCL.CNTL which is exactly like the new data set you want to create, except for the DSORG, which you want to specify as PS. In other words, YOUR.JCL.CNTL is a library, and you want to create a flat file that looks exactly the same in other respects. You code the DD statement something like this:

```
//NEW DD DISP=(NEW,CATLG),
//   UNIT=DISK,
//   SPACE=(TRK,(15),RLSE),
//   DSN=YOUR.FLAT.FILE,
//   DCB=(YOUR.JCL.CNTL,DSORG=PS)
```

Except for DSORG, all of the DCB attributes for the new data set named YOUR.FLAT.FILE will be copied from YOUR.JCL.CNTL except that the DSORG for the new data set will be PS, as you specified.

DCB=*.DDNAME

Similar in spirit to DCB=datasetname above. This one copies the DCB parameters you specified on an earlier DD statement, rather than copying from a data set.

The example below will create a data set named MY.VANDAMME.DATASET on ddname VANDAMME, and use the DCB parameters specified there. On the subsequent DD statement CHOMSKY, it will create another new data set named MY.CHOMSKY.DATASET, which will look exactly like the data set created on the AA DD statement. That is, it will have the same DCB parameters.

Example:

```
//DCBREF JOB 1,MSGCLASS=X
//ONE EXEC PGM=IEFBR14
//*
//AA DD DSN=MY.VANDAMME.DATASET,
//    DCB=(LRECL=80,
//    RECFM=FB,
//    BLKSIZE=23440,
//    DSORG=PS),
//    DISP=(NEW,CATLG),
//    SPACE=(TRK,5),
//    UNIT=SYSDA
//*
//CHOMSKY DD DISP=(NEW,CATLG),
//    UNIT=3380,
//    DSN=MY.CHOMSKY.DATASET,
//    DCB=*.AA,
//    SPACE=(TRK,5)
```

In general anything that uses an asterisk in this way is called a referback. You have already run into this in the section on DSN. If you use referbacks, keep in mind that the DD statement to which you are referring back must precede the statement doing the referring.

This has two other, more complicated forms, just as it did for DSN:

DCB=*.stepname.ddname

and:

DCB=*.stepname.procstepname.ddname

REFDD

Coding REFDD= is basically the same as coding a referback in the DCB parameter, except that, if you use it when creating a new data set, it also copies the SPACE allocation from the referenced data set.

It has the same complicated and simplified versions as the DCB referback form, which were explained in the REFERBACK part of the section on the DCB parameter.

The REFDD parameter is available only if you are using SMS (System Managed Storage) on your MVS system.

Example:

```
//SYSUT2 DD DSN=D.T.SUZUKI,
//    REFDD=*.SYSUT1, etc.
```

is equivalent to:

```
//SYSUT2 DD DSN=D.T.SUZUKI,
//    DCB=*.SYSUT1, etc.
```

ALTERNATE SOURCES OF DCB INFORMATION

Well, you certainly do know how to code the DCB parameter on that DD statement now, don't you? Thought so. You do, in fact. No doubt at all. Even if you skimmed half of this chapter very lightly, you know a good bit.

But before you go off feeling like an expert, you may as well pause to consider that there are two other places where MVS can look to find DCB information, other than the DD statement.

But hold, you say. You know one of them already. The data set itself.

That is, the DCB parameters that were specified when the data set was created. MVS saves those, if the data set resides either on disk or on a Standard Label or ASCII Label tape.

Right. That is why you can say:

```
//HAHA DD DISP=OLD,
//    DSN=GOOD.OLD.DATASET
```

without specifying any DCB information on the DD statement.

So, yes, MVS will look at the DCB parameters that were saved when the data set was created. That is, however, as they say, the last place he will look.

In other words, if you specify the DCB parameter on your DD statement, MVS will take your word for it, and not bother to look at the saved DCB information.

But there is one other place MVS looks, before considering the wishes you have expressed on the DD statement.

The program itself can contain DCB information for the file. If it does, then what the program specifies internally takes precedence over what you specify on the DD statement.

The order, then, is this:

If the program has the DCB coded internally, that is the DCB that is used.

If the program does not have the DCB coded within it, or if the program has only part of the DCB information coded, then MVS will glance over at your DD statement to pick up anything it can use. If you supply anything that the program has not specified, your DD statement information will be merged in with that from the program. This is of course called merging DCB parameters.

If anything is still missing, MVS will look at the DCB information that it has stored for the data set, which is probably what was saved when the data set was created. It will use what it finds there to supply any missing DCB information. That is, it will continue merging DCB parameters, as before. To complete the Data Control Block, as they say.

Of course, if your program then writes into the data set—not an unlikely occurrence—MVS will update its saved information when you close the data set. This update will be done using the complete merged DCB that was put together by the above described process.

That means that the saved information can change.

Occasionally someone messes up a data set by changing the DCB information in this way. IEBCOPY and the Linkage editor are the usual programs that are used, or rather misused, in this capacity. These programs do not specify any DCB information within themselves. They take whatever you give them. They have very little use for DCB information for their own processing. This means that you can specify DCB information on the DD statement accidentally, and your DCB information will be used to update the saved information when the program closes the data set.

Of course, messed up DCB information can also be fixed in this way, using the same programs and the same method. More about this when we come to the section of examples.

Remember the basic order. If the program specifies any DCB information internally, that wins. But the stuff you say in the DCB on the DD statement wins over whatever is saved with the data set itself.

How does your program specify DCB information internally? A couple of quick examples.

In a COBOL program, you can specify the BLKSIZE by using the BLOCK CONTAINS clause on the FD file definition. If your logical records are each 80 bytes long and you specify BLOCK CONTAINS 10 RECORDS then that program will demand that the BLKSIZE of the associated file must be 800. Usually you will not want to do this. You will prefer to omit the clause entirely or to say BLOCK CONTAINS 0 RECORDS. Then MVS will use whatever BLKSIZE is specified on the DD statement or what was saved with the data set itself.

In a PL/I program, you can specify the BLKSIZE in the ENVIRONMENT when you DECLARE the file. For example, you could say:

DCL FOOD FILE RECORD OUTPUT
ENV(FB RECSIZE(80) BLKSIZE(800)) ;

and thereby restrict your program to using, for the file named FOOD, only files with a RECFM FB, an LRECL of 80, and a BLKSIZE of 800. But this is usually a bad idea. The only merit of it is that it saves someone from having to specify DCB information on the DD statement if they DUMMY it out.

Again, the basic order. If the program specifies any DCB information internally, that takes precedence over any other source of DCB information.

Next MVS checks the DCB on the DD statement and uses it to fill in any information it doesn't already have from the internal program DCB information.

Last of all MVS checks what was saved with the data set itself.

BUFNO

Pronounced BUFF NO, meaning number of buffers. You do not need to specify this in general. If someday you happen to have a problem with a limited region size, that is, if you have too little memory available for your program, then you can maneuver a little by specifying BUFNO=1 in the DCB for all of your data sets, to minimize the amount of region used for buffers, and hence to leave more region leftover for your program to use for everything else. If you leave this parameter unmentioned, as you usually will, the system will generally allocate at least two buffers at the moment your program opens the data set, and then unallocate these buffers when your program closes the data set.

OPTCD

Almost useless, but there are two cases where you might conceivably be interested in this.

The first such case is OPTCD=J. You can use this if you are printing your output on a 3800 laser printer and you want to play with the fancy characters available thereon.

When using the 3800, you may select up to 4 fonts with the CHARS parameter. A font is a typestyle. Assuming that you have placed an ASA carriage control character in the first byte of each line you write out to be printed, you will be putting something called a TRC in the second byte of each line. TRC stands for Table Reference Character. It tells the printer which typestyle (font) to use to print that particular line, from among those you have specified in the CHARS parameter. Putting the digit zero in the TRC byte means that you want the first typestyle to be used, the digit one means you want the second font, 2 means the third font, and 3 means the 4th. Four is the limit.

That is the use of OPTCD=J. Read more about this in the section on Other DD Parameters, if you are interested.

OPTCD=Q represents the second case that serves any purpose you are ever likely to have. If you have received a tape from someone working on a non-IBM system, that tape may be written in ASCII.

ASCII, pronounced ASS KEY (really), is a code for representing characters in zeroes and ones. It is not the same as the code you use on the IBM mainframe. The code you use on the IBM is called EBCDIC, pronounced Ebb's a Dick (really).

So, you want to translate. MVS will do this for you automatically it knows the tape is an ASCII standard label tape. You tell MVS this by coding LABEL=(,AL). You do not need to code OPTCD=Q in this instance.

If however you have coded LABEL=(,NL) or LABEL=(,BLP) you need to include OPTCD=Q in the DCB for the input tape. OPTCD=Q will also cause the opposite translation to be performed on output, if you want to write a tape in ASCII to send to someone who wants it.

OPTCD=W means that a fancy write validity check is to be done when writing a tape.

OPTCD=B means end-of-file indicators will be ignored when reading tapes.

DEN

DEN means tape density. How close together the bits are on the tape. There exist some varieties of model 3420 type tape drive unit that can read and write tapes that are recorded either at 6250 bits on each inch of tape (6250 bits per inch, or 6250 BPI) or at 1600 bits per inch (1600 BPI). Such a tape drive is called a dual density tape drive. They also exist in an 800BPI/1600BPI version.

Thus you may someday find yourself in the position of having a dual density 1600BPI/6250BPI tape drive and wanting to write data onto it at 1600 bits per inch to send to someone who does not have the ability to read a tape recorded at 6250. You include DEN=3 in your DCB to cause the tape to be written at the lower density. DEN=3 means 1600BPI, DEN=4 means 6250BPI, and DEN=2 means 800BPI.

Note that all the files on the tape must be written at the same density.

On most systems the tape must also be initialized at that density. You should request that the operators give you a tape that has already been initialized at your chosen value of DEN.

When reading a tape you need not specify DEN.

Chapter 7

CONCATENATION AND SPECIAL DD NAMES

CONCATENATED DD STATEMENTS

By now you have a pretty good idea how to describe a data set using a DD statement.

Also you remember that the DDNAME, which starts in column three of your DD statement, must be the same as the file name within your program. That is, if your program says something like this:

READ FILE(INFILE) INTO(MYRECORD)

Well then you know you need to have a DD statement in your JCL that looks something like this:

```
//INFILE DD DISP=SHR,
//    DSN=MY.INPUT.FILE
```

Makes perfect sense.

But suppose half of your data is in one data set and the other half of it is in another?

Or suppose you are executing a program that looks at the library on the DDNAME called SYSLIB and searches through it for a particular member name, and in fact it looks for several members, and some of them are in one library, and other members are in another library?

Enter the concatenated DD statement.
It looks like this:

```
//INFILE DD DISP=SHR,
//   DSN=MY.ORIGINAL.INPUT.FILE
//   DD DISP=SHR,
//   DSN=SOME.OTHER.INPUT.FILE
```

Or, again:

```
//SYSLIB DD DISP=SHR,
//    DSN=MY.OWN.LIBRARY
//    DD DISP=SHR,
//    DSN=SOME.OTHER.LIBRARY
//    DD DISP=SHR,
//    DSN=SOME.THIRD.LIBRARY
```

You have, of course, noticed that the DDNAME field is blank on the add-on lines, but the operation field, DD, is included. The system assumes you would not do anything so seemingly silly unless you intended to group the lot together and treat them as if they were all one data set really.

Concatenated DD statements. You see them all the time.

A few things to keep in mind about them.

First: If by chance the various data sets in the group have different block sizes, then either specify the one with the largest block size first, or else override the DCB parameter on the first one so that the larger block size will be used for allocating buffers. Example:

```
//SYSLIB DD DISP=SHR,
//   DSN=BIG.BUFFER.LIBRARY
//   DD DISP=SHR,
//   DSN=SMALL.BLKSIZE.LIBRARY
```

Or, again:

```
//SYSLIB DD DISP=SHR,
//   DSN=SMALL.BLKSIZE.LIBRARY,
//   DCB=BIG.BUFFER.LIBRARY
//   DD DISP=SHR,
//   DSN=BIG.BUFFER.LIBRARY
```

The second thing is this. If the data sets you concatenate are libraries, and if they happen to contain some members with the same names, then the member that will be used at any particular time will be the one found first, that is, nearest the top of your concatenated list.

The third thing you want to know here is that order is important when you concatenate data sets on unlike device types.

If you concatenate a disk data set with an instream data set, the disk data set has to come first.

The order is: disk first, tape second, cards last.

There is one notable exception to this. If you are using an MVS/ESA system, it is likely that the ordinary traditional IBM-supplied program IEBGENER has been replaced with an entirely different IBM-supplied program that has the same name but costs extra and will do extra things. One of the extra things it will do is that it will put aside the above restriction on ordering unlike device types. The fancy version of IEBGENER will let you concatenate unlike device types in any order you like.

Now you know about concatenated DD statements.

Special ddnames

In the general case, you have one DD statement for each file your program uses. That is in fact the point of having DD statements. To connect the file names within the program with actual data files outside the program.

MVS, being a set of programs, wants data files too.

Some of these you can specify for it, with specially named DD statements.

133

The ddnames that MVS recognizes as having some particular meaning will now be described. These DD statements tell MVS to do particular special things for you, like produce a dump, or use a different catalog than usual, or look for your program in your own program library rather than in the MVS system program libraries. If you omit these special DD statements, MVS will assume the usual defaults.

STEPLIB and JOBLIB

When you want to execute a program, MVS wants to know where to get the program.

You tell MVS where to look for your programs by means of the STEPLIB and JOBLIB DD statements. STEPLIB applies to one particular step. JOBLIB applies to your entire job.

The JOBLIB statement, if you use one, is placed after the JOB statement but before the first EXEC statement.

A STEPLIB statement follows the EXEC statement for the step to which it applies, in with the rest of the DD statements for that step.

If you happen to include both a JOBLIB and a STEPLIB then MVS will search the STEPLIB and not look in the JOBLIB.

If a specified program is not found in the designated library, MVS will then search its own default libraries to find the program. The names of these default libraries are specified by the systems programmers responsible for MVS system maintenance at your site (They call their main list of default program libraries the LINK LIST, which they spell LNKLST).

Example: MVS will look in AFRICAN.PROGRAM.LIBRARY for the member named KWELA, and then MVS will look in JAPANESE.PROGRAM.LIBRARY for the member TEMPURA. If any member is not found, the default MVS system libraries will be searched.

```
//SMITH3H1 JOB 1,MSGCLASS=X
//STEP1  EXEC PGM=KWELA
//STEPLIB DD  DISP=SHR,
//  DSN=AFRICAN.PROGRAM.LIBRARY
//STEP2  EXEC PGM=TEMPURA
```

```
//SYSPRINT DD SYSOUT=*
//STEPLIB DD DISP=SHR,
// DSN=JAPANESE.PROGRAM.LIBRARY
//SYSIN  DD DISP=SHR,
//     DSN=SUZUKI.DATA
```

Example: MVS will look in AFRICAN.PROGRAM.LIBRARY for the members named KWELA, MBAQANGA, and INNUIT. If one of them is not there, then MVS will look in AMERICAN.PROGRAM.LIBRARY for the missing member. If either is not found, the default MVS system libraries will be searched.

```
//SMITH3H2 JOB 2,MSGCLASS=X
//JOBLIB DD DISP=SHR,
// DSN=AFRICAN.PROGRAM.LIBRARY
// DD DISP=SHR,
// DSN=AMERICAN.PROGRAM.LIBRARY
//STEP1 EXEC PGM=KWELA
//STEP2 EXEC PGM=MBAQANGA
//STEP3 EXEC PGM=INNUIT
```

Notice that, unlike DD statements in general, the JOBLIB DD statement is placed immediately after the JOB statement, before any EXEC statements. It is not associated with a particular step within the job.

If your program calls subroutines and builtin functions, MVS needs to know where to find them. Maybe you use a function that converts the current system date to a printable equivalent, for example, changing something like 022800 to February 28th, 2000. Maybe the function is called CDATE. There could be dozens of programs named CDATE in various libraries on various disks. You need to tell MVS which library or libraries to search.

If these subroutines and functions are not included as part of the load module, they can be brought in from STEPLIB or JOBLIB at execution time, just like the main program that calls them.

If, however, the subroutines are already included as part of the load module, this means that they were brought in from the ddname SYSLIB at the time when the linkage editor produced the load module. (The business of the linkage editor will be covered in Chapter 17.)

The point for you to understand at the moment is simply that these subroutines might be brought in from STEPLIB or JOBLIB at the time when your program executes, or, then again, they might not be, depending on how the options were specified when your program was linked. So you might, at the time your program executes, be able to control where the subroutines are obtained; or you might not. If you are, then STEPLIB or JOBLIB is searched to find the subroutines.

STEPCAT AND JOBCAT

When you specify a data set name on a DD statement, and the data set name is cataloged, MVS will look in its master catalog to find where the data set is. The master catalog may, in turn, refer MVS to some user catalog. For example, all data set names beginning with the prefix SALLY might be cataloged in a user catalog named PAYROLL.PROJECT.CATALOG, and the MVS master catalog may contain only a note saying that, if the high level qualifier of any data set is SALLY, then look for the actual information about it in PAYROLL.PROJECT.CATALOG.

This ought to be transparent to you. You ought never to have to specify a STEPCAT or JOBCAT.

Alas, sometimes reality is different.

In case you ever need to direct MVS to look for your data sets in some particular catalog, you use the STEPCAT and JOBCAT DD statements. STEPCAT applies to one particular step. JOBCAT applies to your entire job.

If MVS searches the STEPCAT or JOBCAT for a reference to a particular data set and fails to find it there, then MVS will search its own master catalog for the data set, just as if there had been no STEPCAT or JOBCAT present.

Notice that, when you use STEPCAT or JOBCAT, any new data sets you catalog during the course of your processing will then be cataloged in the specified catalog, and you will need to refer to that catalog in the future to find those data sets again. Obviously things can, through such methods, go from bad to worse.

Avoid the use of STEPCAT and JOBCAT altogether if you are using SMS (System Managed Storage) for any of your files.

For that matter, avoid the use of STEPCAT and JOBCAT in general whenever possible.

Example: MVS will look in SIAMESE.CATALOG for the data set ORIENTAL.RICE, and then MVS will look in PERSIAN.CATALOG for the data set FALAFEL; If either is not found, MVS will search the MVS master catalog for it:

```
//SMITH3H3 JOB 3,MSGCLASS=X
//STEP1 EXEC PGM=IEFBR14
//STEPCAT DD DISP=SHR,
//    DSN=SIAMESE.CATALOG
//LUNCH DD DISP=SHR,
//    DSN=ORIENTAL.RICE
//STEP2 EXEC PGM=IEFBR14
//SYSPRINT DD SYSOUT=*
//STEPCAT DD DISP=SHR,
//    DSN=PERSIAN.CATALOG
//LUNCH DD DISP=SHR,
//    DSN=FALAFEL
```

Example: MVS will look in SIAMESE.CATALOG for each of the data sets mentioned in the job below. If any are not found, then MVS will look in CALICO.CATALOG for the missing data sets; if they are still not found, MVS will search the MVS master catalog to find them:

```
//SMITH3H4 JOB 4,MSGCLASS=X
//JOBCAT DD DISP=SHR,
//    DSN=SIAMESE.CATALOG
//    DD DISP=SHR,
//    DSN=CALICO.CATALOG
```

```
//STEP1 EXEC PGM=ICHIBAN,
// PARM='/HAJIMEMASHO, KUDASAI'
//BEVERAGE DD DISP=SHR,
//   DSN=WAIN.WO.IPPON
//MAINDISH DD DISP=SHR,
//   DSN=SUSHI
//MUSTARD DD DISP=SHR,
//   DSN=KARASHI.WO.HITOBIN
//SIDEDISH DD DISP=SHR,
//   DSN=POTETO.CHIPPU
//   DD DISP=SHR,
//   DSN=SPRING.ROLLS
//KUDAMOAO DD DISP=SHR,
//   DSN=MOMO.WO.SUKOSHI
//   DD DISP=SHR,
//   DSN=MOMO.WO.ICHIGO
//STEP2 EXEC PGM=APPLEPIE
//DESSERT DD DISP=SHR,
//   DSN=APPLE.PIE
//   DD DISP=SHR,
//   DSN=PEACH.ICE.CREAM
//FRUIT  DD DISP=SHR,
//   DSN=APPLES.ORANGES.AND.BANANAS
//SIDEDISH DD DISP=SHR,
//   DSN=POTATO.CHIPS
//   DD DISP=SHR,
//   DSN=SPRING.ROLLS
//SNACKS  DD DISP=SHR,
//   DSN=PEANUTS.AND.POPCORN
```

Notice that, like JOBLIB, but unlike DD statements in general, the JOBCAT DD statement is placed immediately after the JOB statement, before any EXEC statements. It is not associated with a particular step within the job.

DUMPS

If your program produces an ABEND dump, MVS wants to know what kind of dump to produce, and where to put it.

You have a choice of ddnames for your dump, including SYSABEND and SYSUDUMP. A SYSABEND DD statement will usually get you a bigger dump, sort of an unabridged version. SYSUDUMP is the condensed version. Actually the people who install and maintain MVS at your company—the systems and operations staff—choose how much is included in each of these types of dump, using the operator command CD (which means Change Dump). If you leave out the dump statements entirely, then MVS will not produce a dump for you.

The ddname PLIDUMP is used only by PL/I. If a PL/I program abends, the PL/I routines can write a special PL/I formatted dump onto the ddname PLIDUMP.

SYSPRINT

Not used by MVS itself, the ddname SYSPRINT is, however, used by PL/I to write PL/I error messages. Some other programming languages also use this name. Others may use some other name such as SYSDBOUT or FT06F001.

Most IBM Utility programs also use SYSPRINT for error and informational messages.

SYSIN

Many programs use SYSIN as the ddname from which to read input cards, especially control cards or parameter cards. Most IBM Utility programs use it for control cards, and most compilers use it to read your program statements.

Because SYSIN is so commonly used for input cards, MVS makes an interesting assumption. If MVS is processing your JCL and it comes to an unexpected non-JCL line, it says to itself, Oh; this must be input data for the program; probably SYSIN in fact. And MVS generates—makes up for you—a DD statement named SYSIN, which it inserts just before the first of the unexpected non-JCL lines. MVS tells you that it has done this by including, in your JCL listing, a message saying:

//SYSIN DD * GENERATED STATEMENT

SYSOUT

Not used by MVS itself, the ddname SYSOUT is, however, used by COBOL to write the output of TRACE and DISPLAY statements.

IEFRDER

This will be discussed in Chapter 12, the chapter on procedures. But you should know that it is special.

For one thing, IMS writes its log to the ddname IEFRDER.

But, quite apart from that, MVS uses the name IEFRDER to construct a DD statement in certain cases related to procedures.

Chapter 8

OTHER DD STATEMENT PARAMETERS:

USE OF THE DUMMY PARAMETER AND THE DDNAME PARAMETER

These are contrivances for avoiding the immediate specification of an actual useful data set to be associated with a DD statement.

DUMMY tells MVS to ignore the file.

For example, if you say //SYSIN DD DUMMY when you execute IEBGENER, as you did in the preceding section, then you are telling MVS this:

"Listen, this program I'm executing—IEBGENER—is going to issue an OPEN for a file named SYSIN. Well, I don't really have any SYSIN data to give it. But I don't want it to blow up on me. Do this. When GENER opens the file, just let him open it as if there were really something there. As soon as he tries to issue a READ, tell him he's already at the end of the data. Think it'll work? Ah, go ahead. It'll work." It usually works.

You'll want to learn to call these IBM-supplied programs by their familiar names. GENER for IEBGENER. B.R. Fourteen for IEFBR14. The first three letters, if pronounced, are generally pronounced as if they were initials: I.E.B. COPY for IEBCOPY, which is, for some reason, rarely referred to by the more informal short form of the name. Example of computer humor: If someone suggests executing I.E.B. Eyeball that means take a close look at something.

What else about DUMMY? Two things to know.

One is that you can code other parameters after the DUMMY and most of them will be ignored.

The other is that you can code the DCB parameter and it will be used, if the program expects to find DCB information on that particular DD statement.

Many programs do have this expectation, so you may sometimes need to code DCB information on a DUMMY DD statement.

Example: Program PIRANHA usually reads a file from the DD statement FOOD, which usually looks like this:

```
//F  EXEC PGM=PIRANHA
//FOOD DD DISP=OLD,
//   DSN=DEAD.MEAT
```

In the above example, the data set DEAD.MEAT will be processed by PIRANHA.

Now you want something different.

You want the program to ignore the FOOD DD statement.

However, PIRANHA expects to obtain DCB information from the DD statement when it opens the file, because PIRANHA can process a variety of formats of FOOD file, and it sets up certain things differently internally depending on what type of FOOD it gets.

You decide to use the lazy form of the DCB parameter, since the data set PIRANHA used the last time still actually exists (although you do not want it to be used for FOOD in this case). You code the following instead of the above:

```
//F  EXEC PGM=PIRANHA
//FOOD DD DUMMY,DCB=DEAD.MEAT
```

DUMMY tells MVS to ignore the file.

As with BUFNO, if someday you happen to have a problem with a limited region size, that is, if you have too little memory available for your program, you can save memory by using the smallest possible blocksize for each file that is dummied out.

So much for DUMMY.

What does the DDNAME parameter do?

Example:

```
//F   EXEC PGM=PIRANHA
//FOOD DD DDNAME=SYSIN
//SYSIN DD *
BANANAS
APPLES
TANGERINES
APRICOTS
SPINACH
```

The DDNAME parameter tells MVS to use some subsequent file as a substitute for the first. Yes, you can confuse some versions of MVS by using humorous statements such as

```
//SYSIN DD DDNAME=SYSIN
```

but you are unlikely to obtain any good results from doing so.

The DDNAME parameter may seem a pointless contrivance at this point, but it will prove useful when we come to the chapter on procedures, Chapter 12.

DYNAM

DYNAM means dynamic allocation. What it amounts to is this: You code almost nothing on the DD statement. Even the ddname you choose is unimportant. The program you execute then makes up a DD statement when it wants to use one, using as a base the DD DYNAM you have provided.

Most programs are not smart enough to do this. Most of those that are, are written in assembler language.

TSO uses DD DYNAM a lot. For example, when you use a text editor under TSO, the text editor uses one of the DD DYNAM statements to allocate the data set you want to edit. These dynamic allocation DD statements are provided in the JCL that controls your TSO session. Such a set of JCL is called a LOGON Procedure.

Since all DD DYNAM statements look pretty much the same, IBM added a parameter called DYNAMNBR to the EXEC statement. If you code DYNAMNBR=99 on the EXEC statement, that counts the same as if you had coded 99 separate DD DYNAM statements. Obviously DYNAMNBR is the more widely used method. The following two examples are equivalent, and demonstrate how to code DD DYNAM and DYNAMNBR:

```
//IKJACCNT EXEC PGM=IKJEFT01,
//     PARM=ISPF,DYNAMNBR=5
```

is the same as coding:

```
//IKJACCNT EXEC PGM=IKJEFT01,
//     PARM=ISPF
//NAME01 DD DYNAM
//NAME02 DD DYNAM
//NAME03 DD DYNAM
//NAME04 DD DYNAM
//NAME05 DD DYNAM
```

FREE

Coding FREE=CLOSE on a DD statement causes MVS to deallocate the data set as soon as your program closes the file.

If it is a SYSOUT file, this causes the file to be eligible for printing immediately, rather than waiting until your program ends.

If it is an ordinary data set, it frees the data set for other programs that may be waiting to use it.

If you have FREE=CLOSE on a DD statement, your program cannot open the file again after closing it. It is as if the DD statement disappears as soon as the file is closed.

AMP

This is rarely useful, but you should know what it means when you see it.

You do not use the DCB parameter in JCL with VSAM data sets.

The DCB-like information, such as record length, is always stored in a catalog for VSAM data sets. Consequently you do not need this sort of parameter with VSAM, unless you are trying to override some of the catalog information.

When VSAM was invented, the AMP parameter was invented with it, to take the place of the DCB parameter when VSAM data sets are processed.

AMP subparameters must be specified enclosed in single quotes (apostrophes) if anything more complicated than AMP=AMORG is coded.

The first subparameter you will see for AMP is almost always AMORG. AMORG, in the spirit of DSORG, means that the data set is a VSAM data set.

Since AMP is only ever specified for VSAM data sets, it is difficult to see why the AMORG subparameter was ever thought necessary.

AMP=AMORG is required in the rather unusual circumstance that you are processing a VSAM data set through the ISAM-to-VSAM interface, and overriding the RECFM.

In other words, the program thinks it is getting an ISAM data set but you are giving it a VSAM one instead; and the program expects a record format other than V, that is, varying, which is the default for VSAM. (ISAM is an extinct species of data set. Programs using it were forced to evolve to use VSAM.)

The basic DCB-like things you can specify through AMP are the number of data buffers, specified as BUFND, the number of index buffers, specified as BUFNI, the maximum amount to be used for buffer space altogether, specified as BUFSP, and the record format, specified as RECFM.

You may as well see the ugly example:

    //OLDJCL EXEC PGM=ANCIENT

```
//ISAM  DD DSN=VSAM.KSDS,
//    DISP=OLD,
//    AMP=('AMORG,RECFM=FB')
```

Telling MVS where to put it:
The UNIT, VOL, and LABEL parameters

If you want MVS to create a new data set for you, you will usually want to keep it either on tape or on disk

Only sequential files can be kept on tape, that is, flat files; not libraries, not IMS data bases, not VSAM files, not DB2 tables. Nothing fancy. You can create backup copies of fancy files on tape, but you cannot use the tape copies for anything except recreating the files on disk. Any sort of fancy file has to be on disk to be useful.

If you are creating a flat file that is quite large, and you do not plan to use it very often, then you should put it on tape. If you are creating a backup copy of a data set, that ought to go on tape. When someone in another location asks you to post a copy of some data, put it on a tape. Except for these cases, you should prefer disk rather than tape.

Having decided on either tape or disk, you will inform MVS of your decision through the use of the UNIT parameter. You may be able to say simply UNIT=TAPE or UNIT=DISK.

There are, however, different types of tape unit, and different types of disk unit.

The different models of tape drives that IBM builds, or has built, are identified by different model numbers, such as 3420 and 3480. Your company may have one or the other of these types, or both, or some other types. The most common type at present is the 3480. This can be specified in JCL as UNIT=3480.

The tapes that are used with the 3480 are relatively small and are packaged in rectangular plastic cases, making them look something like oversized audio cassette tapes. Thus 3480 tapes are sometimes referred to in jargon as square tapes. They are also called tape cartridges.

The tapes that are used with the 3420 are called round tapes. If a round tape is distributed containing a copy of some small software package, the tape may be as small as a dessert plate and is sometimes called a DTR which is short for distribution tape reel. However, most round tapes are big, about the diameter of a large dinner plate, each tape reel holding 2400 feet of tape. In appearance they resemble the audio tape used with the old reel-to-reel tape recorders, or reels of Super 8 home movie film. Round tapes are sometimes called half inch tapes, because half an inch is the width of the tape.

Competitors of IBM make tape drives that deliberately resemble the IBM models. These are specified in JCL as the IBM model numbers which they resemble.

There are different model numbers for tape drive units just as there are for disks. The various models differ as to size, speed, cost, and storage capacity. The most common at present is the 3380. You can say UNIT=3380, but this brings us to another snag. Two snags.

The first snag is minor. Suppose you specify UNIT=3380 in all of your JCL and then one day your company decides to ship out all of the 3380 disks and replace them with something else. A new expensive model perhaps, or some old 3350 disks that they acquired for next to nothing. You have to change all your JCL if that happens.

And the other snag?

In all likelihood your company has many 3380 disks. You are not supposed to leave your data sets just lying around anyplace. You are expected to put them on one of the selected disks allocated to your project or group.

MVS allows the people who set up the system configuration at your company to make up arbitrary names to designate different groups of disks. Thus they might set up one group to be called UNIT=PROD and another to be called UNIT=TEST and another to be called UNIT=APOLLO. How do you know what names they have chosen? You have to ask, or else find out by looking at other people's JCL and assuming they have it right.

The name SYSDA is a made up name traditionally used to designate disks that are available for general use on a short term basis. This is a common name, perhaps because IBM distributes a lot of JCL that uses the name SYSDA to describe any disk. SYSSQ and SYSALLDA are other such names.

Some places will therefore have a group named SYSDA defined to include every disk on the system, and some other places will have SYSDA defined as including only some of their disks, and finally a few places might tell you that you are not allowed to use SYSDA at all. You have to find out the local customs.

UNIT=VIO, by the way, means virtual disk. Areas of virtual memory are used as pretend disk. These areas are subject to being paged in and out between real memory and disk, just like the rest of your program's memory, so the pretence is only partial. (You remember paging from chapter 1.)

You can use VIO for temporary data sets only, obviously. All of your areas of memory are lost when your job ends.

Ought you to use VIO? Well, if nothing else much is running on the machine, VIO can be pretty speedy, since there is no competition with other programs for the use of real memory. On a busy machine, VIO is not too useful, except in the case where you happen to be forced to use an itsy-bitsy BLKSIZE, something like BLKSIZE=800. With a tiny BLKSIZE, using VIO is a good trick to minimize I/O and hence make your job run faster.

Of course, the systems programmers at your company can make up names other than VIO, and assign those names to mean VIO. Usually they pick names that begin with V, like V3330, V3380, V2314, V3350, V3390, and so on. But really they can use any arbitrary names.

Disks can be grouped into arbitrary sets and assigned names just as tapes can. Most places will have a group named UNIT=TAPE, but you cannot assume that any particular place does, neither can you assume that it refers to the type of tape unit you need to use. You almost have to ask someone; or look at other people's JCL and assume the same units will meet your needs as have met theirs.

Another point about using the UNIT parameter with tapes. It is a good idea to code the DEFER subparameter. This means that MVS will not issue a message to the operator to mount your tape on the tape drive until your program actually attempts to use it. It saves the operator the trouble of mounting the tape if your job fails before using the tape. It is coded UNIT=(TAPE,,DEFER) rather than simply UNIT=TAPE. Or, of course, it might be coded UNIT=(3480,,DEFER) or UNIT=(3420,,DEFER), or whatever is appropriate to the type of tape unit you are requesting.

DEFER is nonsensical when referring to a disk. In the past there were removable disks. The 2311, the 2314, and the 3330, for example. But modern disks are permanently mounted.

Another good subparameter of UNIT is AFF.

An abbreviation for affinity. To mean that you want a second DD statement to use the same unit as some other DD statement. (A very loose interpretation of the meaning of the word affinity, but there it is) .

For example, suppose that you have the data sets named FEBRUARY.INVOICES and FEBRUARY.BILLS as the first and second data sets on the same tape, a tape called WANDA; and that your program refers to these through the ddnames INVOICES and BILLS. You could specify UNIT=TAPE on the DD statement for FEBRUARY.INVOICES and then specify UNIT=AFF=INVOICES on the DD statement for BILLS. Like so:

```
//GO4IT  EXEC PGM=MYPGM
//INVOICES DD DISP=OLD,
//     DSN=FEBRUARY.INVOICES,
//     VOL=(,RETAIN,
//     SER=WANDA),
//     LABEL=(1,SL),
//     UNIT=(TAPE,,DEFER)
//BILLS  DD DISP=OLD,
//     DSN=FEBRUARY.BILLS,
//     VOL=(,RETAIN,
//     SER=WANDA),
//     LABEL=(2,SL),
//     UNIT=AFF=INVOICES
```

We explain about VOL and LABEL next, contain yourself.

But why do you want to say UNIT=AFF=INVOICES in the above example? Why not just say UNIT=TAPE again?

Saying UNIT=AFF=INVOICES means that BILLS will use the same physical tape drive as INVOICES, with the result that the operator will be asked to mount the tape only once, rather than twice. Consideration for others. Who knows, you might want help from that very computer operator some night when your car fails to start.

Even if you aren't big on consideration for others, you might at least want to consider yourself: you can save considerable time by minimizing tape mounts. Especially if your job uses multiple files on the same tape. Tape mounts take time. Even if you have an automated robot tape library on wheels.

An aside: If you use two data sets from the same tape in your program, remember to CLOSE the first file before you OPEN the second one. You cannot have both open at the same time.

So much for UNIT.

Now about VOL.

As you recall, any particular tape is identified by a volume serial number of up to 6 characters in length. The volume is referred to in JCL as VOLUME or VOL, whichever you prefer to use. VOL has a keyword subparameter called SER which is used to designate the volume serial number. Thus if your tape has ANGELA for its volume serial number, you refer to this in JCL as VOL=SER=ANGELA in the simplest case.

You may also, of course, specify the RETAIN subparameter of VOL to indicate that this particular tape volume is to be retained on the tape drive for use by subsequent steps in your job. This is coded VOL=(,RETAIN,SER=ANGELA) or, in place of ANGELA, the volume serial number (known in conversation as VOL SER, pronounced Vahlsehr) of your particular tape. DERVLA or BARBIE perhaps. You can use shorter vol-sers, but 6 characters is the maximum allowable. FIFI and DIDI, for illustration, are okay, whereas MADONNA and MARILYN are not.

If you fail to code RETAIN and you use the same tape in more than one step of your job, the operator will usually be called upon to mount your tape again for each such step.

Worse, the tape may be called for on a different tape drive each time. For example, if your company has twenty identical 3480 tape drives in the computer room, MVS may call on the operator to mount the tape on a different one each time.

It saves wear on the machines that way.

This ordering, however, is a choice made by the people who set up MVS at your site, and they might have set it up to use the tape drive with the lowest address every time, or start at the lowest and use the next highest each time, or, of course, select one at random each time.

Use RETAIN. It does no harm, even if you use the tape for only one step. If MVS needs the tape drive for another job, and your job has retained a tape but is not using it in the step that is running at the time, then MVS will kick the tape down and allocate the unit to the other job.

Form good habits while you're young. And remember, other people are going to copy your JCL, and you'll be setting a good example. Yes, they will. They will copy it. Maybe not today or tomorrow, but they will. You watch.

The RETAIN subparameter of VOL is nonsensical for disks these days, but you may occasionally see it if you are looking at very old JCL. Just ignore it. MVS does.

VOL is not usually specified for disks, but it can be.

Ordinarily one will specify only the UNIT parameter for disk, and let MVS choose which particular disk volume to use from among those available in the UNIT group that has been requested.

However, you do need to specify the VOL or VOLUME parameter if you refer to an uncataloged disk data set that already exists.

There are a couple of ways this can happen.

Normally, when someone (yourself for example) creates a new data set on disk, the person will specify DISP=(NEW,CATLG) to cause a catalog entry to be created for the data set. The catalog entry will tell the name of the volume where MVS has put the data set. This makes it easy for MVS to find the data set again.

Now you know what a catalog is.

It is a place where MVS keeps a big list of the names of data sets, and where they are.

Disk data sets should generally be cataloged, that is, they should be on the list.

Occasionally, however, someone will create a disk data set saying DISP=(NEW,KEEP) instead of DISP=(NEW,CATLG), by mistake, KEEP being the accepted custom for tapes but not for disks.

In such a case you need to find out the name of the volume where MVS placed the data set, and specify that volume name in the VOL parameter when you go to look for the data set again. Hopefully you will then say DISP=(OLD,CATLG) to rectify the original oversight. (Or catalog it using SPF option 3.2 under TSO.)

A word of warning. Most installations have a policy of automatically deleting, in the dead of night, any uncataloged disk data sets that may be found to exist.

Another example of an uncataloged disk data set situation. Which requires first another definition. Shared DASD.

DASD is an acronym for Direct Access Storage Devices. That means disk. The point is that you can access different parts of a disk directly, in the same way you can pick up a phonograph arm and place the needle down on a different part of the record. Direct access. As opposed to sequential access, which is what you have for computer tapes, which are very like audio cassette tapes in that respect.

Now, Shared DASD:

Suppose you have two computers in your computer room and they are both wired up to some or all of the disks. You can use those disks from either computer. Share them.

That is shared DASD. Pronounced to be a near rhyme for nasty or even daz dee.

Each of your two computers, of course, runs its own separate copy of MVS, and each MVS system has its own separate master catalog. There may be other catalogs (called user catalogs) that are shared, or there might not be. But each MVS always has its own master catalog. Actually, the master catalog of each MVS system can be treated as a user catalog on the other system, but our example involves the case where the catalogs on the two systems are kept sufficiently separate that—you guessed it— you create a new data set and catalog it on one of the systems, but the other system is not able to find it by searching through the catalogs for a pointer to it.

Same simple solution as before. DISP=(OLD,CATLG) combined with VOL=SER= the name of the volume. You find out the name of the volume by looking at the JCL listing from the job that created the data set, or by looking at the data set information under TSO on the system where it was created and is cataloged (for example, using SPF 3.2, if you use SPF).

Now you know the basics of using UNIT and VOL.

If you are using tape, you will also need the LABEL parameter, which we will cover next. If you are using disk you will need the SPACE parameter, which we will cover later in this Chapter in the "How Big Is It?" section.

So what about LABEL?

Two subparameters of LABEL concern us immediately. Both are positional. The default for them is LABEL=(1,SL) which we will now explain.

A computer tape is pretty big. That is, it can hold a lot of data.

In fact the data you will put on the tape at any one time will probably use up only a fraction of the tape. Like recording just one song on a 90 minute cassette tape.

It seems like a shame to waste the rest of the tape.

As luck would have it, you need not waste it.

You can put your next set of data on the tape after the first set. Like recording a second song on a cassette. You can, in fact, put any number of data sets on the same tape, as long as they will fit, just like the songs on the cassette.

Remember the 1 in the LABEL=(1,SL) above? That means the first song on the tape, or, rather, the first data set.

If you said LABEL=(4,SL) what would the 4 mean? Right, it would mean the fourth data set on the tape.

That number is called the file number.

The word file has now acquired at least three separate meanings. It is used as a synonym for ddname. It is sometimes used as a synonym for data set name, although this use is discouraged because of the ambiguity. And now it is also used as the relative number of the data set on tape. Oh well. File. There it is.

Question of order: If you have ten files on a tape, you can read them back in any order you wish. You cannot, however, write a 12th file until after you have written an 11th.

Now what about the SL?

It means Standard Label.

Normally MVS will write some control information at the beginning of the tape, and before and after each data set on the tape. This information includes useful items such as the volume serial number of the tape, the name of the data set, and all of the DCB information for the data set. This can be handy when you are trying to figure out what some antique tape contains. Standard Labels. Good with MVS.

If you are creating a tape to send to someone for use with a non-MVS system, maybe even a non-IBM system, then you might want to omit the standard labels. In this case you had best created a non-labeled tape, specified as NL in place of SL. Unless they specifically requested an ASCII Label or ASCII Standard Label tape, in which case you specify AL.

There are other possibilities, for example you can call an assembler language subroutine that you write yourself to create your own non-standard labels (NSL), but you do not need to bother with that just now. NL and SL are the normal choices. You will usually do best to specify SL if you are creating a tape that will later be read as input on an MVS system, and NL when creating other tapes (unless AL is specifically requested).

BLP means Bypass Label Processing. It means that you treat the labels themselves as data, the same as the data files.

If you omit the LABEL parameter, the default is LABEL=(1,SL). This is fine for the first file. If you have a tape that already has 20 files on it, be careful.

If you write onto the tape and forget to specify the LABEL parameter, LABEL=1 will be assumed—no error message—and you will overwrite your existing data, starting at the beginning of file 1 of the tape. Any data that you do not succeed in overwriting is recoverable only with difficulty and the use of BLP. So, be careful.

One last note about tape labels.

You obtain a tape by requesting it from someone, usually someone in the computer room or the tape library. These tapes will already have been initialized either having or not having standard labels. Tell the person which type you want. Avoid initializing it yourself.

As far as disks go, all are standard labeled, so you can omit the label parameter for disks, accepting the default of (1,SL).

There are two more subparameters of LABEL that are meaningful for disks as well as tapes. EXPDT means expiration date, and RETPD means retention period. The expiration date is expressed as a date in YYDDD format; for example, EXPDT=99365 to indicate the 365th day of year 99, or EXPDT=05005 for January 5th of year 05. The retention period is expressed as a number of days, for example, RETPD=90 for a retention period of 90 days.

Specifying a retention period or an expiration date will not really prevent a data set from being overwritten or deleted before that date. All it does is cause a reply to be requested from the operator as to whether or not it is okay to overwrite the data set. For example, suppose you create a data set on the tape WANDA with an expiration date of 99365, using a DD statement that looks something like this:

```
//SYSUT2 DD DISP=(NEW,KEEP),
//    DSN=FIRST,
//    VOL=(,RETAIN,
//     SER=WANDA),
//    UNIT=(TAPE,,DEFER),
//    LABEL=(1,SL,
//     EXPDT=99365)
```

Now if you try to overwrite the data in the next step of your job by saying:

```
//SYSUT2 DD DISP=(NEW,KEEP),
// VOL=(,RETAIN,SER=WANDA),
// UNIT=(TAPE,,DEFER),
// DSN=MISTAKE, LABEL=(2,SL),
```

Notice the misplaced blank space before the LABEL. All that will happen is that MVS will write a message to the operator enquiring as to whether or not it is okay for you to overwrite the FIRST file. If the operator gives the go-ahead, your program will go ahead and overwrite the file. If the operator does not say it is okay, then MVS will not allow your program to proceed. As you can see, expiration dates and retention periods have limited usefulness.

These dates are even less reliable if used on a tape data set other than the first one on the tape.

Example: Suppose you have written three small files on a tape, and you have put an expiration date on the third one.

The next step of your job writes another file on the tape. You meant to have it write the fourth file, but you made a mistake and omitted the LABEL parameter.

What happens? Correct, MVS assumes you want LABEL=(1,SL), the default. Now suppose you write a very large file. What happens? Correct, you overwrite all of the data on the first three files, regardless of the expiration date you had on the third one. Oh, well. Live and learn. You'll be more careful with that LABEL parameter next time.

Despite the limited usefulness of the expiration date, some tape management systems use it as a sort of secret password. If you specify the right date, you get to do special tape management things. This is a reasonable use of EXPDT. So if you see a funny expiration date in somebody's JCL on an MVS system with a tape management system, that is probably the point of it.

What happens if you ask for a tape unit, but you do not specify a particular volume? MVS asks the operator to mount a scratch tape. This means the operator is free to mount any tape at all. At most sites, the operators have a group of tapes set aside to use in such cases. This group of tapes is known as a pool of scratch tapes.

What happens if your program does ask for a specific tape volume and writes so much data onto the tape that the data fills up the tape, and the program still tries to keep writing more data? In most cases, MVS will ask the operator to mount a scratch tape, and then your program will write the rest of its data onto the scratch tape.

What's wrong with this picture?

When your job ends, the scratch tape you have used is returned to the pool of scratch tapes, meaning any other program that asks for a scratch tape can use the same one you used. It can then overwrite your data, and your data will be lost.

Oh well.

At many companies, the operators automatically assume that, if your program calls for a scratch tape, it must be a mistake. They may ring you on the telephone, and/or they may cancel your job, or they may just mount a scratch tape. Customs vary. If they cancel your job, your job ends with a 222 abend code. Abend 222 means operator cancel.

You now know the basics of the use of the VOL, UNIT, and LABEL parameters. You can create a new data set and tell MVS where to put it.

How Big Is It? SPACE on Disk

General Description

Disk is unlike tape in that locations on disk can be accessed directly, whereas access to a tape is inherently sequential.

In this respect a disk resembles a phonograph record or a CD, while tape resembles audio cassette tape.

One can lift the phonograph arm and place the needle down again at the beginning of a selected song.

With a cassette tape, one must play through, or fast forward through, all of the intervening length of tape before accessing the desired song.

Tape is sequential access.

Disk is direct access. (Those are vocabulary items: sequential access and direct access.)

A disk is, however, unlike a phonograph record or CD in this: a disk has more than one read/write head. (A read/write head on a disk is the equivalent of a needle on a phonograph.)

A 3380 disk has 15 read/write heads.

Sort of as if a phonograph turntable were to have fifteen associated needles.

You might at some time have seen a record changer.

It was a device that would allow one to stack several phonograph records on top of each other, on the same turntable, at a moderate elevation above the playing surface. These were then dropped down one at a time and played by the single phonograph needle.

Imagine that mechanism. A thin rod passed through the holes in the centers of several phonograph records (which we will call platters). Say there are 8 platters.

Now imagine that, instead of each platter lying flush against the next, the platters are slightly separated from one another by spacers. Something like rubber washers or empty spools from cellophane tape or from sewing thread.

Further imagine—you have a good imagination, right?—imagine there are 8 phonograph arms on this turntable, rather than just one. The 8 arms are arranged so that each of the eight needles touches the top of one of the eight platters.

Make it better than that. Imagine each arm has two needles, one on the top and one on the bottom, enabling the bottoms of the platters to be played at the same time as the tops.

Actually, one of the needles is missing, so really there are only 15 of them altogether. (2x8=16;16-1=15.) And they aren't phonograph needles at all, they are of course read/write heads, and the platters are magnetic disk platters rather than phonograph records. And one of the surfaces, like one of the read/write heads, is unavailable, so there are 15 surfaces and 15 read/write heads.

The eight arms do not move independently of each other. All eight move simultaneously. Like a fork with eight tines.

Try this:

Put your fingers between the next few pages of the book you're holding. Index finger between this page and the following page, middle finger between that page and the next, next fingers separating the next pages.

Your fingers are the access arms. The pages are the disk surfaces.

Move your hand up to the top of the page, then down to the bottom of the page, with your fingers between the pages. You can push your fingers in deeper, then pull them back so only the tips are still between the pages.

You can move your hand up and down and your fingers in and out. This is the way the access arms move with a disk.

Well, it would be if this was a round book and you rotated it instead of just moving your fingers up and down from the top to the bottom.

Now you have a sort of a picture of the storage mechanism known as a magnetic disk.

Actually some of the newer disks are not really organized like that at all, but the terminology was developed from that sort of picture.

Old disk volumes were removable from the disk drive units. (As PC floppy disks are removable.) Modern disk volumes are permanently mounted, which means that the read-write mechanism is combined with the platters in the same package, like a PC hard disk.

Remember the phonograph record?

One side of a phonograph record has of course only one groove, a very long spiral.

Magnetic disk is different. The pattern on a surface of a 3380 magnetic disk should be pictured as if it is composed of 885 concentric circles.

Each such circle on a 3380 disk can hold up to 47,476 bytes of data. The circle is called a track, sometimes abbreviated TRK. In JCL it is abbreviated TRK and pronounced track.

On a 3390 disk, a track can hold 56,664 bytes of data. We use 3380 in our examples because they are now the most common type of disk.

With an additional extension of imagination, you can easily see that the outermost track of the topmost available surface, considered together with the outermost track of the lowest available surface, and simultaneously together with the counterpart outermost tracks of each of the 13 intervening surfaces, taken together form an imaginary cylinder.

Pronounced cylinder.

Abbreviated CYL.

Known in JCL as CYL, usually pronounced as cylinder or cylinders but sometimes pronounced sil or sils.

Similarly the innermost tracks taken together form another cylinder, and in the same way the entire disk is composed of a set of 885 concentric cylinders, each cylinder being composed of one track from each surface.

All 15 tracks in any one particular cylinder can be accessed without any movement on the part of the read/write heads. The heads move together like the tips of the tines of a fork.

The tracks that together form a cylinder are referred to as contiguous tracks. Adjacent concentric cylinders are referred to as contiguous cylinders. Two contiguous cylinders are also 30 contiguous tracks. In general these things are called contiguous space.

There are 885 cylinders on an IBM model 3380 disk volume. Each cylinder contains 15 tracks. Each track can contain up to 47,476 characters of data (bytes). Each track on a 3390 can hold up to 56,664 bytes.

The double density disks have twice the number of cylinders, that is, 1770 such cylinders for a 3380 rather than 885.

So a 3380 disk volume is fairly big.

These disk volumes, by the way, come together in boxes of 4, and 4 such volumes are therefore sometimes referred to as a 3380 disk unit, but this is a different meaning of the word unit than the JCL meaning of UNIT. You should know about it only so you can avoid being confused if you hear someone else use it in this non-JCL sense. A string of disks, again by the way, means several disks cabled together one after the next onto the same disk controller (disk control unit, another meaning for unit, again not a JCL meaning). A string of 3380 disks is usually 16 volumes, that is, 4 physical boxes. (If there are fewer than 4 boxes, this is known as a short string.)

But back to the individual disk volume.

Also called a disk pack.

Each and every track has an address.

Many physical records can be contained on each track.

Each physical record on the track has an address.

The disk itself also has an address, called a unit address.

In short, we can locate any data on disk directly by means of these addresses.

How nice.

So, the disks being big and accessible, each disk is normally used to hold a large number of data sets, belonging to various people.

MVS remembers where they all are.

When you set up a new data set, MVS marks out a little place on disk for it.

Like Tom Cruise claiming his plot of land in the film "Far and Away".

The smallest your plot of space can be is one track

The upper limit varies depending on the type of data set, but even the smallest maximum would allow you one entire volume. If one were available.

So, when MVS goes to mark out the little place where your new data set will reside, it needs to know how much territory to reserve for you. Something more definite than the range of 1 track to 1770 cylinders.

You tell MVS this information by means of the SPACE parameter in your JCL.

There are a lot of positional subparameters for SPACE.

THE FIRST AND SECOND POSITIONAL SUBPARAMETERS

The first is easy, something like TRK or CYL.

MVS uses that item to interpret the significance of the number(s) which immediately follow it. For example, SPACE=(TRK,1) would mean one track, whereas SPACE=(CYL,1) would mean one cylinder, which amounts to 15 tracks.

SPACE=(TRK,15) would not necessarily get you a cylinder, of course. It might get you non-contiguous chunks that add up to 15 tracks. MVS is, however, smart enough to try to find contiguous tracks for you when it can.

Specifying CYL rather than TRK is slightly more efficient with respect to the speed with which MVS reads and writes your data. Performance, as they say.

In units of cylinders, as they often say, introducing yet another non-JCL meaning for the word unit.

Back to this first positional subparameter, TRK or CYL.

Sometimes you will see a number in the first position rather than one of these abbreviations.

Such a number, in such a case, is considered to signify a number of bytes. MVS then figures out for you how many tracks that would come out to be, and gives you that many tracks, rounded up to the nearest track naturally.

Hence, the allocation of SPACE=(1024,1) will end up giving you 1 track, as will the specification SPACE=(1024,10) or the specification of

161

SPACE=(TRK,1). Because MVS will round up to the nearest track, and a track on a 3380 is 47,476 bytes long.

The number that is used rather than TRK or CYL is referred to as a block, and this way of allocating space is referred to as allocating space in blocks.

This method of allocating space in blocks rather than in tracks or cylinders can be a handy method if you have a fairly accurate idea as to how many records you will be creating but you don't want to do any arithmetic.

It won't win you any points with the people who want you to allocate things in terms of cylinders. But you can't have everything. Why not, you want to know? Well, okay. You can use ROUND. We'll come to that shortly. Meanwhile back to this idea of allocating SPACE in blocks. It saves you doing arithmetic.

After all, besides not wanting to do any arithmetic, you might not do the arithmetic accurately anyway even if you bothered to do it.

Consider how complicated it can be.

You have to remember to consider the inter-record gap. The what? Yes, that empty space left between physical blocks on disk. Sort of like the empty space between the songs on a record or a CD. Yes, or a tape. There are inter-record gaps on tape as well.

These inter-record gaps vary in size. Some space is wasted due to the 3380 design feature that causes it to round the data block allocation upwards to a multiple of 32; and then you have to add 12 to the block size; and also, if you have keys, you add 12 to the key length; and in general there is a significant fraction of wasted space, all of which means that, as you were just saying, besides not wanting to do any arithmetic, you might not do the arithmetic accurately anyway even if you bothered to do it.

And, after all, doing arithmetic is what the computer does so well, is it not?

So, then, suppose you have chosen to use a BLKSIZE of 23440 for your data set, and the logical records in your file are each 80 bytes long, giving you 293 logical records in each block. (You picked 23440 because it is half a track.)

Suppose you expect your program to write about a thousand records to the file (logical records, that is, records as you intuitively conceive them to be). You figure that, at 293 records per block, that must be close to four blocks. Not much arithmetic there. You can specify SPACE=(23440,4) and let MVS figure out how many tracks that comes out to be.

In this example, 23440 is not only the size you have chosen for your BLKSIZE parameter in your DCB. You have also used 23440 as the size of the block in terms of your space request. In effect you are requesting that MVS figure out how many tracks 23440 multiplied by a 4 would work out to be, and then just give you that number of tracks.

Take an even simpler case.

Suppose you prefer to avoid even the simple calculation just shown.

So, then, you are still pretty sure that your file is going to have a thousand records (logical records, that is, records as you intuitively conceive them to be). Your records are each to be 80 bytes long. Knowing that you are going to have a thousand records, you can specify SPACE=(80,1000) and let MVS figure out how many tracks to give you.

Much easier than figuring out how many tracks or cylinders you want.

Notice that the size of the block you use for requesting SPACE has little to do with the size of the block specified in the BLKSIZE parameter in the DCB.

The BLKSIZE parameter you use in your DCB controls the maximum size of the block of data MVS will actually try to read from or write onto the disk for that data set.

The size of the block you use in your SPACE parameter is only used to calculate how much SPACE on disk will be set aside for that data set.

You see the difference.

When people allocate space in terms of blocks, they usually use the same number for the size of the block in the SPACE parameter as they use for the BLKSIZE parameter in the DCB; but there is no compelling reason for this.

There is a reason, but it isn't compelling.

The size of the block you request in your SPACE allocation has the following relation to your DCB BLKSIZE: MVS will figure out the SPACE allocation for you AS IF the size of the block you are requesting in the SPACE parameter is the same as the size you are requesting as BLKSIZE in the DCB.

In order to make the calculation for you when you allocate SPACE in blocks, MVS has to take into consideration the inter-record gaps, one after each block. To do the calculation, MVS assumes that the number you have specified in the first subparameter of SPACE is the size of a physical block, that is, that this number is the same as your DCB BLKSIZE. It doesn't have to be, but that is one of the assumptions that influence the calculation. So the calculation will be off a bit if the block size you specify for allocating SPACE is different from your DCB BLKSIZE.

This means that, considering the inter-record gaps (between adjacent blocks), MVS will over-estimate your SPACE allocation if you use a smaller size block for allocating SPACE than the actual BLKSIZE you specify in your DCB.

How badly does MVS overestimate? This is really the same question, you notice, as: How much SPACE are you wasting if you choose a small BLKSIZE?

It's like this. If you ask for a thousand blocks of 80 in your SPACE parameter, MVS will make the SPACE calculation for you as if you had specified

SPACE=(80,1000),DCB=(RECFM=FB,LRECL=80,BLKSIZE=80)

which means that, on a 3380 disk, you will get 13 tracks. If you then proceed to write one thousand 80-byte records into that data set with the DCB parameter specified as

DCB=(RECFM=FB,DSORG=PS,LRECL=80,BLKSIZE=23440)

you will use only 2 tracks. (Two blocks per track.)

Suppose you want to be frugal about your SPACE allocations, and suppose you do not expect to modify the data set subsequent to running your program. You can compensate for the overestimate by adding RLSE at the end of your SPACE request for 1000 eighty-byte records. Like this:

SPACE=(80,1000,RLSE) rather than just SPACE=(80,1000). (We will come to RLSE again shortly; it releases leftover SPACE when your program closes the data set).

Let us press on to the next aspect of SPACE.

SECONDARY EXTENTS

The secondary extent.

That is the next subparameter.

Take an example.

Suppose you saw a space allocation specified as SPACE=(TRK,(3,10)) and you wondered what the 10 meant.

The 10 in this example is the secondary allocation. The proper English-like interpretation of the above space request is this:

"Give me three tracks of disk space for this data set, and, if I fill that up but yet my program attempts to write more data into the data set anyway, well, give me a break, let me have another 10 tracks."

As a matter of fact you will be allowed to run out of space and get another allotment 15 times altogether, for a total of 16 extents, subject to availability of space on the disk; or, if you have a more recent release of MVS, you can have up to 123 extents. No, that isn't a typo. We'll say it again. 123 extents. Subject to availability of space on the disk, as always.

An example.

You ask for a 3 track primary extent and a 10 track secondary extent, that is, you specify SPACE=(TRK,(3,10)) in your JCL when you create your data set. As if you opened an account and were handed 3 tracks as an advance. You begin writing into your data set. You continue to write into the data set until you are informed that this will no longer be possible, no more SPACE is available. Rather as if you had run up to your overdraft limit on your account. How much SPACE would you have used by this time? Answer: 153 tracks. A 3 track primary extent, plus 15 secondary extents of 10 tracks each. And you didn't even have to do any arithmetic.

Subject to availability. There has to be SPACE on the disk when you try to get a new secondary extent, just as the bank itself must have funds before it can advance them to you.

If you happened to use up the last 3 tracks on that particular disk volume, or all the money belonging to that particular bank, you would be out of luck. Fair is fair. If you were going to need that much space, you should have estimated your primary allocation better. The 3 in the above example is the primary allocation.

As a matter of fact MVS may not be able to get you the primary allocation you request. At least he may not be able to get it as one big lump. In that case, before he gives up, he will try to get you three separate lumps that, taken together, add up to the amount you requested as a primary. In this case what ought to be your primary will really be composed of up to three extents rather than one. The number of secondaries you can later obtain will be reduced accordingly. Luckily this doesn't happen too often, and generally only on quite large SPACE requests. By the way, when it does, it makes the SPF 3.2 data set information screen look rather strange.

You ought to estimate your primary allocation as well as you can. If you get several separate chunks of space (if your data set "goes into extents", as they say) then the various chunks probably will not be contiguous. They could be anyplace on the volume. They could be far apart. That implies arm movement, that is, the read/write heads have to move physically from one place on disk to another. Time consuming. A leading cause of slow response times and long running jobs.

There are one or two very handy uses of the secondary extent subparameter, however, as follows.

Suppose you have a program that sometimes creates a very large file (a dump for example, or some tremendous error reporting trace). Usually the program does not create this output file at all. What do you say for a space allocation? You can profitably say something like this:

SPACE=(CYL,(0,50),RLSE)

and what do you suppose that does? It allocates zero space if the program does not write to the file. If, however, the program does write to the file, it allocates 50 cylinders.

Releasing unused SPACE

RLSE is JCL talk for release. It means that MVS is to release the unused portion of the allocated space when the program is through writing into it. So, in the example, 50 cylinders would be allocated, but, if only 32 of them were used, then the other 18 cylinders would be unallocated and left for someone else to use. If 31 and a half were used, still only 18 would be released, because MVS rounds upward to the nearest cylinder if space is requested in terms of cylinders.

Do yourself a favor and never use RLSE on a library. (You know, a partitioned data set, a data set with members.) If your data set has members, it is a library, and RLSE in the JCL is a mistake.

But as far as sequential files are concerned, RLSE is usually the right thing to do. Moral, ethical, correct, well-mannered, responsible. Demonstrates JCL Savoire-faire.

More about secondary extents

Will there be 50 cylinders available on that disk when your program tries to get its secondary extent?

There ought to be.

When MVS allocates a data set for you, it checks the available disk volumes within the unit class you have specified until it finds one that has enough space available to satisfy your request for the primary plus one secondary. So, in this case, MVS would find a disk volume with at least 0+50=50, that is, fifty cylinders available. Of course someone else could come along and grab that 50 cylinders while your job was running, since the secondary extent isn't really allocated to your data set until the program starts to write into it. So there is a slight risk. Nevertheless it can be a handy trick where disk space is tight. A particularly useful application of it occurs when you have a program that will write to one out of three or four files, depending on conditions, but you don't know which one.

Now, one more trick about secondary extents.

Suppose you are dealing with a data set that has been allocated by some clown like myself who dislikes secondary extents in general. On performance grounds. Data sets built for speed, don't you know.

So this particular data set has been allocated with just a primary and no secondary.

You find that you want to add some data into the data set, and the data set is full.

Moreover, a dozen other people have the data set allocated to their apparently permanent terminal sessions with DISP=SHR. These people are widely dispersed geographically and are apparently beyond the reach of telephone.

Consequently the time-honored procedure of allocating a new, bigger version of the data set, copying the old data into it, and then renaming the two versions around, is not applicable to the present case.

You have tried something of the sort perhaps, and been rewarded with some cheerful message such as "Data set in use, please try again later."

You are, for whatever reason, desperate to add your data into this data set. Perhaps it is a library which contains HELP messages that the terminal users read frequently, and someone has put an embarrassing message into it, and that was the last thing that would fit.

You cannot allocate the data set DISP=OLD because the unreachable terminal users all have it allocated DISP=SHR. You understand this, and you have overcome your natural disinclination to update a data set using DISP=SHR. You would gladly accept that risk. In fact, you tried, and your job abended with a D37 or a B37, and that is how you know the thing is full. Moreover your telephone rings every five minutes with another complaint about the problem, and your boss is due back from lunch in 15 minutes.

Assume moreover that you have no outstanding job offers from other companies.

Your ideological and philosophical disposition quickly shifts very far in favor of a secondary extent.

Lucky you. You have read this book.

You use the trick of specifying a SPACE allocation with a secondary extent, on the DD statement for that data set, in the JCL for the program that is trying to update the data set. When the program attempts to write into the data set, this time, the secondary extent will be allocated. The data set will be updated. Good will have triumphed over evil.

Notice that, if the data set had originally been allocated with a secondary extent specified, it would have used up 16 extents before being declared full. In this case you really would have been out of luck. You could not at that point have requested additional secondary extents.

You ought to be aware of one problem here.

If you have given yourself, say, a secondary extent of 27 extra tracks in the JCL that updated the data set using the above trick, but you only used up one or two of those tracks really, and of course you did NOT code RLSE, you may thereafter merrily edit the data set using the text editor of your choice, saving your updates on disk until the full measure of that one secondary extent of 27 tracks is used up.

But you only get one secondary extent of 27 tracks, you cannot have fifteen of them, because the number 27 has not been permanently saved away for future reference. Consequently the editor cannot use that number to allocate additional secondaries for you.

Of course, you could resort to the above described trick again, 14 more times before being truly out of luck; or, over a hundred times on a newer MVS system; but what you ought to do is to reallocate the data set with a realistic primary as soon as you can, for performance if nothing else.

Maybe one more warning about secondary extents is in order before we proceed to the last subparameter of SPACE that we will cover in this section, that is to say, the third number you sometimes see inside the inner parentheses, which specifies the number of directory blocks for a library.

First, the warning about secondary extents.

Some programs are very smart. IMS for example. Some parts of MVS itself. Parts of TSO.

These examples just enumerated are smart in a particular way.

When they start their processing—when they come up, as we say— they look at some of the data sets they know they will be using, and they find out exactly where on disk those data sets are located. They make notes as to the addresses. If a data set has five extents, well and good, a note of those five locations is made. Whatever the allocation is, fine. It is noted.

The program in question does not then search again for this information. It refers to its own internal notes. This makes it run faster.

But suppose that you wrote something into that data set that had the five extents, and, as chance would have it, you caused the data set to go into a sixth extent. Well and good. But it does lead to the following problem.

The smart program does not know where the new extent is, and it does not look for it.

That being the case, anything in the sixth extent is not accessible to this very clever, fast program.

The error message you will get in such a case will generally not be extremely informative.

Sometimes for example the smart program will tell you that it found a hardware error on the disk. Not very smart in that case, is it? There is no telling quite what error message you might get from some of these smart programs, but the suggestion that it must be a hardware error is quite a common erroneous error message.

You can spot this type of error most easily if you notice that it is happening only with data that has been added recently, and that all such data experiences the same error. Take a simple case. You replace an IMS screen and suddenly IMS cannot find that screen anymore. Okay, fine. You and other people replace ten more screens, and IMS cannot find any of them. Very likely a data set has acquired an extra extent that IMS has not noticed. How and when can IMS be made to notice it?

Well, you can take IMS down and bring it up again. (Restart it, recycle it, bounce it). If it is MVS itself that has trouble recognizing something, you need to IPL. These are things that are best scheduled in the dead of night. If the problem occurs under TSO only, you are lucky. You can LOGOFF and then LOGON again, and the world will be beautiful again.

So that was your warning about secondary extents. Now onward to those directory blocks.

DIRECTORY BLOCKS - LIBRARIES, PARTITIONED DATA SETS

If you have a partitioned data set—a library, a data set with members, you know—then MVS has to keep a list of the names of the members someplace, and a little note as to where exactly each member starts, and some other little notes like that. SPF statistics for some data sets, IDR data for others. Where is this information kept?

In the directory portion of the data set.

Where is that? At the beginning.

How big is it? You decide.

It is allocated in terms of directory blocks. Each directory block is 256 bytes long. You can hold enough information for about half a dozen members in one directory block, depending.

Depending on? On how much information you keep there. If you keep SPF statistics, well, that uses up a good little piece. Load module information uses up a good little chunk as well, if your members are load modules, that is, if the data set is a load library. Relatively, that is. None of it really amounts to much. Figure on six members to a directory block in general. You can experiment and see how many you get for particular sorts of libraries if curiosity motivates you.

When you have decided on a number, use it as the third subparameter within those inner parentheses.

When you request directory blocks for your library and you do not request a secondary extent, you denote the absence of the missing positional subparameter by including the usual comma.

Example: You want a 5 track primary, no secondary, and 16 directory blocks. You say: SPACE=(TRK,(5,,16)) and you have it.

If you request too few directory blocks, then you will get an E37 abend when you try to add or replace a member. Put another way, it means the directory is full.

At that point you can delete some members if you want to make room in the directory.

Or you can create a new library that is identical to the first one except that it has a different name and more directory blocks, and then copy all of the members from the first data set into the new data set, then rename the old one to some other name, and finally rename the new one to the old name.

If you happen to run into this problem when you are editing something under SPF, and you don't want to lose your work, save your member temporarily into some other library using the CREATE subcommand. Find out how to use it by typing the two words "HELP CREATE" on the COMMAND line.

By the way, about that E37...

It doesn't always mean your directory is full.

It can also mean that the disk volume where your library is sitting is full, and your library tried to get a secondary extent, but it couldn't get one because the disk itself was full. It is also possible to get an E37 by running off the end of a tape reel, but this is rare.

95 times out of a hundred, an E37 means the directory of a library is full.

LESS COMMONLY USED SUBPARAMETERS OF SPACE

Our discussion of the basics of SPACE is now concluded.

There are other subparameters of SPACE, but none of them are what one would call basic.

Well, okay, I'll tell you just one more.

ROUND.

It rounds the allocation upward to a cylinder boundary, so your data set will be allocated in terms of cylinders.

Example:

SPACE=(80,(1000),,,ROUND)

What will the example do? Right. MVS will figure out how many tracks it would take to store one thousand 80-byte records. Then he will round that number upwards to get the nearest number of cylinders, and allocate your SPACE for you in cylinders. Nice? Hey, MVS isn't so bad.

Thus in the above example you would get 1 cylinder. Had you left off the word ROUND you would have gotten 13 tracks.

You may of course combine RLSE with ROUND:

SPACE=(80,(5000),RLSE,,ROUND)

Bet you never pictured yourself doing THAT when you first picked up this book.

The above SPACE request will get you 5 cylinders. Unused cylinders of SPACE will be released when your program closes the data set. Had you left off the word ROUND, you would have gotten 61 tracks, with all unused tracks released when the data set is closed.

Are you starting to feel like an expert yet? Notice the silly mistakes you begin to see other people making, increasingly more as you continue to read this book. What could it mean?

Chapter 9

FILES THAT DO NOT NEED NAMES

There are two types of files that do not need names assigned through the DSNAME parameter. These files are handled by MVS and are known as System Input and System Output files.

DD * AND DD DATA

You remember something about this from Chapter 2.

MVS knows whether something is JCL or not by looking at the first two columns on the line, called the ID field.

If you want to include lines containing data mixed in with your lines containing JCL, then each such set of data (instream data) should be preceded by a DD statement telling MVS that the following data is to be considered as associated with some particular ddname.

If you omit such a DD statement, then SYSIN is assumed, which is usually a pretty good guess coming from an unimaginative thinker like MVS.

So, the following two jobs are equivalent:

```
//JOB1 JOB acct-number,
//      JOHN.SMITH,
//      MSGCLASS=X etc
// EXEC COBUCLG
//SYSIN DD *
   ... input COBOL program source
/*
```

JOB2 is equivalent to JOB1 above:

```
//JOB2 JOB acct-number,
//    JOHN.SMITH,
//    MSGCLASS=X etc
// EXEC COBUCLG
   ... input COBOL program source
```

JOB2 has omitted the //SYSIN DD * statement, and MVS has assumed that the following non-JCL lines must be meant for SYSIN. Similarly, MVS has assumed that the non-JCL lines have ended at the end of the simulated deck of cards.

Really each line in a JOB is a simulated card, unless you are using real punched cards. So the non-JCL lines within the deck of simulated cards are obviously simulated card input.

Let's use a more interesting example. An example that actually does some simple thing. Let's print something.

The IBM-supplied program IEBGENER, which comes included in the price of MVS, can copy a flat file from one place to another. From a tape to a disk, for example, or from one disk data set to another. Or from simulated cards to real paper. Let's do that.

IEBGENER reads its input from the ddname SYSUT1. Whatever it reads from SYSUT1 it writes to SYSUT2. You can remember this easily, should you wish to do so, by imagining that you have misspelled the phrase by saying it writes two SYSUT2, get it, two instead of to, well, anyway, about IEBGENER ... it also expects a SYSPRINT DD statement, where it will write a few messages, and it also expects a SYSIN DD statement, which can be DUMMY. Okay, so let's tell IEBGENER to print something for us:

```
//JOB3 JOB acct-number,
//    JOHN.SMITH,
//    MSGCLASS=X etc
// EXEC PGM=IEBGENER
```

175

```
//SYSPRINT DD SYSOUT=*
//SYSIN  DD DUMMY
//SYSUT1  DD *
```

To: Somebody
From: John Smith
Date: Today

Look, I actually printed something.
Using JCL. and IEBGENER. I'll bet
you don't even know what that means.

It means you are going to get memos
from me printed on this cheap computer
paper, and soon I will be demanding a
nice laser printer.

 Have to be careful when you mix lower
case letters in with JCL like this,
though. If you type any of your JCL in
lower case, that gets you a JCL error.

```
//SYSUT2  DD SYSOUT=A
//
```

What if you want to include real JCL statements within your instream data?

This is not worth doing 99 times out of 100, and you should re-think whatever led you to consider it. However, if you are interested, read the rest of this section, rather than skipping ahead as you might otherwise do.

You use DD DATA rather than DD * and you may include, within your instream data, JCL statements containing // in columns one and two. You terminate the input data with a line that contains only a /* in columns one and two.

JCL generally has // in columns one and two. A line which contains

/* in columns one and two, rather than //, signals the end of an input data file. As in JOB1 above. Simple enough concept, except for this:

If your input data file contains a /* statement, it messes up the whole thing.

In fact this very condition often occurs, even in modern times. It has the consequence that the remainder of the lines after the /* are actually executed as JCL. This can be inconvenient if you hadn't planned for it.

So you use the DLM parameter.

For example, if you say:

//SYSUT1 DD DATA,DLM=@@

Then MVS will vacuum up all of the following lines until it comes to a line that says @@ in columns one and two:

@@

You can use other characters instead of @@. For example you could use ## or anything else as long as you remember to have a card with ## or whatever you defined as the delimiter.

This used to lead to a lot of good times in the days of real punched cards. From time to time someone would forget the ending delimiter, and MVS would continue to suck up all of the following card decks containing everyone else's jobs, and all those other jobs wouldn't be jobs at all, they would be part of that one person's large instream data file. Pretty funny. Well, it doesn't happen much anymore. But people still like to be careful with DLM delimiters. But then you have to be careful with the /* too.

It's like this. A DLM delimiter can cause problems if it is unexpectedly absent, whereas the /* delimiter generates its own particular havoc by being unexpectedly present.

In fact you almost never need to use DD DATA unless you are using real punched cards, but you will see DD DATA used in existing JCL decks so you may as well know what it means.

DD * is much more useful. As already discussed. Now you know how to use simulated cards as input.

Telling MVS Where to Put Printed Output: SYSOUT and DEST

SYSOUT

SYSOUT can be equal to A or B or any letter or digit, and can have positional subparameters to designate special paper.

The meaning of SYSOUT=A, SYSOUT=B, and so forth, is decided by the people responsible for MVS at your site. They are able to set things up in such a way that SYSOUT=1 is printed on one particular printer; SYSOUT=2 and SYSOUT=Q are printed on some other printer from 9 a.m. to 5 p.m., but SYSOUT=H is printed on that printer at night; and so forth, to the limits of their imaginations and the available equipment and character set.

By a convention that is very widely but not universally followed, SYSOUT=A means ordinary printed output, SYSOUT=B means punched cards, and SYSOUT=X means simulated output that will be viewed at a TSO terminal rather than being printed.

SYSOUT=* means that the * is to be replaced by whatever value is assigned on the MSGCLASS parameter on the JOB statement.

Thus if your JOB statement says MSGCLASS=A, all occurrences of SYSOUT=* within your JCL will be replaced by SYSOUT=A. If your JOB statement says MSGCLASS=X, all occurrences of SYSOUT=* within your JCL will be replaced by SYSOUT=X. And so on.

There are positional subparameters to SYSOUT.

The first is the output class. As just discussed. If you say SYSOUT=A, then the output class, sometimes called the sysout class, is A.

The second is the name of a program, called a writer. If such a program is specified, your output is given to that program rather than being printed. Such a program might be used to write your output to tape, to edit and then print it, to copy your output to some special device, and so on. We will come back to this.

The third parameter is the name of the special paper you want to use. Special forms. Stationery. It could specify three-part paper, gummed labels, paychecks, or any other sort of special stationery available for use at your site.

How do you know what form name to use for which paper? You ask someone. Each site assigns names to their own forms.

When it is time for your output to be printed, MVS will write a message to the operator's console asking that the required stationery be mounted on the proper printer.

Since this creates additional work for the operations staff, most places will request that you put your SYSOUT into a special held class if it is to use special forms. Here a held class is an output class that is not printed immediately, but waits in an unserviced queue. At intervals, or perhaps if the operator wants to do you a special favor, the operator will mount the special forms and release the jobs in the held queue for that particular stationery.

For example, suppose that the people responsible for such things at your site have set up SYSOUT=H to be a held class.

Suppose that you want to print some of your output on a special form named CHEX. Say this output is produced by your program on the file-name OUTFILE. You would specify, on the DD statement for that output file:

```
//OUTFILE DD SYSOUT=(H,,CHEX)
```

You could additionally specify other parameters such as DCB, of course. For example, if the lines in your output file are generated by the program as fixed length records, each 131 bytes in length, with the first byte of each line containing an ASA carriage control character, and if there are 100 such records per block, you might say:

```
//OUTFILE DD SYSOUT=(H,,CHEX),
//       DCB=(LRECL=131,
//       RECFM=FBA,
//       BLKSIZE=13100)
```

There is more about DCB in the Chapter 6. Also mentionable on a DD statement for a SYSOUT file are such parameters as CHARS, FCB, or UCS, to designate a particular character set to be used, sometimes called a font. Which parameter is used depends on what type of printer is to be used for printing the output. If you want to use special character sets, check with someone at your site who has actually used them there. Different fonts will be available at different sites and for different printer types. Some printer types have no special fonts at all. Some in fact will not even print lower case letters. Parameters specific to SYSOUT are discussed further in this chapter.

Another word about held output. You may deliberately specify that your output be held, regardless of its output class. You do this by adding HOLD=YES to the statement. This is useful if you are uncertain whether you will really want it to be printed or not.

Now you know about the output classes and special forms. What about that missing positional parameter, where you can specify the name of a program?

Such a program is usually an external writer. An external writer will usually write the output to someplace other than a printer, for example to tape or microfiche or some archiving device. If such a program is used at your site, you need to find the name of it by asking or snooping.

Rather than specifying an external writer, the name of the program can specify the internal reader. The internal reader is a standard part of the MVS system. It is called INTRDR and can be specified, obviously, as SYSOUT=(A,INTRDR) on the DD statement. So what does that accomplish, you ask?

A program can actually submit a job, that is, a set of JCL to be executed. For example, when you use the SUBMIT command under TSO, that program hands your JCL over to MVS to be run as a background job. How is this wonder accomplished? The SUBMIT program copies your JCL to a DD statement specifying SYSOUT=(A,INTRDR) and MVS takes it from there.

Your own programs can, of course, do the same thing. You can write an output file consisting of lines of JCL. If the DD statement for the related file specifies the internal reader, then the JCL will be processed by MVS as a submitted batch job.

Here is an example of the use of the internal reader.

The program IEBGENER copies a flat file (or one member of a library) from one place to another. Whatever is specified on the ddname SYSUT1 is copied to SYSUT2. The IEBGENER program also requires that you supply DD statements for SYSIN and SYSPRINT. It uses SYSPRINT to write error messages and that sort of thing. SYSIN is usually unused and is specified as DUMMY. The following example uses IEBGENER to copy six lines of JCL into the internal reader, to be processed by MVS as a job.

```
//MYJOB JOB (account),
//      'MY.NAME',
//      MSGCLASS=X etc.
//PRINT EXEC PGM=IEBGENER
//SYSIN DD DUMMY
//SYSPRINT DD SYSOUT=*
//SYSUT2 DD SYSOUT=(A,INTRDR)
//SYSUT1 DD DATA
//* COMMENT - FIRST LINE OF INPUT
//INPUT JOB (account),
//      'MY.NAME',
//      MSGCLASS=X etc.
//INPUT EXEC PGM=IEFBR14
//INPUT DD DSN=JUNK.DATA.SET,
//      DISP=(OLD,DELETE)
//
//* COMMENT - LAST LINE OF INPUT
/*
//* THE "/*" ENDS THE "DD DATA"
```

Now you know.

DEST

DEST is short for destination.

Suppose, for example, that you have 200 different printers at your site, all set to print output class A. How can you make your output print on one particular printer rather than another? You specify DEST.

The printers in the main computer room are generally designated as DEST=LOCAL and other printers are considered to be remote. Remote is the opposite, somehow, of local.

Remote printers are designated with arbitrary numbers by the people responsible at your site. Hence one printer might be RMT1 (remote one) and another might be RMT200 (remote 200). Sometimes pronounced as R.M.T. followed by the number.

For example, suppose you want to execute the program named IEBGENER to print the member named MEMBER from the data set named MY.INPUT.LIBRARY, and you want your SYSUT2 (pronounced siss yewt 2, or siss yew tee 2) to be printed in output class A, on remote printer 409; however, you want to view the JCL from the job at your TSO terminal, which you specify on the JOB statement as MSGCLASS=X; and you want the SYSPRINT file to go to the same place as the MSGCLASS output. You would code the JCL as follows:

```
//MYJOB JOB (account),
//      'MY.NAME',
//      MSGCLASS=X etc.
//PRINT EXEC PGM=IEBGENER
//SYSIN  DD  DUMMY
//SYSPRINT DD SYSOUT=*
//SYSUT1  DD DISP=SHR,
// DSN=MY.INPUT.LIBRARY(MEMBER)
//SYSUT2  DD SYSOUT=A,
//      DEST=RMT409
```

See how easy it is?

How Big Is The Printed Output:
OUTLIM and COPIES

OUTLIM (output limit)

OUTLIM means OUTput LIMit. The value is expressed in terms of number of lines. Thus, if you want to limit the quantity of output allowable on SYSPRINT to 15 thousand lines, you specify:

```
//SYSPRINT DD SYSOUT=A,
//     OUTLIM=15000
```

If your program attempts to write more than the specified number of lines to that DD statement, the program will terminate with ABEND code 722.

If you do not code OUTLIM on your DD statement, the system default is assumed.

The MVS systems programmers at your company can change the system default value for OUTLIM.

They are also free to arrange things in such a way that your program will not actually abend if it exceeds the system default for output, but, rather than abending, will simply cause a message to be written to the MVS operator console saying ESTIMATED LINES EXCEEDED for your job. This message will be redisplayed there at intervals as your job continues to exceed the default for the allowable number of lines of SYSOUT. The frequency of the message is also set at the discretion of the MVS systems programmers at your company.

The MVS operators, at their discretion, may cancel your job if it appears to be producing so much sysout that it seems to threaten to use up most of the SPOOL (new word: spool. Spool space is the area on disk where all the sysout is kept before it is actually printed.)

If your job manages to fill up the entire spool without anyone noticing the messages, the system crashes. Oh well.

If they cancel your job, you get a 222 abend code.

At most places the operators prefer to avoid canceling jobs if at all possible.

183

Thus you have another opportunity to embarrass yourself with the dreaded infinite loop.

Your job might experience some unusual error that causes it to print the same error message repeatedly in a loop.

Eventually the program will use up all of the CPU time that has been allowed for it, and finish in a flash of brilliance with a 322 abend, having sent to the print queue the equivalent of several boxes of paper. The MVS operators may, at their discretion, refrain from allowing this sysout to actually print. They can purge the print while it is still in the print queue. They can purge the print from the printer when they observe that they are being called upon repeatedly to feed more boxes of paper into the printer to print the same error message a few hundred thousand more times.

Don't count on it.

You can end up with someone delivering a large stack of sysout to your desk on a hand truck.

Why do they allow it to print? I don't know. Perhaps their idea of a joke. Perhaps once a long time ago they cancelled some print that someone really wanted and they were impolitely reprimanded. In any case, they are as likely as not to print any inconceivable garbage you happen to direct toward the printer, unless you ring them up and explicitly request that they refrain.

Some programmers, particularly those who learned programming on PCs, have a tendency to write blank lines to the printer when they want to get double or even triple spacing between the lines that contain printable information. In an MVS system there is a much more efficient method to get double or triple spacing. It is by using ASA Carriage Control Characters, these carriage control characters will allow a programmer to skip to the top of a page before printing a line, and to move the paper one, two, or even three lines before printing a line.

Why would you want to know about this?

Suppose you have to print a report using triple spacing. That is to have two blank lines between each printed line. This report would be much more readable than a report with the lines all crunched up together. Anyway, each page will have 20 lines of printed information. If the program were written to print two blank lines between each line of information then each page would need 58 lines written to the SYSOUT SPOOL. However if the program uses ASA Carriage Control Characters then each page would only need 20 lines written to the SYSOUT SPOOL.

You are not going to reach the OUTLIM nearly as quickly using ASA Carriage Control Characters. OUTLIM is a count of the lines written to the spool. It really does not matter if anything is there.

COPIES (NUMBER OF COPIES)

If you want multiple copies of a report, specify the number of copies you want with the COPIES parameter. For example, specify the following to generate three copies of the report your program writes to the ddname INVOICES:

```
//INVOICES DD SYSOUT=A,
//      COPIES=3
```

At some companies the operators don't like it if you use the COPIES parameter because they have no way of seeing how much sysout your job has actually produced. They might let your job start printing, thinking it only has a thousand lines of sysout to print, which is what the system tells them it has. Unknown to them, you have specified COPIES=10 and you really have ten thousand lines to print. So it takes longer for the printer to finish printing your job than what the operators thought it would take. Some places they don't care, some places they do. It's a print scheduling thing. As long as your sysout is small and you only request a few copies, it isn't normally noticed. With large reports and large numbers of copies it can be a problem. In that case the thing for you to do is to talk to someone in operations about whether or not it will be a problem for them. They might just let you put it in a different sysout class, say SYSOUT=5 or something rather than SYSOUT=A, and then they will set the printer to print that class when they have time for it.

OUTPUT

This is a useful one if you print a lot of complicated sysout.
You know there are EXEC statements, JOB statements, and so forth.
Another sort of statement is called the OUTPUT statement.
It has the word OUTPUT in the operation field, like this:

```
//JONES OUTPUT CLASS=A,
//     DEST=RMT409,
//     COPIES=2
```

Later, from a DD statement, you can refer to this OUTPUT statement
by coding the OUTPUT= parameter on the DD statement. For example,
you would refer to the above OUTPUT statement by coding
OUTPUT=JONES on the DD statement.

Let's take an example. You are familiar with using the program
IEBGENER to print a file. Let's use IEBGENER to print the one line
message " Notice: Service Department will close at noon this Friday ".
This line will be read from SYSUT1 and printed to SYSUT2. The follow-
ing example will print two copies of the SYSUT2 output on the printer at
RMT409, and also one copy on the LOCAL printer:

```
//SAMPLE JOB (9999),XXXXX,
//     CLASS=T,MSGCLASS=X
//RMT409 OUTPUT DEST=RMT409,
//     COPIES=2
//LOCAL OUTPUT DEST=LOCAL
//PRINT EXEC PGM=IEBGENER
//SYSPRINT DD SYSOUT=*
//SYSIN   DD DUMMY
//SYSUT1  DD *
Notice: Service Department will
close at noon this Friday
//SYSUT2  DD SYSOUT=A,
//     OUTPUT=(*.RMT409,
//       *.LOCAL)
```

The parameters available on the OUTPUT statement are much the same as those available on a DD statement specifying SYSOUT. They are not completely identical, although the ones on the OUTPUT statements in the above example are. A few are different. For example, CLASS=A on the OUTPUT statement is the same as SYSOUT=A on the DD statement. In this case you code SYSOUT=(,) on the DD statement to indicate that the SYSOUT class is to be taken from the OUTPUT statement.

The following more complicated example has two steps. The first step will print one copy of the SYSUT2 output on the printer at RMT409, and also one copy on the LOCAL printer, just like the example above. The second step will print one copy of the SYSUT2 output on the printer located in the Sales department at Remote 102, one copy on the printer located in the Service department at Remote 123, and one copy on the LOCAL printer:

```
//SAMPLE JOB (9999),XXXXX,
//     CLASS=T,
//     MSGCLASS=X
//RMT409 OUTPUT CLASS=A,
//     DEST=RMT409
//LOCAL OUTPUT CLASS=A,
//     DEST=LOCAL
//SALES OUTPUT CLASS=A,
//     DEST=RMT102
//SERVICE OUTPUT CLASS=A,
//     DEST=RMT123
//STEP1 EXEC PGM=IEBGENER
//SYSPRINT DD SYSOUT=*
//SYSIN   DD DUMMY
//SYSUT1  DD *
Notice: Service Department will
close at noon this Friday
//SYSUT2  DD SYSOUT=A,
//     OUTPUT=(*.RMT409,
//       *.LOCAL)
```

```
//STEP2  EXEC PGM=IEBGENER
//SYSPRINT DD SYSOUT=*
//SYSIN  DD DUMMY
//SYSUT1  DD *
Notice: Service Department will
close at noon this Friday
//SYSUT2  DD SYSOUT=(,),
//    OUTPUT=(*.SALES,
//    *.SERVICE,*.LOCAL)
```

CHARS, BURST, FOLD, and TERM -
MORE PARAMETERS ON THE DD STATEMENT

Although other parameters exist for the DD statement, you will rarely run into any of them, except for those to do with printed output. The ones that control printed output are used to specify special character sets (fonts) and so on. These character sets and other parameters are specified differently depending on the type of printer you have. Beyond that, for any given printer type, you may or may not be able to specify any particular character set. In other words, producing fancy output is very site dependent, and the best way to do it at your own particular site is to find other people who have it working and copy from them. Consider also in this regard that many places have non-IBM printers, such as the HP LaserJet, connected to the IBM via network links. The requirements for these special printers may not even be specifiable in JCL.

However, just so you can see how little you're missing, let's sample a few of the special output handling parameters that JCL does provide. If you have no interest in this, please skip ahead to the next section.

Consider the laser printer. Many laser printers accept plain sheets of paper identical to the paper used in photocopiers. Some laser printers, however, will accept continuous fan-folded paper with perforated edges, the kind of paper generally thought of as computer paper. This paper can then be separated into individual sheets and the outer edges removed along the perforation lines.

If you are routing your output to an IBM model 3800 laser printer, that printer may have an optional burster/trimmer/stacker feature which can perform the just-described operation for you. You may request that it do so by specifying BURST=YES or BURST=Y, or you may request that it refrain from so doing by specifying BURST=NO or BURST=N on the DD statement. The BURST parameter may be specified on the OUTPUT statement rather than on the DD statement, if you are using an OUTPUT statement.

We continue with parameters related to the IBM 3800 laser printer.

The CHARS parameter is used to specify selected character sets. The name of the character set you select can be from 1 to 4 characters in length. Examples:

> CHARS=ESTR requests a font known as Essay Standard
> CHARS=EITR requests a font known as Essay Italic
> CHARS=EBTR requests a font known as Essay Boldface
> CHARS=BITR requests a font known as Boldface Italic
> CHARS=BRTR requests a font known as Boldface Regular

You can specify up to 4 special character sets enclosed in parentheses; for example:

> CHARS=(ESTR,EITR,EBTR,BRTR)

would select the four character sets of those four names.

In this case you would also need to specify OPTCD=J in your DCB, and you would need to supply a TRC (table reference character) in each line of output to be written to the printer. The TRC would determine which of the four character sets (fonts, or typestyles) would be used to print that particular line.

Putting 0 in the TRC byte on any particular output line means that you want the first typestyle to be used for printing that line, which would get you the ESTR character set if you had specified CHARS=(ESTR,EITR,EBTR,BRTR) as shown above.

Putting 1 in the TRC byte means that you want the second typestyle to be used, which would get you the EITR character set if you had our example setting of CHARS=(ESTR,EITR,EBTR,BRTR) as shown above.

Putting 2 in the TRC byte means that you want the third typestyle to be used, which would get you the EBTR character set if you had our example setting of CHARS=(ESTR,EITR,EBTR,BRTR).

Putting 3 in the TRC byte means that you want the fourth typestyle to be used, which would get you the BRTR character set if coupled with CHARS=(ESTR,EITR,EBTR,BRTR).

Where do you put the TRC byte?

If your RECFM if FBA, FA, VBA, VA, or UA, then the first byte of each output line should contain an ASA carriage control character, and the second byte of each output line should contain your TRC character. You remember that the A appended at the end of your RECFM means that you will be using ASA carriage control.

For any RECFM that does not specify carriage control, you will put your TRC byte in the first position of each line.

MVS uses the library named SYS1.IMAGELIB to store all of the available character sets. The ones available for use with the 3800 via the CHARS parameter are stored with member names beginning with XTB1 or XTB2, XTBn, etc. For example, SYS1.IMAGELIB (XTB1DUMP) contains the definition MVS uses when you specify CHARS=DUMP in your JCL, and SYS1.IMAGELIB (XTB1GT10) has the definition for CHARS=GT10. You can look at a list of the member names of SYS1.IMAGELIB using some tool such as SPF option 1 or option 3.1, just to get an idea of the names of the character sets you have available. If, for example, you see a member named XTB1GT15, then you ought to be able to specify CHARS=GT15 in your JCL. Like BURST, CHARS may be specified on the OUTPUT statement if you prefer.

For the sake of example, suppose now that things at your place are set up in such a way that all SYSOUT=G output goes to an IBM 3800 printer for which the BURST feature is operational and for which the GT10 character set is available. You can direct your SYSPRINT to be printed with character set GT10, and separated into pages with the edges trimmed, by specifying:

```
//SYSPRINT DD SYSOUT=G,
```

```
//      CHARS=GT10,
//      BURST=YES
```

So much for the 3800 IBM high speed laser printer.

The parameter FOLD=YES means that lower case letters are to be converted to upper case before printing. It is not available on all printer types. This is rarely useful, but you might want to be aware of the vocabulary item FOLD. Folding means converting lower case to upper case.

If the printer you are using does not use the CHARS parameter, for example if it is a model 3211 or some other impact printer, then it probably uses either the FCB or the UCS parameter as a substitute.

These also refer to images stored in SYS1.IMAGELIB, and the names start with UCS1, UCS2, FCB2, FCB3, and so on. For example, specifying UCS=PN would get you the character set defined in SYS1.IMAGELIB (UCS1PN) if it were available for that printer, or SYS1.IMAGELIB (UCS3PN) perhaps, depending on the type of printer. FCB is short for Forms Control Block and it defines the length of each page and where the first line is to be printed. You will only need to specify this if you are using Special Forms such as Pay Slips. You might code it like this FCB=PAY.

There are numerous printer types. The best thing to do, if you want to mess around with this sort of thing, is to find people who have done it before at your present site, and copy their JCL. Try the various possibilities you have available and see what you get.

One last example of an obscure parameter you may come across on the DD statement. TERM=TS. It is used in TSO LOGON procedure JCL, and it specifies that data for that DD statement should be read from and/or written to the TSO terminal. For example, you might see the following in a TSO LOGON procedure:

```
//SYSIN  DD TERM=TS
//SYSPRINT DD TERM=TS
```

It just means that SYSIN data will be read from the terminal, and SYSPRINT output will be displayed on the terminal screen.

Chapter 10

Examples and Concluding Remarks about Data Definition

Just a few examples, to clarify everything and bring it all together. Then you can start considering yourself a local expert on DD statements. If you haven't started already.

Most of our examples will use one of two programs. The first program, which you have already encountered, is IEBGENER. It copies any flat file specified on SYSUT1 to SYSUT2. Any one single member of a library, taken alone, counts as a flat file. Of course several flat files concatenated together through the use of concatenated DD statements also count as one flat file.

The second program we will use is IEFBR14. It does absolutely nothing. It is a one instruction program, and that instruction is RETURN or END or however you prefer to think of it in the programming language of your choice. Actually it is written in Assembler language, and the one instruction is BR 14. BR means branch, which is like GO TO. Register 14 is the address for return. So it means: go back to from whence you came. RETURN, in other words. END. Why would anybody have such a silly program? To take advantage of JCL facilities without actually doing anything else. Take our first example:

```
//SMITH0 JOB 1,MSGCLASS=X
//BR14 EXEC PGM=IEFBR14
```

```
//NEW  DD DSN=SMITH.NEW.DATASET,
//    DISP=(NEW,CATLG),
//    DCB=SMITH.OLD.DATASET,
//    SPACE=(TRK,5),
//    UNIT=SYSDA
```

What will happen in the above example? The program will do nothing. The data set named SMITH.NEW.DATASET will be created on a disk volume of MVS's choice. It will be given 5 tracks. It will be a sequential file (a flat file) because no directory blocks were specified. A catalog entry will be created for it, so MVS will be able to find it again in the future. It will have DCB parameters identical to SMITH.OLD.DATASET. The do-nothing program will do nothing with it, the job will end, and the data set will remain.

More examples.

Suppose you have just received a tape in the post. With it has come a letter informing you that you have received a sequential file named NIGERIAN.SALES.DATA on a Standard Labeled (SL) tape named APRIL.

You look at the tape. If it was round, you would guess you could mount it on a 3420 tape drive, but since it is rectangular you decide it will require a 3480. You want to copy it to disk so you can look at the data from TSO.

At the company where you work in the current example, you refer to disk as UNIT=3380. Nice straightforward company.

This is just a sequential file, and you know IEBGENER will copy a sequential file, so you decide to use IEBGENER to copy it to disk.

You happen to know that the Nigerian Sales Data is not likely to be a very big file. Maybe the letter even tells you that the file contains only a thousand records. You aren't sure of the record length. This doesn't bother you, because you know that you have a Standard Labeled tape and IEBGENER will copy the DCB information from the tape labels. You decide to overestimate your space requirement and use the RLSE subparameter to get rid of the extra space. A track on a 3380 was close to 50,000 bytes in length, was it not? 47,476. Let's overestimate wildly, you say, and give it 30 tracks with the excess released. Assuming that your TSO userid is SMITH, you code either of the following:

```
//SMITH1 JOB (account-number),
//      SMITH,
//      MSGCLASS=X
//**
//*  Thorough example, ought to
//*  work on nearly any
//*  MVS system.
//**
//COPYSTEP EXEC PGM=IEBGENER
//SYSIN   DD DUMMY
//SYSPRINT DD SYSOUT=*
//*
//SYSUT1  DD DISP=SHR,
//      DSN=NIGERIAN.SALES.DATA,
//      UNIT=(3480,,DEFER),
//      VOL=(,RETAIN,SER=APRIL),
//      LABEL=(1,SL)
//*
//SYSUT2 DD UNIT=3380,
//      DISP=(NEW,CATLG,DELETE),
//      DSN=SMITH.NIGERIAN.SALES.DATA,
//      DCB=(*.SYSUT1,DSORG=PS),
//   SPACE=(TRK,30,RLSE)
```

The following simplified JCL does the same thing:

```
//SMITH2 JOB (account-number),
//      SMITH,
//      MSGCLASS=X
//**
//* Simplified version
//* of the above examplee
//**
//   EXEC PGM=IEBGENER
```

```
//SYSIN   DD DUMMY
//SYSPRINT DD SYSOUT=*
//SYSUT1  DD DISP=OLD,
//   DSN=NIGERIAN.SALES.DATA,
//   VOL=SER=APRIL,
//    UNIT=3480
//SYSUT2  DD DISP=(,CATLG),
//   DSN=SMITH.NIGERIAN.SALES.DATA,
//   SPACE=(TRK,15,RLSE),
//   UNIT=3380
```

As a TSO user, you probably already realize that, unless you tell it not to do so, TSO tends to append your userid as the high level qualifier whenever you specify a data set name not enclosed in quotes. The point is, if you are logged onto TSO under the userid SMITH, and you refer to a data set named NIGERIAN.SALES.DATA, then TSO will look for a data set named SMITH.NIGERIAN.SALES.DATA, because it has assumed your userid as a prefix. Similarly, if you refer to a data set named SMITH.NIGERIAN.SALES.DATA, then TSO will look for a data set named SMITH.SMITH.NIGERIAN.SALES.DATA, because it has again tacked on your userid.

This tendency of TSO to add your userid at the beginning of a data set name is something you need to keep in mind when using the same data sets both under TSO and in JCL. TSO assumes your userid as the high level qualifier of the data set name, unless told not to do so. JCL makes no such assumption.

Next example.

You want to delete the data set SMITH.NIGERIAN.SALES.DATA, which is a cataloged disk data set that really exists. You created it in the last example. Your userid is still SMITH.

```
//SMITH3 JOB (account-number),
//   SMITH,
//   MSGCLASS=X
```

```
//**
//* Delete a data set
//**
//     EXEC PGM=IEFBR14
//SYSUT2 DD DISP=(OLD,DELETE),
//     DSN=SMITH.NIGERIAN.SALES.DATA
```

You may, of course, specify any ddname of your choice when you execute IEFBR14. In the above example, you have used the ddname SYSUT2 because you copied the JCL from your earlier IEBGENER, and just left the ddname as it was, since it didn't matter.

Next example.

You want to amuse your friends and annoy people in responsible positions. You decide to create an uncataloged disk data set with a name that contains funny characters. To make it more difficult to delete, you include an embedded blank space towards the end of the name, because you know that this confuses SPF 3.4, and you hope it may confuse other programs as well. Of course, to accomplish this annoying project, you will need to specify the data set name enclosed in quotes:

```
//SMITH JOB (acct-num),
//**
//*
//* Create an uncataloged data
//* set with an odd name
//*
//**
//     EXEC PGM=IEFBR14
//DD1 DD DISP=(NEW,KEEP),
//     DSN='*+..hello..+* *',
//     UNIT=SYSDA,
//     SPACE=(TRK,0),
//     DCB=(DSORG=PS,
//     LRECL=80,
```

```
//  RECFM=FB,
//  BLKSIZE=23440)
```

Perhaps this will not really annoy anyone. Perhaps it will be automatically deleted by a program that runs in the middle of the night. On the other hand, perhaps it will not. Perhaps it will be more annoying than you intended. Perhaps your friends will not be amused. You decide to delete the thing.

First you have to figure out where it went. Which disk volume.

It isn't cataloged, of course.

You decide you'll have to look at the output listing.

Well. So you look at the output listing. It looks something like the following:

```
        JES 2 JOB LOG—SYSTEM A B C
0
        17.29.45 JOB07944 £HASP373 SMITH STARTED -
        INIT 7 - CLASS I
        17.29.45 JOB07944  IEF403I SMITH - STARTED -
        TIME=17.29.45
        17.29.47 JOB07944  IEF404I SMITH - ENDED -
        TIME=17.29.47
        17.29.47 JOB07944 £HASP395 SMITH ENDED
        0—— JES2 JOB STATISTICS ———
        -  21 JUN 93 JOB EXECUTION DATE
        - 10 CARDS READ
        - 41 SYSOUT PRINT RECORDS
        -  0 SYSOUT PUNCH RECORDS
        - 2 SYSOUT SPOOL KBYTES
        - 0.02 MINUTES EXECUTION TIME
        1 //SMITH JOB 0,MSGCLASS=X
        2 //S1  EXEC PGM=IEFBR14
        3 //DD1 DD DISP=(NEW,KEEP),
        // DSN='*+..hello..+* *',
        // UNIT=SYSDA,SPACE=(TRK,0),
```

```
//   DCB=(DSORG=PS,LRECL=80,
//   RECFM=FB,BLKSIZE=23440)
IEF236I ALLOC. FOR SMITH S14
IEF237I C89 ALLOCATED TO DD1
IEF142I SMITH S14 - STEP WAS EXECUTED - COND
    CODE 0000
IEF285I  *+..hello..+* * KEPT
IEF285I  VOL SER NOS= ABC001.
IEF373I STEP /S1 / START 93172.1729
IEF374I STEP /S1 / STOP 93172.1729 CPU 0MIN
    00.01SEC SRB
IEF375I JOB /SMITH/ START 93172.1729
IEF376I JOB /SMITH/ STOP 93172.1729 CPU 0MIN
    00.02SEC SRB.
```

You are utterly charmed by this, of course, but you hide your feelings. You eventually notice, however, the name of your data set on a line that says "KEPT" off to the right.

To the left of the name of your data set you notice it says IEF285I, which is called the message number. You can look up these numbers in a set of books something like a dictionary. The set of books is called Messages and Codes. That isn't its name. That is what people call it. You don't need to look up your message this time. Just realize that you could.

You look at the next line on your listing, and it is also an IEF285I message, but, rather than telling you the name of your data set again (you already know that), and saying "KEPT" (you know that too), this time it says "VOL SER NOS= ABC001." Ah, you say. It has KEPT the data set on disk volume ABC001. Very good.

Well and good. Now you are going to delete this data set. You first try SPF option 3.4, and SPF option 3.2, but they refuse to do the job. You decide to delete it the same way you created it: with JCL. You copy the JCL you used before, add the VOLUME and change the DISP. Being conscientious, you also change the job name and the comments, although you are not required to do so. You also realize that you could remove the

DCB and the SPACE, which are no longer needed, but you don't bother to do so. You run the following job, and the data set disappears:

```
//SMITH6 JOB (account-number),
//    MSGCLASS=X
//*
//* Delete an uncataloged
//* data set with an odd name
//*
//    EXEC PGM=IEFBR14
//*
//DD1 DD DISP=(OLD,DELETE),
//   VOL=SER=ABC001,
//   DSN='*+..hello..+**',
//   UNIT=SYSDA,SPACE=(TRK,0),
//   DCB=(DSORG=PS,LRECL=80,
//   RECFM=FB,BLKSIZE=23440)
```

Okay, but now you want to do something useful. Maybe change DCB information for a data set, that sort of thing.

In fact you have a data set with an LRECL of 320, and the SPF editor refuses to let you edit it, because the record length (320) exceeds the SPF editor's acceptable maximum of 256 bytes per line. You don't like that.

You say to yourself that one 320 byte record is obviously equal to four 80 byte records. Can you not chop them up and treat each 320 byte record as four 80 byte records?

Hey, okay. You know that the LRECL has no real physical existence. The BLKSIZE, okay, that is physical record size. There are real physical inter-record gaps between blocks. But the division into logical records is purely arbitrary. MVS will take your word about what you want to use for the length of the logical records, as long as an integral number of logical records will fit into each block.

Furthermore you instantly recall that MVS looks at the DCB information on the DD statement in the JCL before looking for DCB information that is stored with the data set itself.

So, you decide to use IEBGENER to create a copy of the data set that has LRECL=80 in the DCB information that is stored with the data set itself.

Your data set is named SMITH.LRECL320.DATA and it was created with DCB attributes of LRECL=320,RECFM=FB, and BLKSIZE=6400.

You can make a copy of this that looks identical but has DCB attributes of LRECL=80,RECFM=FB, and BLKSIZE=6400. Each of the old 320 byte records will be mapped as four 80 byte records. Very easy to do. You run the following IEBGENER:

```
//SMITH7 JOB (account-number),
//    SMITH,
//    MSGCLASS=X
//*
//*  Copy a data set with
//*  LRECL=320
//*  to one with LRECL=80
//*
//COPYSTEP EXEC PGM=IEBGENER
//*
//SYSIN   DD DUMMY
//*
//SYSPRINT DD SYSOUT=*
//*
//SYSUT1  DD DISP=SHR,
//  DSN=SMITH.LRECL320.DATA,
//  DCB=(RECFM=FB,BLKSZE=6400,
//  DSORG=PS,LRECL=80)
//*    yes, MVS will accept your
//*    word on this LRECL=80
//*    and not look any closer
//*
//SYSUT2 DD UNIT=SYSDA,
//  DISP=(NEW,CATLG,DELETE),
//  DSN=SMITH.LRECL80.DATA,
```

```
// DCB=(RECFM=FB,BLKSZE=6400,
// DSORG=PS,LRECL=80),
// SPACE=(CYL,(1,20),RLSE)
//* ... specify the
//* appropriate disk
//* unit if not SYSDA
```

Now you go to SPF option 2 or any other text editor of your choice and happily edit your new data set, SMITH.LRECL80.DATA, making all of the changes you want to make. When you are finished editing it, you copy the corrected version back into the original data set as follows:

```
//SMITH8 JOB (account-number),
//      SMITH,
//      MSGCLASS=X
//*
//* Copy a data
//* set with LRECL=80
//* to one with LRECL=320
//*
//COPYSTEP EXEC PGM=IEBGENER
//SYSIN   DD DUMMY
//SYSPRINT DD SYSOUT=*
//SYSUT1  DD DISP=SHR,
// DSN=SMITH.LRECL80.DATA,
// DCB=(RECFM=FB,BLKSZE=6400,
// DSORG=PS,
// LRECL=320)   yes, MVS
//*   will accept your
//*   word on this
//*   LRECL and not
//*   look any closer
//SYSUT2 DD DISP=OLD,
// DSN=SMITH.LRECL320.DATA
```

Of course, the whole thing relies on the fact that 320 is a multiple of 80. If your original data set had possessed an LRECL of 312, you would have needed to use 78 rather than 80 to make it work the same. If it had originally been 1024, you could have used 128 or 64 for your new record length. You get the idea.

Another example. We will move on to a new program for this example. IEBCOPY. IEBCOPY is similar to IEBGENER, except that it copies libraries rather than flat files.

There are a lot of fancy options with IEBCOPY, and we will talk more about it in the chapter on Utility Programs, Chapter 17. In its simplest form, IEBCOPY copies an entire library from SYSUT1 to SYSUT2.

When a library becomes full, one can recover some space by compressing the library. This is done with IEBCOPY. If you specify the same library for both the input and the output, IEBCOPY compresses the data set for you. As follows:

```
//SMITH9 JOB (account-number),
//    SMITH,
//    MSGCLASS=X
//COMPRESS EXEC PGM=IEBCOPY
//**
//*  Compress the library
//*  named SMITH.LIBRARY1
//**
//SYSPRINT DD SYSOUT=*
//SYSIN   DD DUMMY
//SYSUT1 DD DISP=OLD,
//    DSN=SMITH.LIBRARY1
//SYSUT2 DD DISP=OLD,
//    DSN=SMITH.LIBRARY1
```

You will not see the above simple straightforward example used very often. People generally prefer the following setup, which accomplishes exactly the same thing:

```
//SMITH10 JOB (account-number),
//      SMITH,
//      MSGCLASS=X
//COMPRESS EXEC PGM=IEBCOPY
//**
//* Compress the library
//* named SMITH.LIBRARY1
//**
//SYSPRINT DD SYSOUT=*
//DD1   DD DISP=OLD,
//      DSN=SMITH.LIBRARY1
//SYSIN DD *
      COPY I=DD1,O=DD1
```

In the above example, you give IEBCOPY some instructions via the SYSIN file. You tell IEBCOPY that you want to copy input from the ddname DD1 and write it as output to the ddname DD1. This SYSIN information would not be required if you used the default ddnames of SYSUT1 and SYSUT2 for input and output.

WARNING: Run your compress in a Job class that allows enough time for it to complete. Consider making a backup copy of the library before running the compress. If your compress fails part way through, your data set will be mangled.

Frequently you will see the following even less straightforward setup, which also accomplishes exactly the same thing:

```
//SMITH11 JOB (account-number),
//      SMITH,MSGCLASS=X
//COMPRESS EXEC PGM=IEBCOPY
//**
//* Compress the library
//* named SMITH.LIBRARY1
//**
//SYSPRINT DD SYSOUT=*
//DD1   DD DISP=OLD,
```

```
//    DSN=SMITH.LIBRARY1
//DD2   DD DISP=OLD,
//    DSN=SMITH.LIBRARY1
//SYSIN DD *
    COPY I=DD1,O=DD2
```

All of which is no doubt very interesting and useful, you now say, but what does it have to do, really, with DD statement examples? Glad you asked.

Now that you know how to use IEBCOPY compress, you can use it to change the DCB information on a data set. Yes, you can now repair that data set that had its DCB information mangled when someone wrote a load module into a procedure library by mistake. Or a procedure into a load library. Or whatever they did. Now you want the exact details of how to repair this data set.

It happens from time to time that someone makes a mistake by writing the wrong kind of member into a data set. When the program is finished writing the misplaced member, the DCB the system stores with the data set is re-written with the DCB information that would be appropriate to the mistaken member, but is inappropriate to all of the pre-existing members.

An aside: Assuming this is a disk data set, the stored DCB information is kept in the Volume Table of Contents (VTOC, pronounced VeeTahk) in an area called the DSCB (Data Set Control Block). Changing this information is referred to as rewriting the DSCB. But this is very technical talk, so you should be careful about using it in mixed company.

Anyway, the data set has had its DSCB mangled by mistreatment. All of the old members are still there, but you get ugly messages about I/O errors when you try to use them.

Step 1: Delete the member that caused the problem, using SPF 3.1 or any convenient tool. This is necessary if the offending member has a larger actual block size than the size you intend for the data set to have.

Step 2: Run an IEBCOPY compress, explicitly specifying, on the DD statement(s), the DCB information as you wish it to be.

Explicit example: You have a data set named USER.PROCLIB which once had DCB attributes of LRECL=80,RECFM=FB,BLKSIZE=3120, until someone wrote a load module into it. Since then it seems to have BLKSIZE=19069,RECFM=U,LRECL=80 or something equally odd. The load module is named TEMPNAME. First you use any convenient tool to delete TEMPNAME, for example SPF 3.1; this preliminary step of deleting the miscreant member is necessary only if the BLKSIZE of that member is larger than the BLKSIZE you intend to specify. Having done this, you run the following job:

```
//SMITH12 JOB (account-number),
//      SMITH,MSGCLASS=X
//**
//*  Repair the DCB
//*  attributes of a library
//**
//COMPRESS EXEC PGM=IEBCOPY
//SYSPRINT DD SYSOUT=*
//PROCLIB DD DISP=OLD,
//      DSN=USER.PROCLIB,
//      DCB=(LRECL=80,
//      RECFM=FB,BLKSIZE=3120)
//SYSIN DD *
    COPY I=PROCLIB,O=PROCLIB
```

As if by magic, the mangled DSCB will be repaired when the above is executed.

These are practical examples. They are supposed to cover cases that you may actually encounter in real life.

What else might you want as an example here for reference? You might want to change the record format (RECFM) of a mangled FBS data set to unmangled FB.

Perhaps you remember that an FBS data set is exactly like an FB data set, except that, for an FBS data set, all blocks except the last block must be the same size, that is, the maximum size, the size specified in the BLKSIZE. The last block may be short. This means that an FBS data set becomes mangled if anyone adds records onto the end of it using DISP=MOD.

In case this ever happens to you, you will want to copy the mangled data set to a new FB data set using IEBGENER. You will tell IEBGENER, in the DCB parameter on the DD statement, that the existing FBS data set is really RECFM=FB. As FB, it will be perfectly readable.

Assuming that the input data set is named MANGLED.FBS.DATASET and it has DCB attributes of RECFM=FBS, BLKSZE=3120, DSORG=PS, and LRECL=80, your JCL will look like this:

```
//SMITH14 JOB (account-number),
//      SMITH,MSGCLASS=X
//*
//*  Copy a mangled FBS data
//*  set to a new FB data set
//*
//UNMANGLE EXEC PGM=IEBGENER
//SYSPRINT DD  SYSOUT=*
//SYSIN   DD  DUMMY
//*
//SYSUT1  DD DISP=SHR,
//  DSN=MANGLED.FBS.DATASET,
//  DCB=(LRECL=80,BLKSZE=3120,
//  DSORG=PS,RECFM=FB)      yes, MVS
//*  will accept your
//*  word on this RECFM
//*
//SYSUT2 DD UNIT=SYSDA,
//  DISP=(NEW,CATLG,DELETE),
//  DSN=SMITH.NEWFB.DATASET,
//  DCB=(LRECL=80,BLKSZE=3120,
//  DSORG=PS,RECFM=FB),
//  SPACE=(TRK,(500),RLSE)
```

After the above job completes, you may rename the old data set to some other name, and then rename the new data set to the original name. Then any other JCL that refers to that data set will not need to be changed.

After a while you can delete the mangled data set, that is, after you are happy that the new one is everything you hoped it would be.

Why, you ask, have you specified DISP=(NEW,CATLG,DELETE) for the new data set? And how did you come up with 500 tracks as a SPACE request? Related questions.

You're guessing about the SPACE. You don't know how big the thing is and you don't feel like looking at SPF option 3.2 to find out. You feel that 500 is a big number. If you guessed too large, the RLSE parameter ensures that any unused tracks will be liberated when the program closes the data set. If you guessed too small, the job will ABEND with a D37 abend code; in this case the conditional DISP of DELETE will take effect, and the new data set will be deleted. You can then increase the SPACE and run it again. Is there anything else that could go wrong in regards to your very versatile SPACE planning? Yes, it could happen that 500 tracks are not available anywhere on disk. In that case you would get a JCL error telling you that the requested space is not available. You would then need to reduce the size of your space request and try again.

This Chapter on examples would scarcely be complete without an example of the use of the TRC byte and OPTCD=J on the 3800 laser printer. Suppose you want to print a page containing a title in the bold-face typestyle EBTR followed by a short paragraph in the essay standard font ESTR. You are including ASA carriage control characters in the first byte of each line. Suppose that, at your company, SYSOUT=3 goes to the 3800 laser printer. You can use the following sort of JCL:

```
//SMITH15 JOB (account-number),
//      SMITH,MSGCLASS=X
//*
//*  Print something fancy on
//*  the 3800 laser printer
//*
//PRINT   EXEC PGM=IEBGENER
//SYSPRINT DD  SYSOUT=*
//SYSIN   DD  DUMMY
//*
```

```
//SYSUT2 DD SYSOUT=3,
//  DCB=(OPTCD=J,
//  RECFM=FBA),
//  CHARS=(ESTR,EBTR)
//SYSUT1  DD *
```

10

−0

-1 **T H I S   I S   T H E**

01 **B O L D F A C E   T I T L E**

+1 _____

00 Here we have a short

0 paragraph to be printed

0 in a different font from

0 the above title, as you can

0 see from the different

0 TRC codes. A trick, by the

0 way, is that a blank in

0 the TRC column is treated

0 as if it were a zero. So you

0 don't really need to put all

   those zeroes in column 2.

   This is a good reason to put

0 your primary typestyle first

0 in the list in the CHARS parm.

0 Well, have fun with it.

+0 _____

-0

//* END OF THE EXAMPLE

You now know more than enough about DD statements to get by.

SECTION 3.

RUNNING THE PROGRAMS

Chapter 11

EXEC: THE EXECUTE STATEMENT

THE EXEC STATEMENT FOR EXECUTING PROGRAMS

The EXEC statement, in its basic form, is pretty simple. In this chapter we will discuss the basic use of the EXEC statement for executing a program.

The other way you can use an EXEC statement is for executing a procedure. A procedure is a set of JCL statements. Procedures will be discussed in Chapter 12 in more detail.

First, the basics.

PGM

To execute a program, you code PGM= as the first parameter on the EXEC statement. The PGM parameter has the unusual attribute of being both a keyword parameter and a positional parameter at the same time.

Example:

Tell MVS that you want to execute program IEFBR14:

    // EXEC PGM=IEFBR14

It can't be that simple really, right?

Right. There is also another form, the referback form. The PGM=*. to match the referback available with DSN and DCB. You do not need to use it, but it is there if you want it. And you should have a passing familiarity with it so you can make sense of it when you see it. You may do the following, should you ever wish to do so, or you may encounter existing JCL where someone else has done the following:

```
//SMITH4A1 JOB  MSGCLASS=X
//STEP1  EXEC COBUCL
//SYSIN  DD  DISP=SHR,
//  DSN=SMITH.COBOL.SOURCE(PGM1)
//R EXEC PGM=*.STEP1.LKED.SYSLMOD
//STEPLIB  DD DISP=SHR,
//  DSN=*.STEP1.LKED.SYSLMOD
```

So those are the basic forms.

What happens if the system cannot find the program you ask it to execute? You get an 806 Abend.

Generally this means either that you need to correct your spelling of the name of the program, or else that you need to find out the name of the library where it is—it must be someplace, right?—and include that library on a STEPLIB or JOBLIB DD statement.

Related abends you can get are the 047 and the 306.

This means that MVS found the program you wanted, but the program wanted to do special authorized things and it wasn't in a special authorized library (047 means the main program wasn't in an authorized library, and 306 means a subroutine wasn't).

This kind of authorization, called APF authorization, is different from RACF-type security authorization. Basically MVS keeps a list of program libraries that are authorized to do special operating system type things such as backup entire disk volumes without being asked for the passwords for any of the data sets on the disks; and, possibly, unload and reload IMS data bases. If you try to execute such a program—to reload a data base, say—and the data sets in your STEPLIB or JOBLIB concatenation are not in the APF list, your program will abend in this way.

Usually this problem comes up when you have concatenated libraries on STEPLIB or JOBLIB, and some of them are in the list of APF authorized libraries, but others are not. MVS decides to play it safe and treat the lot as unauthorized. It's called losing authorization.

You then need to remove from your concatenated STEPLIB or JOBLIB those libraries that are authentically not APF authorized, leaving only those that are. Then it should work.

How do you know which are in the list?

Try looking in SYS1.PARMLIB(IEAAPF00), the place where the list is usually kept. Of course, you might not be authorized to look at it. Or it might be called IEAAPF27 or IEAAPF86 or some such variation. If you do get to look at it, note that the volume names are specified explicitly for each data set on the list. That means that a data set can lose authorization if somebody moves it and forgets to update the list. The lists are usually pretty long, so hunting down an 047 or a 306 this way can be tedious. If you are not (RACF-)authorized to look at the list, or if you don't particularly feel like going through it, you can always just guess, or ask one of the people responsible for MVS maintenance at your place. If you decide to ask, especially if you take this decision because you're too lazy to go through the list, pretend you don't know about the list. They don't expect you to know. Another point in favor of just asking, besides laziness, is that, if they have recently moved some data sets and forgotten to update the list, they will probably realize it immediately as soon as you ask, and maybe even remember which data sets they moved. Notice that after they update the list, the updated version will normally not go into effect until after an IPL (Initial Program Load) (like re-booting a PC).

Ninety per cent of these errors are caused by having included a non-APF-authorized library in the STEPLIB or JOBLIB concatenation. Check that out before you risk embarrassing yourself enquiring about the APF list only to have it pointed out that your concatenation includes the library SMITH.GAMES.LOAD, most pointedly not in the APF list.

TIME

The TIME parameter limits the amount of CPU time your program may use.

It is expressed in units of minutes comma seconds. Thus TIME=(1,30) means one minute and thirty seconds of CPU time; TIME=5 means five minutes of CPU time; TIME=(0,45) means forty-five seconds of CPU time.

If you specify such a time limit and your program uses that amount of time before completing, the program will fail with a 322 ABEND. If the program is an IMS BMP, the abend code is U002.

Notice that the time in question is CPU time, not wall clock time.

You realize that computer time (CPU time, processing time) is different from elapsed time (real time, wall clock time). Your program may begin processing at 4:00 and end at 4:15 but use only a few seconds of CPU time during that interval. The CPU time is the time that your program was actually using the CPU, that is, doing computations and manipulations. The rest of the interval was spent waiting. Part of the time your program may have been waiting for its turn to use the CPU, since the CPU is shared between all the tasks that are running concurrently. Part of the time may have been spent waiting for I/O to complete, or waiting for a data set someone else was using. None of that time counts towards the accumulation of CPU time. Only actual processing time counts, not waiting time.

Your program can run out of waiting time, but you cannot control the amount of waiting time you are allowed. That is controlled by the people who set up MVS for you. When would you run out of waiting time? Suppose MVS issues a message to the operator requesting some reply (such as permission for you to overwrite a data set with an EXPDT expiration date) or requesting some action (such as mounting a tape). If the operator never responds, your program will eventually abend with a 522 abend code.

Why would you want to specify a limit on the amount of CPU time your program is allowed?

Generally only in one of these two cases: Either you want to increase the default, or you want to specify a small limit because you fear your program may go into a dreaded infinite loop (which happens too often).

The default time limit is set up at the discretion of the people responsible for setting up MVS at your site. It can and usually does vary depending on job class. The people who set up these time limits have farther reaching powers. They can prevent you from specifying the TIME parameter at all; or, to be more precise, they can arrange things in such a way that your job will fail with a JCL error if you attempt to specify the TIME parameter. A fairly common practice is for them to specify an upper limit as to what you are allowed to request.

Specifying TIME=1440 means that the program is to be permitted to run for all eternity. On some systems, it also means that the accounting routines will lose track of the program and you will not be charged for your CPU time.

TIME=NOLIMIT means the same as TIME=1440, but it is only available as of MVS/ESA version 4 and thereafter.

TIME=MAXIMUM is similar but not identical. Available as of MVS/ESA version 4 and thereafter, this nuance does place an eventual limit on the amount of CPU time that the job is allowed, something short of eternity. Short of a year, in fact; about eight months. What's the point? The point is that MVS does actually keep track of the time, although you can have all you want; as opposed to not keeping track at all.

To achieve a similar effect with less advanced software, code TIME=1439 (just short of 1440).

A word of caution. If your program ABENDS with a 322, that does not necessarily mean you ought to increase the TIME you allow it. It more often means that your program has gone into an infinite loop. Check the program before you increase the time limit.

Examples:

Execute the program IEFBR14, and allow it an hour of CPU time (Most of the time will not be used):

```
//BR14 EXEC PGM=IEFBR14,TIME=60
```

Execute the program IEFBR14, and allow it only 1 second of CPU time (which should be plenty):

```
//BR14 EXEC PGM=IEFBR14,
//   TIME=(0,1)
```

Execute the program IEFBR14, and allow it 3 minutes and 27 seconds of CPU time (to create an aura of precision):

```
//BR14 EXEC PGM=IEFBR14,
//   TIME=(3,27)
```

Execute the program IEFBR14, and allow it to run forever (It won't take advantage of your generosity):

```
//BR14 EXEC PGM=IEFBR14,
//   TIME=1440
```

Do not code TIME=0. This used to mean zero. Now it means that the step is allowed to use whatever CPU time is leftover from the previous step.

(Note that TIME and REGION on the JOB statement work much the same as on the EXEC statement, except that TIME on the JOB statement specifies a total time for the entire job, and TIME=0 works differently . This is covered in Chapter 14.)

REGION

The REGION parameter specifies the maximum amount of memory your program may use. Virtual memory. Virtual storage. Region.

It is expressed in units K or M. K, short for kilobytes, is about a thousand bytes (1024 really). M, short for Megabytes, is about a million bytes (actually 1024 multiplied by 1024).

The default region size is specified at the discretion of the people responsible for setting up MVS at your site. It can but rarely does vary depending on job class. The people who set up these region sizes have the same far reaching powers for REGION as for TIME: They can arrange things in such a way that your job will fail with a JCL error if you attempt to specify the REGION parameter. More often they make no such restriction, but rather you find yourself limited by the amount of virtual memory MVS actually has available. The people responsible for setting up MVS don't like it any better than you do. In fact they probably feel the pinch of the shortage much more acutely than you, if that makes you feel any better.

If your program requires a larger REGION than you give it, that is, if it needs more memory than it can get, it will abend, usually with an 878 or 80A abend code. Occasionally it can be an 0C4 memory. Which particular Abend code it gets depends on what exactly it was trying to do.

Examples:

Execute the program IEFBR14, and allow it about 6 million bytes of virtual storage (virtual memory):

```
//BR14 EXEC PGM=IEFBR14,
//   REGION=6M
```

Execute the program IEFBR14, and allow it about 6 million bytes of virtual storage and 20 minutes of CPU time:

```
//BR14 EXEC PGM=IEFBR14,
//   REGION=6M,TIME=20
```

Execute the program IEFBR14, allowing it about half a Megabyte (500 Kilobytes) of virtual storage and 20 minutes of CPU time; Reverse the order of TIME and REGION relative to the preceding example, just to show that you understand that these are true keyword parameters (as opposed to that mongrel PGM parameter, which always has to come first even though it has the appearance of a keyword parameter):

```
//BR14 EXEC PGM=IEFBR14,
//   TIME=20,REGION=500K
```

This is as good a time as any to introduce a few vocabulary items related to REGION.

The first of these words is partition. It has nothing to do with MVS, but you hear it used as if it were a semi-synonym for REGION. The history is this. IBM distributes other operating systems besides MVS. Notably

VM and DOS/VSE. Also, many years ago, MFT and mainframe DOS non-VSE (no relation to PC DOS). Under MFT, and under (mainframe) DOS, the system takes all of the available memory and divides it into separate areas of fixed size. If it had 6 Megabytes of memory, for example, it might reserve 3 Meg for itself and then divide the remainder into areas where programs could run, maybe 4 areas of 500K each plus one area of 1 Meg. These areas for programs to run are called partitions. Each is some fixed size, determined by the people who set up the system. It doesn't work that way with MVS. With MVS the size of the program memory is variable and is requested by the REGION parameter. Nevertheless, you will often hear the word partition used to refer to region size, and it is pedantic to insist on correct use. You know what they mean. Well, now you do. Just to complete the history of that era, there was another operating system called MVT. MVT did use the REGION parameter and therefore was the direct ancestor of MVS.

The other vocabulary item you will encounter in this connection is address space. The area of memory where your program runs is called its Address Space. Address Spaces are assigned numbers, called Address space ID numbers, abbreviated ASID. One job might have Address space 27 while another might have ASID number 43, for example. The numbers are assigned sequentially. Job numbers are also assigned sequentially, but the Address space number is a different number from the job number. Do you care about the ASID number? Very unlikely. The size of the Address space is the region. In practice the word region is most commonly used to mean both the area in memory (the Address space) and the size of the area (the region). Still you ought to be passingly familiar with the term Address space so you won't feel ignorant if you happen to hear it used..

(Note that REGION on the JOB statement works much the same as on the EXEC statement, except that the REGION on the JOB statement overrides the REGION on the EXEC statement. This is covered in Chapter 14.)

PARM

The PARM parameter is used to pass information to a program at the time the program executes.

Why not just have the program read data from a data set? You could. The PARM parameter is just a way of passing a small amount of information to the program without using a data set.

You can write your own programs to obtain information from the PARM parameter, but you probably never do. Probably the only programs you use that read the PARM information are IBM-supplied programs such as the compilers and the Linkage Editor.

So, how do you do it?

You can pass a string of up to 100 characters, enclosed within single quotes (apostrophes). PARM='Summer rain' for example, or PARM='LIST,LET,XREF,AMODE(31),RMODE(ANY),AC(1)' for another example. The quotes are optional if the string contains only letters, numbers, and hyphens.

PARM=OKAY would be valid, but PARM='OKAY.FINE.' would require quotes.

Parentheses will do instead of quotes if the string contains only letters, numbers, matched parentheses, hyphens, and commas. For example, PARM=(LIST,LET,XREF,AMODE(31),RMODE(ANY),AC(1)) is valid.

Special characters require the quotes.

A question mark is an example of a character that is considered special in this context, as are the full stop, the exclamation mark, asterisks, most mathematical symbols, packed decimal and all other unprintable characters, and the entire lower-case alphabet, to name a few.

Two questions perhaps now spring into your mind.

One, how do you include an apostrophe within the string? Two, how do you pass a quoted string of 100 characters when a card - a line of JCL - is only 80 columns wide?

Easily done.

One: an apostrophe is represented as two consecutive apostrophes within the quoted string. For example, if you code PARM='You''re joking.' then the program will receive this string: You're joking.

Two: To continue a quoted string onto a second line, you need to use both parentheses and quotes. Begin with a left parenthesis. Then put an opening single quote mark followed by as much data as fits. Add an ending single quote mark followed by a comma. On the next line, begin with an opening single quote mark again. Follow this with the rest of your data. End with an ending single quote mark followed by a closing right parenthesis. The only problem with this method is that the comma that signifies a continuation of the line also becomes embedded in the string that is passed to the program. Fortunately most of the IBM-supplied programs ignore these extra commas. (IMS does not ignore them.)

Example:

```
//SMITH4D1 JOB 0,MSGCLASS=X
// EXEC PGM=IEFBR14,
//    PARM=('You"re',
//        'joking.')
//*
//* What the program sees:
//* You're, joking.
//*
```

Additional examples:

```
//SMITH4D2 JOB 0,MSGCLASS=X
//*
//A EXEC PGM=IEFBR14,
// PARM=OKAY
//*
//B EXEC PGM=IEFBR14,
// PARM=(OKAY,FINE)
//*
//C EXEC PGM=IEFBR14,
// PARM='SURE, WHY NOT?'
//*
//D EXEC PGM=IEFBR14,
```

```
// PARM='YOU"RE JOKING.'
//*
//E EXEC PGM=IEFBR14,
//    PARM=(LIST,LET,
//    XREF,AMODE(31),
//    RMODE(ANY),AC(1))
//*
//F EXEC PGM=IEFBR14,
//    PARM=(LIST,LET,
//    XREF,AMODE(31),
//    RMODE(ANY),AC(1))
//*
//G EXEC PGM=IEFBR14,
//*
// PARM=(LIST,LET,XREF,
//    'AMODE(31)',
//    'RMODE(ANY),AC(1)')
//*
//H EXEC PGM=IEFBR14,
// PARM='LIST,LET,XREF'
//*
//I EXEC PGM=IEFBR14,
//    PARM=702-6143
//*
//J EXEC PGM=IEFBR14,
// PARM=('Help! I"ve been ',
//    'kidnapped by',
//    ' space aliens and',
//    ' am being bored to',
//    ' death; also',
//    'there"s a bad smell.')
//*
```

Maybe you wonder what XREF and LIST mean in the above PARM strings.

In the above cases, they don't mean anything, since they are passed to IEFBR14. IEFBR14, as you know, does nothing. Part of the nothing it does consists of not looking at the PARM.

Okay, you say, but what if it was some other program instead of IEFBR14? You see XREF and LIST all the time, being passed to programs like the linkage editor and the compilers.

Well, yes, there is a curious and comforting sameness in the PARM parameters accepted by many of the IBM-supplied programs. LIST generally means you want a listing of some sort. XREF, if it is valid for any particular program, generally expresses the idea that you want a cross reference listing to be printed. X is short for cross. REF is short for reference.

Other parameters, such as AMODE (addressing mode) and RMODE (residence mode) will be discussed in the section on the linkage editor.

On second thought, maybe you DO want to pass information to your own programs through the PARM parameter. The following sample PL/I program shows the basic process.

Notice that when you pass a PARM to a PL/I program you should include a single slash within the quoted string just prior to the actual data you wish to pass. Anything within the string prior to this slash is examined by PL/I to see whether it might be a run-time instruction to PL/I itself, something meaningful like ISASIZE(10K). If you omit the slash, PL/I will attempt to make sense out of your string; failing to do so, it will give you an IBM003I error message, "ERRONEOUS PARM OPTION HAS BEEN IGNORED". The IBM003I message is harmless, but if you dislike it, remember to include the slash, as is done in the example.

Just for your information, COBOL uses the slash in exactly the opposite way, so that parameters passed to COBOL come AFTER the slash, and those passed to your program precede the slash.

The example:

```
//SMITH4D3 JOB 0,MSGCLASS=X
//COMPILE EXEC PLIXCL
//SYSPRINT DD SYSOUT=*
```

```
PSAMPLE: PROC(PARM)
OPTIONS(MAIN);

DCL PARM CHAR(100) VARYING;
DECLARE LINE CHARACTER(100);

LINE = PARM;
PUT SKIP LIST(LINE);

END PSAMPLE;

//LKED.SYSLMOD DD DISP=SHR,
//   DSN=SMITH.LOAD(PSAMPLE)
//LKED.SYSPRINT DD SYSOUT=*
//*
//PSAMPLE EXEC PGM=PSAMPLE,
// PARM=('/YOU"RE NOT SERIOUS',
//     ' ARE YOU?')
//*
//STEPLIB DD DISP=SHR,
// DSN=*.COMPILE.LKED.SYSLMOD
//SYSPRINT DD SYSOUT=*
```

The above program produces the following output on the ddname SYSPRINT:

```
YOU'RE NOT SERIOUS, ARE YOU?
```

Perhaps you prefer COBOL rather than PL/I. If so, use the following example instead:

```
//SMITH4D4 JOB 0,MSGCLASS=X
//COMPILE EXEC COBUCL
    IDENTIFICATION DIVISION.
    PROGRAM-ID.  PSAMPLE.
    ENVIRONMENT DIVISION.
```

223

```
CONFIGURATION SECTION.
SOURCE-COMPUTER. IBM-370.
OBJECT-COMPUTER. IBM-370.
 DATA DIVISION.
 WORKING-STORAGE
  SECTION.
 01 OUTPUT-PRINT-LINE.
  05  PRINT-LINE
    PIC  X(100).
 LINKAGE SECTION.
 01 PARM.
  05  LENGTH-OF-TEXT
    PIC S9(4) COMP.
  05  TEXT-STRING
    PIC  X(100).
 PROCEDURE DIVISION
  USING PARM.
  MOVE TEXT-STRING
    TO PRINT-LINE.
  DISPLAY PRINT-LINE.
  STOP RUN.

//LKED.SYSLMOD DD DISP=SHR,
//    DSN=SMITH.LOAD(PSAMPLE)
//*
//PSAMPLE EXEC
// PGM=*.COMPILE.LKED.SYSLMOD,
//*
//  PARM=(' IF IT ISN"T FUN',
//  'YOU"RE NOT DOING IT RIGHT.')
//*
//STEPLIB DD DISP=SHR,
// DSN=*.COMPILE.LKED.SYSLMOD
//    DD DISP=SHR,
//    DSN=SYS1.VSCLLIB
```

```
//     DD DISP=SHR,
//     DSN=SYS1.VSCOLIB
//SYSPRINT DD SYSOUT=*
//SYSOUT  DD SYSOUT=*
```

The above program produces the following output on the ddname SYSOUT:

IF IT ISN'T FUN, YOU'RE NOT DOING IT RIGHT.

Notice that COBOL uses the ddname SYSOUT rather than SYSPRINT here, and that you do not precede the PARM string with a slash (/) as you do in the PL/I example.

Notice another nuance before you plan to write programs that accept information via the PARM.

In order to obtain the PARM, your program must be a main program. A subroutine does not receive the PARM.

And when is a main program not a main program?

Oftener than you might think.

Most especially, it is treated as a subroutine when it executes under IMS, either as a batch DLI or a BMP.

In other words, if your program will use an IMS data base, your program will probably be treated as a subroutine of DFSRRC00, a part of IMS. In such a case, if your program is named, say, JIPIJAPA, then your EXEC statement will look something like this:

```
//JIPIJAPA EXEC PGM=DFSRRC00,
//     REGION=6M,
//     PARM=(DLI,
//     JIPIJAPA,
//     JIPIJAPA,,,,,,,,,,,N)
```

As you can see, the program named DFSRRC00 is going to get the PARM, and your program, JIPIJAPA, is never going to see it.

So it's no use to your programs that use IMS databases.

Nevertheless, the PARM string can be handy when you write procedures. Do this. Make an approximate copy of one of the examples above and run it on your own real life MVS system. You may have to change a few things in the JCL to conform to local customs. Possibly your userid is not really SMITH, for example. So rearrange it to make it work for you. Play around with it until you're comfortable that it's really yours, like a new car. Then we'll use it when we come to the chapter on procedures, Chapter 12.

COND

The COND parameter specifies conditional execution of a step. That is, the step might or might not actually execute, depending. Depending on what?

On the results of previous steps. Whether they abended or not and/or what condition codes (return codes) they got.

Notice that COND is an old and unpopular parameter. In more recent times the IF-THEN-ELSE construct has been introduced into JCL as an optional substitute for COND. However, this section is about COND, which you need to know about even if you don't use it in JCL you write yourself; because you want to understand it when you see it on other people's JCL that you might have to run sometime; and because you might want to override the setting.

Take a simple example. If you say COND=ONLY on some EXEC statement, that means that you want that particular EXEC statement actually to be executed only if some previous step abended.

Another simple example: if you say COND=EVEN on some EXEC statement, that means that you want that particular EXEC statement actually to be executed even if some previous step abended.

That almost exhausts all of the possibilities for simple examples of COND.

Nobody likes COND, did I tell you that? Well, nobody we've ever run into as far as we know.

Maybe that's why IBM gave us the IF-THEN-ELSE-ENDIF construction in JCL as of ESA MVS/SP Version 4. Nice enhancement. We'll discuss it in Chapter 13.

Meanwhile, you see the COND parameter used all the time.

Don't feel bad about it if you have trouble remembering the exact syntax. Don't annoy people by moaning about how badly designed it all is, but then again don't feel that it reflects any shortcoming in yourself.

People tend to find it a bit counter-intuitive. I forget the exact words they use to describe it.

But the situation is like this.

Except for the cases of EVEN and ONLY, just given, the COND parameter is used to express some condition under which the current step is to be skipped.

For example, if your EXEC statement said COND=(0,NE) on it, then it would be skipped if any preceding step had ended with a condition code that was not equal to zero. (NE means not equal). Okay so far.

Let's explain condition codes before we go any further.

Also known as return codes.

There exist special areas of memory called registers. MVS uses the different registers for different purposes.

When your program starts to execute, for example, Register 14 contains the address in memory of the next program statement to which control is to be returned when your program ends.

If your program is a subroutine, then Register 14 contains the address of the next statement in the program that called it. So the subroutine ends, and the main program continues with the next statement.

Not to get too metaphysical with this, but ordinary main programs are, in some sense, all subroutines of the big main program in the sky, which in this case is MVS. So IEFBR14, a program you already know, just immediately ends by branching to the address in register 14.

Yeah, fine. So where does the return code come into this?

It's in Register 15.

Whatever happens to be in Register 15 when your program ends (when your program returns to its caller), well, that's the return code. Also called the condition code.

You will often see condition code abbreviated CC and return code abbreviated RC, and they all mean the same thing.

By convention, most programs put a zero into register 15 if all went well during execution. In other words, they set the return code to 0.

227

PL/I, COBOL, and other high level languages do this for you automatically.

By the same convention, programs set the condition code to 4 if things went fairly well, 8 if things didn't go too well, 12 if things went rather poorly, 16 if the situation is bad.

They don't usually go above 16 in this arrangement, but sometimes they do. PL/I often uses numbers in the thousands. Occasionally you run into programs that don't bother to set a return code at all; they end with a return code equal to whatever leftover rubbish happens to be in Register 15.

But most programs follow the little 0-4-8-12-16 system just described.

So, if you have a job that contains two EXEC statements, that is, two steps, then you can arrange things so that the second step is skipped if the first step goes wrong.

Consider the following example. LT means Less than. All three steps will in fact be executed.

```
//SMITH4E1 JOB 1,MSGCLASS=X
//*
//STEP1  EXEC PGM=IEFBR14
//*
//NE0 EXEC PGM=IEFBR14,
//  COND=(0,NE,STEP1)
//*
//*  SKIP STEP NE0 IF 0 IS NOT
//*  EQUAL TO THE CC FROM STEP1
//*
//LT8 EXEC PGM=IEFBR14,
//  COND=(8,LT,STEP1)
//*
//*  SKIP STEP LT8 IF 8 IS LESS
//*  THAN THE CC FROM STEP1
//*
```

What's wrong with this picture? People generally would find it easier to follow and to remember

(1) if the syntax were arranged in exactly the reverse order,

AND

(2) if the conditional contingency specified by the COND parameter were the execution of the conditional step, rather than the skipping of it.

That is, it would be satisfactory enough if one could specify (STEP1,LT,8) and have it be taken to mean that the condition code from STEP1 had to be less than 8 in order for the contingent step to execute. Well, you cannot.

The two problems with COND combine to make a sort of double negative that the human mind naturally strives to resolve in a dream-like twist.

Combining the two negatives, the mind tends to look at the situation as if it meant that the conditional step (step LT8 in our example above) will be executed if the return code from the relevant preceding step (STEP1 in our example) meets the specified condition (is less than 8).

As you see, this appears to work for step LT8 in the above example. It will be executed if the condition code from STEP1 is less than 8.

This is just another way of saying that STEP LT8 will be skipped if 8 is less than the return code from STEP1.

So, what's the problem, you ask, with remembering it the easier, intuitively compelling, doubly reversed way?

The problem is that it is not correct to reverse the thinking in this way when dealing with equality.

In the above example, step NE0 will be skipped if zero is not equal to the condition code from STEP1.

In other words, step NE0 will be executed. (IEFBR14 always returns a zero return code.)

If you start thinking that COND=(8,LT) means go ahead and execute this step if all preceding condition codes were less than 8, don't fall into the trap of thinking that COND=(0,EQ) means go ahead and execute this step if all preceding condition codes were equal to zero.

It doesn't mean that.

That meaning is conveyed by COND=(0,NE) as in the above example.

The brutal part is over now. If you've made it this far, you can't be stopped.

There are complicated forms of the COND parameter, with execution depending on more than one step and so forth. We should probably cover these just briefly. They're nothing compared to the basic concept we just went through, though. Go ahead and take a short break at this point if you want. No human being can be expected to concentrate on the COND parameter for a long period at one sitting.

Are you back with me now?

Okay.

So, here is a complete set of the values you can use as you used NE and LT in the preceding discussion:

LT   means Less Than

LE   means Less than or Equal to

EQ   means Equal to (skip step if equal to)

NE   means Not Equal to as already discussed

GE   means Greater than or Equal to

GT   means Greater Than

Fine.

Obviously LE and GE, which involve a test for equality, can get you into the same trouble as EQ and NE. Avoid them. Even if you have no trouble keeping the meaning of COND clear in your head (I doubt this seriously), have some consideration for the other people who may use or copy your JCL.

In the above discussion, we specified a step name, STEP1, so that execution of the conditional step was dependent only on the result of STEP1.

If you leave off the step name, then execution of the conditional step is dependent on the return codes from all previous steps.

So the following two jobs are equivalent:

```
//SMITH4E2 JOB 2,MSGCLASS=X
//STEP1  EXEC PGM=IEFBR14
//NE0 EXEC PGM=IEFBR14,
//  COND=(0,NE)


//SMITH4E3 JOB 3,MSGCLASS=X
//STEP1  EXEC PGM=IEFBR14
```

```
//NE0   EXEC PGM=IEFBR14,
//     COND=(0,NE,STEP1)
```

Also you can specify multiple conditionals:

```
//SMITH4E4 JOB 4,MSGCLASS=X
//STEP1  EXEC PGM=IEFBR14
//STEP2  EXEC PGM=IEFBR14
//*
//NE0   EXEC PGM=IEFBR14,
// COND=((0,NE,STEP1),
//     (0,NE,STEP2))
```

Next example:

```
//SMITH4E5 JOB 5,MSGCLASS=X
//*
//STEP1  EXEC PGM=IEFBR14
//STEP2  EXEC PGM=IEFBR14
//STEP3  EXEC PGM=IEFBR14
//*
//NE0 EXEC PGM=IEFBR14,
// COND=(0,NE)
//*
//* SKIP STEP NE0 IF 0 IS
//* NOT EQUAL TO THE RETURN
//* CODE FROM ANY PRECEDING STEP.
//*
//* WHICH IS TO SAY, SKIP
//* STEP NE0 IF ANY PRECEDING
//* STEP HAD A RETURN CODE NOT
//* EQUAL TO ZERO
//*
//* EXECUTE STEP NE0 ONLY IF
//* EVERY SINGLE PRECEDING
```

```
//* STEP ENDED WITH RETURN
//* CODE ZERO.
//*
//LT8 EXEC PGM=IEFBR14,
//   COND=(8,LT)
//*
//*   SKIP STEP LT8 IF 8 IS
//*   LESS THAN THE CC FROM
//*   ANY PRECEDING STEP.
//*
//*   IF 8 IS LESS THAN THE
//*   RETURN CODE OF SOME
//*   PRECEDING STEP, THEN THE
//*   RETURN CODE FROM THAT STEP
//*   WAS GREATER THAN
//*   (OR EQUAL TO) 8.
//*
//*   SO, PUT ANOTHER WAY,
//*   SKIP STEP LT8
//*   IF ANY PRECEDING STEP
//*   ENDED WITH A RETURN CODE
//*   GREATER THAN OR EQUAL TO 8.
//*
//*   IN OTHER WORDS,
//*   EXECUTE STEP LT8 ONLY IF
//*   ALL PRECEDING STEPS ENDED
//*   WITH RETURN CODES
//*   LESS THAN 8.
//*
```

You notice that this is almost identical to the example given earlier with job name SMITH4E1, except that here the step name has been left off within the value assigned to the COND parameter. Thus step NE0 will be skipped if any preceding step - STEP1, STEP2, or STEP3 - ends with a non-zero return code.

Naturally your tormentors need not confine their conditional executions to anything so simplistic. They can specify complicated multiple conditions.

You might encounter a version of the above JCL refined in such a way that step NE0 will be skipped if either the return code from STEP1 was non-zero or the return code from STEP3 was non-zero, and step LT8 will be skipped either if 8 is less than the return code from STEP2, or the return code from STEP3 is non-zero.

It looks like this:

```
//SMITH4E6 JOB 6,MSGCLASS=X
//*
//STEP1  EXEC PGM=IEFBR14
//STEP2  EXEC PGM=IEFBR14
//STEP3  EXEC PGM=IEFBR14
//*
//NE0 EXEC PGM=IEFBR14,
//  COND=((0,NE,STEP1),
//      (0,NE,STEP3))
//*
//*  SKIP STEP NE0 IF 0 IS NOT
//*  EQUAL TO THE CC FROM
//*  EITHER STEP1 OR STEP3.
//*
//*
//LT8 EXEC PGM=IEFBR14,
//  COND=((8,LT,STEP2),
//      (0,NE,STEP3))
//*
//*  SKIP STEP LT8 IF 8 IS LESS
//*  THAN THE CC FROM STEP2, OR
//*  IF THE RETURN CODE FROM
//*  STEP3 WAS NON-ZERO
//*
```

Delightful. What else can be done with this ridiculous toy? You can use it in combination with procedures, specifying qualified names. You know, things like COND=(8,LT,PLIXCL.LKED) and COND.LKED=(8,LT) and so on. But we'll save that for the chapter on procedures, Chapter 12.

Nobody likes the COND parameter, but most people seem to end up using it.

One word of warning if it falls to your luck that you are required to change a JCL procedure that already exists. If you are contemplating changing the names of any steps, first check carefully for the COND parameter in subsequent steps.

Many places use very long JCL procedures for production work, and follow a standard for JCL that requires steps within those procedures to be named with ascending sequential numbers, like STEP1, STEP2, STEP3, or S001, S002, S003, ... S024 and so on. In this case, if you ever need to insert a step in the middle someplace and consequently renumber all subsequent steps, you need to make sure you modify any subsequent COND checks accordingly.

Chapter 12

JCL PROCEDURES PROC, PEND, AND SYMBOLIC PARAMETERS

USING THE EXEC STATEMENT FOR EXECUTING PROCEDURES

The chapter on procedures! We've finally come to it!

A procedure, as you recall, is a collection of JCL.

The first statement in a procedure is the PROC statement. PROC (pronounced prahk) is one of those abbreviations you have now come to expect from JCL.

If the set of JCL that constitutes the procedure is kept in a library, then it is a cataloged procedure. The name makes no apparent sense, but that is what it is called.

The member name of a cataloged procedure should be the same as the name in the name field on the PROC statement.

Example:

```
//SHIP  PROC
//SHAPE EXEC PGM=IEFBR14
```

This would be stored in a procedure library as the member SHIP.

Sure, okay.

Now suppose you don't have a procedure library handy, but you still want to have a procedure.

No problem. You use an instream procedure, also called an instream PROC. You put it right in the same deck with the rest of the JCL for your JOB. End the instream procedure with a PEND statement. PEND means Procedure END, get it? (P. END). Anyway.

It looks like this:

```
//SHIP PROC
//SHAPE EXEC PGM=IEFBR14
//    PEND
```

If you want the PROC actually to be executed, then you add an EXEC statement specifying the name of the PROC.

This job executes the instream PROC named SHIP twice:

```
//SMITH5A1 JOB 0,SMITH,
//    MSGCLASS=X
//SHIP    PROC
//SHAPE   EXEC PGM=IEFBR14
//    PEND
//FIRST   EXEC SHIP
//SECOND  EXEC SHIP
```

Pretty easy so far.

Now symbolic parameters

Let's look at a really simple example. Then we'll talk about the example.

The really simple example:

```
//SMITH5A2 JOB 0,SMITH,
//    MSGCLASS=X
//*
//INSTREAM PROC PIECE=CAKE
//*
//PSAMPLE EXEC PGM=PSAMPLE,
//    PARM='/&PIECE '
```

```
//*
//STEPLIB DD  DISP=SHR,
//     DSN=SMITH.LOAD
//SYSPRINT DD  SYSOUT=*
//*
//     PEND
//*
//STEP1  EXEC INSTREAM
//*
//STEP2  EXEC INSTREAM,
//     PIECE=PUZZLE
//STEP3  EXEC INSTREAM,
//     PIECE=COD
```

You remember that PSAMPLE is the program you wrote at the end of the section that explained the PARM parameter. Well, okay, maybe you didn't write it yourself. Maybe you copied it out of a book and changed the variable names a little so it wouldn't be too obvious a copy. This book, maybe. Well, if you didn't, you should. Then you can play along on your own MVS system as we go through this stuff in the book here. Suit yourself. Anyway, let's say you did, and you put it in SMITH.LOAD so that when you executed it from there, it printed whatever PARM string you gave it.

So now, if you execute your program PSAMPLE out of your load library SMITH.LOAD, and you pass it a PARM string when you execute it, then it prints the PARM string.

(You still have the same load library, and PSAMPLE is still in it. Why not? We haven't given an example of deleting it, have we? So we can use it now in our procedure.)

What do you suppose the really simple example above does? If you run it as a job, I mean to say.

After the JOB statement is digested, the first next thing MVS finds is your PROC statement. Okay, says MVS, this must be the beginning of an instream procedure. MVS begins shuffling all of the following cards off into a separate little imaginary pile until he comes to the PEND (Procedure END) statement. MVS calls that pile of cards INSTREAM because INSTREAM is the name you have in the name field on the PROC statement.

After the PEND statement is a blank comment card. Not required. Actually I just put it there to make the example easier to read.

Next comes a statement that says //STEP1 EXEC INSTREAM and now MVS has the first bit of actual work to do. You've told him to execute something. So MVS wonders what this INSTREAM thing is that you want him to do, and goes off looking for it.

It can't be a program, because you didn't say PGM=INSTREAM, you just said INSTREAM. If it isn't a program it must be a PROC, because those are the only two things MVS knows how to do for you on a JCL EXEC statement. So MVS starts looking around for a procedure named INSTREAM. The very first place MVS looks, wouldn't you know it? There it is. That little pile of cards MVS started setting aside when your PROC statement was seen. There it is, INSTREAM, an instream procedure.

If MVS had not been able to find it as an instream PROC, then the system procedure libraries would have been looked at; but since it was included instream, there is no need to look further.

Now MVS examines the PROC statement a little more closely. MVS finds one (count it, 1) symbolic parameter, named PIECE. Yes, PIECE in this example is a symbolic parameter.

The word PIECE is a word you get to make up, within the usual rules of course. And, uh, there is the additional restriction that you cannot use one of the words that JCL already uses as a parameter on the EXEC statement. You cannot call it PGM or TIME, for instance.

If your procedure contains a DD statement named IEFRDER, then avoid using symbolic parameter names that are the same as DD statement parameter names, although you are not in all cases strictly forbidden from doing this. Avoiding using a word like DSN or DCB, for example. We'll talk about this more in this Chapter in the section Merging DCB Parameters and particularly when using IEFRDER.

That's correct, you refer to the symbolic parameter PIECE as &PIECE within the PROC itself.

From outside the PROC, you refer to it simply as PIECE.

Put another way, when your symbolic parameter, PIECE, occurs on the left hand side of an equals sign, it is known by its proper name of PIECE. However, when it occurs on the right hand side of an equals sign, it is a value being assigned to something else, and is known as &PIECE.

You have assigned the symbolic parameter PIECE the default value of CAKE on the PROC statement.

The default value of PIECE is CAKE.

Thus when you say PARM='/&PIECE ' later within the procedure, the value of CAKE is used, and it is the same as if you had said PARM='/ CAKE '.

By the way, if you are using the COBOL version, leave out the slash, that is, make it PARM='&PIECE ' rather than /&PIECE.

If COBOL is not the primary language in use at your company, you may also need to concatenate SYS1.VSCOLLIB and/or SYS1.VSCLLIB and/or some other data sets onto your STEPLIB if you are using COBOL. This depends on exactly how COBOL is installed at your site.

Similarly, if PL/I is not the primary language in use at your company, you may need to concatenate some PL/I libraries onto your STEPLIB.

If you need to concatenate extra libraries onto your STEPLIB in this way, you will have to ask someone at your company for the exact names of the libraries there.

Now, let us pause a moment to contemplate the awesome power you have achieved up to this point.

(1) You get to make up the name of the procedure.

You can call it SHIP or INSTREAM or anything you like, so long as you follow the usual rules: it must be less than or equal to eight characters in length, the first character must be either an uppercase letter or one of the three national characters, and the remainder of the characters must be upper-case letters, digits, or national characters. The usual rules. MBAQANGA and KWELA, also KYAT, QUETZAL, and QINDAR are valid names, as are MXYZPTLK, PARIS, FM104, @2PM, @#3 and LONDON; whereas 10%, ONE-OFF, 98FM, McCULLIN, O'BRIEN, X-MEN, CARCLAMPER and CROCODILE are not.

(2) You get to make up the names of the symbolic parameters.

Subject to the usual naming rules, but with the restriction that you cannot use a name for one of your symbolic parameters that is the same as a word JCL already uses for ordinary EXEC statement parameters (You cannot have a symbolic parameter called COND or REGION, for example).

(3) You get to assign default values.

Subject to the usual rules, except that you can assign long and/or weird strings of non-standard characters if you want to, provided you enclose the long weird strings within single quotes (apostrophes). More nuances of this soon.

I just want you to pause to reflect on your power.

You actually can, should you wish to do so, have a procedure with a symbolic parameter DOG and a default value of BLACK. The point is that you have some control here. You may find yourself making up procedures that other people will end up using. Don't make it hard for them. Give a little thought to your choices of names.

But back to the example.

When STEP1 executes, the default value for PIECE is used, because PIECE has not been coded on the STEP1 EXEC statement. Thus the first invocation of the INSTREAM PROC in the above example will use the default value of CAKE. (Executing a procedure is sometimes called invoking a procedure.)

The program will receive the word CAKE in the PARM string, and it will print one line, saying only the word CAKE. Hey, I admitted it was a simple example.

On STEP2 the same procedure will be invoked, but this time the value of PIECE will be set to PUZZLE. The program will print the word PUZZLE.

You get the picture.

Now that you have mastered this concept of symbolic parameters, there are two more little quirks you need to know about.

One is that you sometimes need to put a period after the name of the symbolic parameter when it is used on the right hand side of the equals.

Example: You could, had you wished to do so, have said, within the above simple example:

```
//PSAMPLE EXEC PGM=PSAMPLE,
//    PARM='/&PIECE.'
```

Rather than what you actually said, which was:

```
//PSAMPLE EXEC PGM=PSAMPLE,
//    PARM='/&PIECE '
```

What's the point, you ask?

In case there is any possibility of confusion, the period tells MVS where the symbolic parameter ends.

For example, suppose you wanted the program to print the word CAKEWALK whenever the PROC was executed with the parameter PIECE set to the value of CAKE. You could do this:

```
//PSAMPLE EXEC PGM=PSAMPLE,
//    PARM='/&PIECE.WALK'
```

That makes sense, right? The &PIECE.WALK will be resolved into CAKEWALK when PIECE=CAKE comes in on the EXEC statement.

Suppose CAKE.WALK was the name of a data set someplace, and you wanted something that would resolve into CAKE.WALK rather than CAKEWALK. You'd have two full stops. &PIECE..WALK will resolve into CAKE.WALK for you.

No doubt you now wish to use your newfound knowledge to do something more complex.

Let's pretend you still have the imaginary data set named SMITH.NIGERIAN.SALES.DATA with members named JANUARY, FEBRUARY, and MARCH, (alias ENERO, FEBRERO, and MARZO), containing the print reports of the sales statistics for your current employer for AK47 assault rifles in Nigeria during those months.

You have another data set just like it for JAMAICAN sales named

SMITH..JAMAICAN.SALES.DATA and not only that but you have two more data sets containing shipment data rather than sales data. These, not surprisingly, you have named SMITH.NIGERIAN.SHIPPING.DATA and SMITH.JAMAICAN.SHIPPING.DATA, and they contain members named for the months also.

You want somebody to be able to print any selected report from one of these data sets by using a simple statement such as this:

```
// EXEC AK47,COUNTRY=NIGERIA,
// MON=MARCH,DATA=SHIPPING
```

Easy enough. You make a procedure named AK47 and put it in one of the system procedure libraries (a PROCLIB). Probably someone else will copy it into the PROCLIB because you won't be authorized to do it. Under MVS/ESA Version 4 and later you will be able to test using the JCLLIB statement, which works much like JOBLIB except that it's for JCL. We'll cover JCLLIB in Chapter 13. Meanwhile you test AK47 as an instream procedure. As follows:

```
//SMITH5A3 JOB 0,SMITH,
//       MSGCLASS=X
//*
//AK47   PROC MON=JANUARY,
//  COUNTRY=JAMAICA,DATA=SALES
//*
//PRINT   EXEC PGM=IEBGENER
//SYSPRINT DD  DUMMY
//SYSIN  DD  DUMMY
//SYSUT2 DD SYSOUT=*
//SYSUT1 DD DISP=SHR,
// DSN=SMITH.&COUNTRY.N.&DATA..DATA(&MON.)
// PEND
//*
//STEP1  EXEC AK47
//STEP2  EXEC AK47,
```

```
//    COUNTRY=NIGERIA,
//    MON=FEBRERO
```

What happens here? On STEP1, all of your defaults are used. &COUNTRY. becomes JAMAICA, so &COUNTRY.N becomes JAMAICAN and the word JAMAICAN is used for the second level qualifier of the data set name on SYSUT1. &TYPE. becomes SALES, the default you specified on your PROC statement. &MON. becomes JANUARY and the entire data set name changes from SMITH.&COUNTRY.N.&TYPE..DATA(&MON.) into SMITH.JAMAICAN.SALES.DATA(JANUARY) with the result that the January report is printed as a result of STEP1.

On STEP2, the EXEC statement specifies COUNTRY and MON, so the specified values are used. The EXEC statement does not specify DATA, so the default value of SALES is obtained from the PROC statement and used.

Thus, for STEP2, &COUNTRY. becomes NIGERIA so &COUNTRY.N becomes NIGERIAN and the word NIGERIAN is used.

&TYPE. becomes SALES and &MON. turns into FEBRERO, an alias name for the member FEBRUARY.

The data set name used for SYSUT1 as a result of STEP2 is thus SMITH.NIGERIAN.SALES.DATA(FEBRERO) and that is printed.

Okay. You have the basic picture. You can, obviously, carry this into very complex patterns should you so desire.

One more point about symbolic parameters. Assigning a value to a symbolic parameter is much like assigning a value to a PARM string. If the value you assign is the least bit strange, then you need to enclose it within single quotes (apostrophes), like a PARM value. (Parentheses are handled poorly for symbolic parameters, being passed along as in the following example.) The really simple example made slightly less simple:

```
//SMITH5A4 JOB 0,SMITH,
//    MSGCLASS=X
//INSTREAM PROC PIECE=CAKE
//PSAMPLE EXEC PGM=PSAMPLE,
//    PARM='/&PIECE '
```

```
//STEPLIB DD  DISP=SHR,
//    DSN=SMITH.LOAD
//SYSPRINT DD  SYSOUT=*
//    PEND
//*
//A EXEC INSTREAM,
// PIECE='Mozart''''s piano concerto 24 in D minor'
//*
//B   EXEC INSTREAM,
//    PIECE='de Resistance'
//*
//C EXEC INSTREAM,PIECE=PIE
//*
//D   EXEC INSTREAM,
//    PIECE=(57, CHANNELS)
```

The above causes the following 4 lines to be printed:

```
Mozart's piano concerto 24 in D minor
 de Resistance
PIE
(57, CHANNELS)
```

Another example:

```
//SMITH5A5 JOB 0,SMITH,MSGCLASS=X
//*
//AK47 PROC D='SMITH.JAMAICAN.SALES.DATA(JANUARY)'
//*
//PRINT   EXEC PGM=IEBGENER
//SYSPRINT DD  DUMMY
//SYSIN  DD  DUMMY
//SYSUT2 DD  SYSOUT=*
//SYSUT1 DD  DISP=SHR,DSN=&D
//*
```

```
//  PEND
//*
//STEP1 EXEC AK47,
//   D='SMITH.JAMAICAN.SALES.DATA(JANUARY)'
```

The example shown as job SMITH5A5 above will accomplish exactly the same thing as executing the AK47 procedure in STEP1 of job
SMITH5A3 above. The symbolic parameter &D on SYSUT1 will be resolved into SMITH.JAMAICAN.SALES.DATA(JANUARY) with the result that the January report is printed as a result of STEP1.

You can take either version of the AK47 procedure, remove the PEND
statement, put the procedure into one of the system procedure libraries,
and people will be able to invoke it saying // EXEC AK47 on their EXEC
statements.

The difference is this.

People will find it easier to use the earlier version, which they can
invoke to print, say, the February shipping report from Nigeria, with a
statement such as this:

```
// EXEC AK47,MON=FEBRUARY,
// DATA=SHIPPING,COUNTRY=NIGERIA
```

rather than the statement that would be required of them if they wanted to
print the same report using the later version:

```
// EXEC AK47,
// D='SMITH.NIGERIAN.SHIPPING.DATA(FEBRUARY)'
```

So, depending on your attitude towards people, take your choice.

What if you decide—in an utterly misguided, pointless and ill-ad-
vised attempt to impress an attractive French person who now runs the
print jobs—that even MON=FEVRIER is too unfriendly; you want this
person to be able to say MOIS=FEVRIER or even LEMOIS=FEVRIER
while other people continue to execute the same PROC saying
MON=FEBRUARY or even MES=FEBRERO if they like.

Easily done, provided you forego having a default month.

Your procedure (which is now in a procedure library, and hence needs no PEND statement) will look like this:

```
//AK47 PROC COUNTRY=JAMAICA,
//      DATA=SALES,
//      LEMOIS=,
//      MES=,
//      MOIS=,
//      MON=
//*
//PRINT  EXEC PGM=IEBGENER
//SYSPRINT DD  DUMMY
//SYSIN  DD  DUMMY
//SYSUT2 DD  SYSOUT=*
//SYSUT1 DD  DISP=SHR,
//DSN=SMITH.&COUNTRY.N.&TYPE..DATA (&MON.&MES.&MOIS.&LEMOIS.)
//*
```

What happens here? The people invoking this PROC can accomplish their purpose by specifying either LEMOIS, MES, MOIS, or MON, but not all four.

Actually, someone could specify more than one, and an occasional clown will do so and then complain about the results. It is socially acceptable for you to tell them simply that they are not allowed to specify more than one of these parameters. If they continue to make trouble, tell them that the keyword parameters MES and MON are mutually exclusive, rather like SYSOUT and DISP on the DD statement.

This is true. If you code a ridiculous DD statement like the following:

```
//SYSPRINT DD SYSOUT=*,DISP=OLD
```

you will get an error message such as this:

IEFC009I KEYWORD DISP IS MUTUALLY EXCLUSIVE
WITH KEYWORD SYSOUT ON THE DD STATE-
MENT

So, as a creator of JCL procedures, you are perfectly within your rights to
follow in the great tradition of having mutually exclusive keywords. You
won't have a nice IEFC009I error message to back you up, of course. You
could have any variety of messages. For example, suppose the month
happens to be February, and the user (the person who runs the job that
invokes your procedure) uses the following EXEC statement:

// EXEC AK47,MES=FEBRERO,MON=FEBRUARY

What happens? The data set name is resolved into:

DSN=SMITH.JAMAICAN.SALES.DATA(FEBRUARYFEBRERO)

and the following messages are found in the listing:

IEFC653I   SUBSTITUTION   JCL   -
DSN=SMITH.JAMAICAN.SALES.DATA(FEBRUARYFEBRERO)
IEF642I EXCESSIVE PARAMETER LENGTH IN THE DSNAME
FIELD

and the JOB fails with a JCL error (IEF642I being the error).

On the other hand, suppose the month in question is May, and the
user says this:

// EXEC AK47,MON=MAY,LEMOIS=JUNE

What do they get for their troubles? An actual Abend, code 013. Also
called S013, where the S means System. Why did this happen? Because
this:

DSN=SMITH.&COUNTRY.N.&TYPE..DATA(&MON.&MES.&MOIS.&LEMOIS.)

247

is now resolved into this:

DSN=SMITH.JAMAICAN.SALES.DATA(MAYJUNE)

which is a legal data set name. The system goes ahead and tries to execute your procedure, looking for a member named MAYJUNE. This it fails to find, because no such member exists; so an Abend 013 results.

By the way, all of the abends that end in 13—013, 213, 613, 813, that sort of thing—have, with rare exceptions, something to do with the data set name being wrong somehow. Usually misspelled.

So the user comes to you with a nice abend dump and says your print program isn't working. The messages aren't too nice, but someplace near the top of the listing you should see a message that contains the phrase:

SYSTEM COMPLETION CODE=013

And a little later you will see a message containing this remark:

ABEND=S013

All you really need to do is to remember that, if the abend code ends with 13, there is almost certainly something wrong with the data set name. In this case, it referred to a member that did not exist.

The same Abend would result if the user had simply misspelled the name of the member:

// EXEC AK47,MON=FEBERARY

Bingo, Abend 013. You spot this easily now of course.

Suppose they misspell one of the other parts of the name, or ask for a country you don't have? This sort of thing:

//STEP1 EXEC AK47,
//   COUNTRY=SERBIA,MON=MAY

The job will fail with a JCL error. You will find messages something like these in the listing:

IEFC653I SUBSTITUTION JCL -
DSN=SMITH.SERBIAN.SALES.DATA(MAY)

IEF212I jobname PRINT STEP1 SYSUT1 - DATA SET
NOT FOUND
IEF272I jobname PRINT STEP1 - STEP WAS NOT EX-
ECUTED

You will notice that the English-like parts of these messages, taken together, tell you that MVS went looking for SMITH.SERBIAN.SALES.DATA(MAY) and could not find the data set. Therefore it did not execute the step, that is, it did not print the report. How could it? You don't have any data for Serbia.

This is exactly the same thing that will happen if they misspell NIGERIA or JAMAICA, or, for that matter, SHIPPING or SALES.

Correct spelling is always an important consideration in JCL. Tell them that if they make trouble. Affect an air of complete self assurance without any trace of arrogance.

Okay.

You realize that this whole scheme will fall apart somewhere around September, because the word September is 9 letters long, too long for a library member name. You don't care too much because you expect to find another job before then. Let them call it SEPT or whatever they like. You count yourself lucky there weren't any Japanese in the company, since ICHIGATSU is already 9 letters long in January.

You have changed employment for the next example. The United Nations, or perhaps the International Red Cross or CARE, offered you a similar job making only slightly less money, which you accepted, more for social reasons than out of any actual problem with your conscience. The work is astonishingly similar, but now you keep track of the distribution of food and medical supplies rather than assault rifles. You do see the connection between the two occupations, but you don't reflect on it too much. Astonishingly, they have given you the userid SMITH, since they actually did not already have someone else with that name.

Your first project is to create a cataloged procedure that will print the distribution reports both for medical supplies and for vitamin supplements for any given month and country. It's like Deja Vu all over again. You're on solid ground.

First you decide not to add the letter N onto the end of the country when you name your data sets. You call them:

SMITH.JAMAICA.VITAMINS.OUTGOING
SMITH.JAMAICA.MEDICINE.OUTGOING
SMITH.ALBANIA.VITAMINS.OUTGOING
SMITH.ALBANIA.MEDICINE.OUTGOING

and so on. Next you decide to make a two step PROC:

```
//REPORTS   PROC COUNTRY=,
//        LEMOIS=,
//        M=MEDICINE,
//        MES=,MOIS=,MON=,
//        O=OUTGOING,
//*
//        PAIS=,
//        S=SMITH,
//        V=VITAMINS
//*
//MEDICINE EXEC PGM=IEBGENER
//SYSIN  DD  DUMMY
//SYSPRINT DD  DUMMY
//SYSUT1  DD  DISP=SHR,
//DSN=&S..&COUNTRY.&PAIS..&M..&O.(&MON.&MES.&MOIS.&LEMOIS.)
//*
//SYSUT2  DD  SYSOUT=*
//*
```

```
//VITAMINS EXEC PGM=IEBGENER
//SYSIN  DD  DUMMY
//SYSPRINT DD  DUMMY
//SYSUT1  DD  DISP=SHR,
//DSN=&S..&COUNTRY.&PAIS..&V..&O.(&MON.&MES.&MOIS.&LEMOIS.)
//*
//SYSUT2  DD  SYSOUT=*
```

Good job. Why did you put the names of the parameters in alphabetical order on the PROC statement? That isn't required. Oh. You want to make maintenance easy. You think that other people may someday modify this procedure of yours, and you think it will be easier for them to spot any particular parameter on the PROC statement quickly if the parameters are in alphabetical order. Especially the bigger the procedure gets. Well, we ARE getting socially conscious here, aren't we though? Okay. fine. Alphabetical order it is. But it isn't an actual requirement.

And you rearranged the DD statements to be in alphabetical order as well. What's the thinking behind that? More of the same?

Yes, but this also makes it easy on the users when they execute your procedure. You, being bright and alert, have realized that you will soon be reading the section on overriding DD statements, and you have peeked ahead. You noticed that, on older MVS systems, overriding DD statements will be overridden in exactly the same order as they appear within the procedure. You think that if you put all of your DD statements in alphabetical order within the procedure, then users can override them in alphabetical order, without having to think too much or do any research.

Give me a break. A few pages ago you were distributing AK-47 assault rifles to Third World countries, and now you're getting particular about your poor users having to figure out the order of your DD statements. Well, I don't know about you, really I don't. But okay, alphabetical order it is.

Keep this in mind, though. If you have a program that prints several reports all in one step, the printed reports will come out onto the printer in the order in which you have the DD statements arranged. If you have your SYSPRINT DD statement prior to your SYSUT2 DD statement, and they both specify the same SYSOUT class, then the SYSPRINT will appear on the printer before the SYSUT2 output. In most cases order of printed reports does not matter much to anyone, but in a few cases it does.

Now, what's the idea behind the symbolic parameters S, M, V, and O in the above? Ah, yes, to get the data set name to fit onto one 80-byte line. &O. is shorter than OUTGOING, and so on. With all your alternate ways of saying MON and COUNTRY, the DSN line is getting fairly long, and you have to get it all to fit onto that one 80-character line.

Suits me. The DSN length limit of 44 characters applies only to the final DSN that results after all of the symbolic parameters are substituted. The member name and the parentheses don't count towards the 44 character limit either.

Now you need to write another procedure.

This one will print a few pages of standard text, say a title page, a copyright notice, a secrecy classification warning, and some hyperbole about the good work of your current organization. All this is kept as member BLURB1 in the card image data set U.N.EARTH.PROJECT, so you refer to it as U.N.EARTH.PROJECT(BLURB1) in JCL.

A card image data set is of course one whose LRECL is 80.

You want the people who execute this procedure to be able to print the standard text contained in BLURB1 followed by any additional text they supply. Preferably they will supply their text as SYSIN data following the EXEC statement for your procedure.

After due thought you decide to name your procedure PUBLISH. Well, the hard part is done. You thought of a reasonable name.

The printing will be handled by IEBGENER as usual.

Unfortunately, the ddname SYSIN is already used by IEBGENER, so you reluctantly choose another ddname for the additional text that the users will supply on cards. You decide on the ddname TEXT.

SYSUT1 will obviously be a case for the concatenated DD statement. You will concatenate your BLURB1 with the cards the user supplies.

How do you do that?

The DDNAME=some-other-ddname construction. In this case,

DDNAME=TEXT will have to do. You wanted DDNAME=SYSIN, but the name was already taken.

Your procedure looks something like this:

```
//PUBLISH PROC WHERE=LOCAL
//*
//PRINT  EXEC PGM=IEBGENER
//SYSIN   DD DUMMY
//SYSPRINT DD DUMMY
//SYSUT1  DD DISP=SHR,
// DSN=U.N.EARTH.PROJECT(BLURB1)
//     DD DDNAME=TEXT
//SYSUT2  DD SYSOUT=A,DEST=&WHERE
```

You have someone place the above procedure in one of the system procedure libraries as member PUBLISH and then people can execute your procedure like this:

```
//ANYBODY1 JOB 0,'ANYBODY CAN DO IT',
//       MSGCLASS=X
// EXEC PUBLISH
//TEXT DD *
```

Devastation of the rain forest
continues unabated. Marmosets
may go extinct but crocodiles
probably won't.
Holes in the ozone
layer continue to
forestall that
threat of a new ice
age that the
scientists were so apprehensive
about back in 1976. Smith has
proposed a plan to
combat droughts

and floods simultaneously by
shipping floodwaters
to the drought
areas in recycled
plastic bottles,
however most of us
on the committee
agree this looks even
less feasible
than Svensen's plan to harness
whales to tow icebergs.
End of report.
/*

What happens when PUBLISH is executed in job ANYBODY1 above?
The input to the program IEBGENER is taken from SYSUT1. SYSUT1
consists of two data sets concatenated together. First
U.N.EARTH.PROJECT(BLURB1) is brought in, and then the second data
set. The second data set is defined on DD statement TEXT, because the
concatenated DD points to DDNAME=TEXT. The user includes an EXEC
statement for the procedure PUBLISH, followed by a TEXT DD statement, followed by the non-JCL cards that comprise TEXT.

This procedure is a big success for you and you think you're getting
along well at the new job. Then your boss asks you to modify the PUB-
LISH procedure so that it works exactly the same way except that now it
will also append a stock trailer page at the end.

Sounds like a simple request.

The trailer page is in member TRAILER of the same library.

Sadly, you find that you are running with the cheap version of
IEBGENER which will not allow you to concatenate a disk data set
following a card input data set. The order has to be disk first, cards last.

After pondering your situation, you decide to make PUBLISH into a
two-step PROC. The first step will be an IEBGENER that will copy the
input cards to a disk data set. Then another IEBGENER step will concatenate the three disk input data sets together on SYSUT1.

The procedure now looks like this:

```
//PUBLISH PROC WHERE=LOCAL
//*
//STEP1  EXEC PGM=IEBGENER
//SYSIN   DD DUMMY
//SYSPRINT DD DUMMY
//SYSUT1  DD DDNAME=TEXT
//SYSUT2  DD DISP=(NEW,PASS),
//    SPACE=(TRK,(1,15),RLSE),
// DCB=(U.N.EARTH.PROJECT,DSORG=PS),
//    UNIT=SYSDA,DSN=&&TEXT
//STEP2  EXEC PGM=IEBGENER
//SYSIN   DD DUMMY
//SYSPRINT DD DUMMY
//SYSUT1  DD DISP=SHR,
// DSN=U.N.EARTH.PROJECT(BLURB1)
//     DD DISP=(OLD,DELETE),
//     DSN=&&TEXT
//     DD DISP=SHR,
// DSN=U.N.EARTH.PROJECT(TRAILER)
//SYSUT2 DD SYSOUT=A,DEST=&WHERE
```

It is executed exactly as it was before in the job named ANYBODY1. The change you have made to the procedure is, as they say, transparent to the user, meaning that a person using it sees no difference. Except, of course, in this case, that the trailer page you wanted to append will now be appended.

When your company installs the fancy version of IEBGENER you can use the following simpler PROC instead of that above:

```
//PUBLISH PROC WHERE=LOCAL
//PRINT  EXEC PGM=IEBGENER
//SYSIN   DD DUMMY
//SYSPRINT DD DUMMY
```

```
//SYSUT1  DD DISP=SHR,
//  DSN=U.N.EARTH.PROJECT(BLURB1)
//  DD DDNAME=TEXT
//  DD DISP=SHR,
//  DSN=U.N.EARTH.PROJECT(TRAILER)
//SYSUT2 DD SYSOUT=A,DEST=&WHERE
```

So, shall we move on to the next topic?

OVERRIDING EXEC STATEMENT PARAMETERS WHEN EXECUTING A PROCEDURE

Suppose you want to execute a procedure that contains the TIME parameter on the EXEC statement within the procedure, and suppose you want to change the time limit.

Maybe the EXEC statement says TIME=(0,30) and you want to make it TIME=5.

If the PROC statement said T='(0,30)' and the EXEC statement said TIME=&T then you would have no problem. You could simply specify T=5 on your EXEC statement when executing the procedure.

But it doesn't.

The picture:

```
//CATTLOGD PROC D='JONES.STUPID.DATASET'
//JONES   EXEC PGM=JAMES,
//      TIME=(0,30)
//INPUT  DD  DISP=OLD,DSN=&D
```

The above pictured set of JCL statements resides as member CATTLOGD in the data set OFFICIAL.PROCLIB and you execute it as follows:

```
//SMITH5B1 JOB 0,MSGCLASS=X
//TIMEOUT EXEC CATTLOGD
```

The problem you have with this is that you have recently started getting 322 abends when you execute it, indicating that the program is running out of time. So, what do you do? You modify your JCL as follows:

```
//SMITH5B2 JOB 0,MSGCLASS=X
//TIMELY  EXEC CATTLOGD,
//     TIME.JONES=5
```

So what is this TIME.JONES? It's the TIME parameter that you want for the JONES step.

Suppose a more complicated example, where the procedure has several steps.

For this example, the below pictured set of JCL statements resides as member SWIM4IT in the data set OFFICIAL.PROCLIB:

```
//SWIM4IT  PROC D='JONES.STUPID.DATASET',
// LUNCH='DEAD.MEAT',
// DINNER='SYS1.PROCLIB'
//*
//BRUNCH  EXEC PGM=PIRANHA,
//     TIME=(0,30)
//FOOD    DD  DISP=OLD,DSN=&D
//SYSPRINT DD  SYSOUT=*
//*
//LUNCH   EXEC PGM=PIRANHA,
//     TIME=(0,30)
//FOOD    DD  DISP=OLD,
//     DSN=&LUNCH
//SYSPRINT DD  SYSOUT=*
//*
//DINNER  EXEC PGM=PIRANHA,
//     TIME=(0,30)
//FOOD    DD  DISP=OLD,
//     DSN=&DINNER
//SYSPRINT DD  SYSOUT=*
```

Now, you want to execute the above procedure, but you want to allow the program PIRANHA a little more time for the DINNER step, say five minutes. Simple enough:

```
//SMITH5B3 JOB 0,MSGCLASS=X
//*
//GO4IT EXEC SWIM4IT,
//   TIME.DINNER=5
```

What if you want to allow five minutes for DINNER and only 15 seconds for LUNCH? It used to be that you had to specify the TIME for LUNCH prior to the TIME for DINNER. They became positional. That is, they became simultaneously keyword and positional, like PGM. This is no longer the case, unless you happen to be working on an old version of MVS.

```
//SMITH5B4 JOB 0,MSGCLASS=X
//*
//GO4IT EXEC SWIM4IT,
//   TIME.LUNCH=(0,15),
//   TIME.DINNER=5
```

Suppose you decide that both BRUNCH and LUNCH need a bigger REGION parameter, in addition to the above alterations to the TIME? If you're working on an old version of MVS, then all of the parameters applicable to the earliest step must come first, and from then on in order, with the parameters applicable to the final step coming last. The following example gives BRUNCH 6 Megabytes for a region size, gives the same to LUNCH, gives LUNCH 15 seconds of CPUtime in which to process, and gives DINNER five minutes:

```
//SMITH5B5 JOB 0,MSGCLASS=X
//*
//GO4IT EXEC SWIM4IT,
//   REGION.BRUNCH=6M,
```

```
//    REGION.LUNCH=6M,
//    TIME.LUNCH=(0,15),
//    TIME.DINNER=5
```

What if all you want to do is to make DINNER conditional on the successful execution of all preceding steps? Easily done:

```
//SMITH5B6 JOB 0,MSGCLASS=X
//*
//GO4IT EXEC SWIM4IT,
//    COND.DINNER=(0,NE)
```

Remember we said we would come to these complicated forms of COND in the chapter on procedures, Chapter 12. There are two items of interest here.

First, COND is subject to the same rules as TIME and REGION, as just shown.

Second, it is possible to specify a qualified step name within the COND value. An example is in order.

The following example executes the same cataloged procedure SWIM4IT we were just using. The execution of STEP3 in job SMITH5B7 below is made contingent on the successful prior completion of the DINNER step in the SWIM4IT procedure executed by STEP1.

It looks like this:

```
//SMITH5B7 JOB 0,MSGCLASS=X
//*
//STEP1 EXEC SWIM4IT
//STEP2 EXEC PGM=IEFBR14
//STEP3 EXEC PGM=IEFBR14,
//    COND=(0,NE,STEP1.DINNER)
```

The next example demonstrates the use of both of the complicated forms of the COND parameter we have just seen. In this example

(a) the execution of the LKED step within the PLIXCL procedure executed by step CLINK is made conditional on the moderately successful completion of all preceding steps,

(b) the execution of the step FOLDIT is made conditional on the prior completion, at least moderately successful, of the LKED step within the PLIXCL procedure executed in step CLINK:

```
//SMITH5B8 JOB  0,MSGCLASS=X
//*
//CLINK EXEC PLIXCL,
//     COND.LKED=(8,LT)
//*
//SYSPRINT DD SYSOUT=*

TSAMPLE: PROC (PARM)
    OPTIONS(MAIN);

DECLARE PARM CHAR(100) VARYING;
DECLARE LINE CHAR(100)
    VARYING INIT(' ');
DECLARE TRANSLATE BUILTIN;
DECLARE UC  CHARACTER(26)
INIT('ABCDEFGHIJKLMNOPQRSTUVWXYZ');
DECLARE LC  CHARACTER(26)
INIT('abcdefghijklmnopqrstuvwxyz');

LINE = PARM;
 /* SET LINE EQUAL TO PARM */

LINE = TRANSLATE(LINE,UC,LC);
 /* TRANSLATE LINE */
 /* TO UC FROM LC  */
```

```
    PUT SKIP LIST(LINE); /* PRINT
     TRANSLATED LINE ON SYSPRINT */
    END TSAMPLE;
    //LKED.SYSLMOD DD DISP=SHR,
    //   DSN=SMITH.LOAD(TSAMPLE)
    //*
    //FOLDIT EXEC PGM=*.CLINK.LKED.SYSLMOD,
    //*
    // COND=(8,LT,CLINK.LKED),
    //*
    // PARM='/Translate me to Upper Case'
    //*
    //STEPLIB  DD DISP=SHR,
    // DSN=*.CLINK.LKED.SYSLMOD
    //SYSPRINT DD SYSOUT=*
```

OVERRIDING AND ADDING DD STATEMENTS

When you execute a procedure, you need not accept in its entirety the set of DD statements that the procedure contains.

You can replace any of them you wish. This is called overriding DD statements.

When you override DD statements your replacements must appear in exactly the same order as the originals if you are running on one of the older MVS systems. On the new version of MVS/ESA, the correct order is not required in simple cases.

Consider the first example:

```
    //SMITH5C1 JOB 1,SMITH,MSGCLASS=X
    //JOGGER PROC
    //STEP1 EXEC PGM=JOG
    //HILL   DD DISP=SHR,
    // DSN=BLACK.HILLS.OF.SOUTH.DAKOTA
    //DALE   DD DISP=SHR,
    //   DSN=OVER.HILL.OVER.DALE
```

```
//TRAIL  DD DISP=SHR,
// DSN=WE.SHALL.HIT.THE.DUSTY.TRAIL
//GROVE  DD DISP=SHR,
//     DSN=SHADY.GROVE
//LAKESIDE DD DISP=SHR,
//     DSN=SMITH.LAKESIDE.COTTAGE
// PEND
//RUN4IT EXEC JOGGER
//HILL  DD DISP=SHR,
//     DSN=HOLLY.WOOD.HILLS
//DALE  DD DISP=SHR,
//     DSN=DALE.ARDEN
```

What happens in the above simple example?

For HILL and for DALE, the data sets HOLLY.WOOD.HILLS and DALE.ARDEN are used, rather than the data sets BLACK.HILLS.OF.SOUTH.DAKOTA and OVER.HILL.OVER.DALE which were named within the procedure. For all other ddnames, the DD statements within the procedure are used.

What would have happened if you had put your DD statement for DALE.ARDEN prior to your DD statement for HOLLY.WOOD.HILLS?

On the most recent version of MVS/ESA, it would have worked exactly the same.

On old versions of MVS/ESA, DALE.ARDEN would have been accepted, but HOLLY.WOOD.HILLS would have been ignored. For the ddname HILL you would have gotten OVER.HILL.OVER.DALE, the data set named within the procedure for that ddname.

Which means that you have to be careful to override DD statements in the same order as they appear within the Procedure if you do not have a relatively recent version of MVS.

Obviously it is an inconvenience for you to have to look at the actual procedure to see the order of the DD statements before you can override more than one.

Unfortunately, that's the way it is, was.

For procedures you write yourself, however, you can put the DD statements within them into alphabetical order within each step. Then at least you will know automatically what the order of the DD statements within them is, and other people who use your procedures will know also.

The above example would then look more like this:

```
//SMITH5C2 JOB 1,SMITH,MSGCLASS=X
//JOGGER PROC
//STEP1 EXEC PGM=JOG
//DALE   DD DISP=SHR,
//   DSN=OVER.HILL.OVER.DALE
//GROVE  DD DISP=SHR,
//      DSN=SHADY.GROVE
//HILL   DD DISP=SHR,
// DSN=BLACK.HILLS.OF.SOUTH.DAKOTA
//LAKESIDE DD DISP=SHR,
//   DSN=SMITH.LAKESIDE.COTTAGE
//TRAIL  DD DISP=SHR,
// DSN=WE.SHALL.HIT.THE.DUSTY.TRAIL
//  PEND
//RUN4IT EXEC JOGGER
//DALE   DD DISP=SHR,
//      DSN=DALE.ARDEN
//HILL   DD DISP=SHR,
//      DSN=HOLLY.WOOD.HILLS
```

Obviously when it is rearranged in this way it is easy to override as many DD statements as you wish to override without looking at the procedure at all.

Note that there is one potential disadvantage to this approach. If you have more than one printed report produced by a particular step, and they are in the same sysout class, use the same forms, and are directed to the same printer, then the reports will generally come out on the printer in the order of occurrence of the DD statements in the JCL. If you want the report on ddname ZEBRA to precede the report on ddname AMAZING, then the DD statement for ZEBRA should precede the DD statement for AMAZING in the JCL.

If that doesn't bother you, then you can try to convince your company to adopt a policy of putting DD statements within procedures into alphabetical order.

Since everyone else (IBM included) does not adhere to this custom, however, you may sometime be faced with the question of finding out the order of the DD statements within the procedure you wish to execute.

I suggest making a preliminary run using TYPRUN=SCAN on your JOB statement. We'll come to that in the Chapter 14, on the JOB statement of course, but basically TYPRUN=SCAN on the JOB statement tells MVS that you don't really want your JCL to be executed at all, you just want it checked for JCL errors. A nice service. Request it, and then look at the listing to see the order of the DD statements. Then override them in the same order as they appear in the listing.

Now the next level of complexity.

If the procedure contains more than one step, then the ddnames you use on your overriding DD statements should be qualified ddnames, that is, they should consist of the step name followed by a full stop followed by the ddname. Also they must appear in the same order as within the PROC if you are using an older version of MVS.

An example:

```
//SMITH5C3 JOB 1,SMITH,MSGCLASS=X
//JOGGER PROC
//STEP1 EXEC PGM=JOG
//DALE   DD DISP=SHR,
//   DSN=OVER.HILL.OVER.DALE
//GROVE   DD DISP=SHR,
// DSN=TRAIL.GOES.THROUGH.A.GROVE
//HILL   DD DISP=SHR,
// DSN=TRAIL.RUNS.OVER.A.HILL
//LAKESIDE DD DISP=SHR,
// DSN=TRAIL.WINDS.BY.THE.LAKE
//TRAIL   DD DISP=SHR,
// DSN=JOGGING.TRAIL.OF.YOUR.CHOICE
//STEP2 EXEC PGM=REST
```

```
//BATH   DD DISP=SHR,
// DSN=SHOWER.SAUNA.AND.JACUZZI
//BEDROOM DD DISP=SHR,
// DSN=NICE.BED.WITH.CLEAN.SHEETS
//STEREO  DD DISP=SHR,
//   DSN=MUSIC.OF.YOUR.CHOICE
// PEND
//RUN4IT EXEC JOGGER
//STEP1.DALE  DD  DISP=SHR,
//   DSN=DALE.OF.YOUR.CHOICE
//STEP2.BEDROOM DD  DISP=SHR,
// DSN=BEDROOM.OF.YOUR.CHOICE
```

If you do not use qualified ddnames, then the DD statements you supply will be considered to apply to the first step of the procedure.

Obviously that means they will be ignored if they were intended for some other step.

This is true even with the latest and greatest MVS/ESA.

Actually the situation is a little more complicated than that.

If you specified, say, in the above example, a DD statement for STEP2.BEDROOM (properly qualified) and then a DD statement for STEREO (unqualified) it would work, because STEREO follows BED-ROOM within STEP2 within the PROC. The point is that, once MVS starts processing the JCL for STEP2, there is no consideration for the possibility that anything you give him might apply to STEP1. STEP1 has gone at that point. MVS sort of just plows straight through the JCL from top to bottom without much sophistication.

In the case of the newest version of MVS/ESA, you may, however, intersperse overriding DD statements indiscriminately provided that they are fully qualified; that is, the following will work in the new version of MVS/ESA:

```
//NEWMVS EXEC  JOGGER
//STEP2.BEDROOM DD DISP=SHR,
//   DSN=BEDROOM.DATA.SET
```

```
//STEP1.DALE   DD DISP=SHR,
//   DSN=CHIP.AND.DALE
//STEP2.STEREO DD DISP=SHR,
//   DSN=STEREO.DATA.SET
//STEP1.TRAIL  DD DISP=SHR,
//   DSN=TRAIL.OF.THE.LONESOME.PINE
```

You can also add DD statements.

If you are running on an older version of MVS, any DD statements you add for any step must appear in your JCL after any overriding DD statements applicable to that step.

Example:

```
//SMITH5C5 JOB 1,SMITH,MSGCLASS=X
//JOGGER PROC
//STEP1 EXEC PGM=JOG
//DALE   DD DISP=SHR,
//     DSN=OVER.HILL.OVER.DALE
//LAKESIDE DD DISP=SHR,
//     DSN=TRAIL.WINDS.BY.THE.LAKE
//TRAIL   DD DISP=SHR,
//     DSN=JOGGING.TRAIL.OF.YOUR.CHOICE
//STEP2 EXEC PGM=REST
//BATH    DD DISP=SHR,
//     DSN=SHOWER
//     DD DISP=SHR,
//     DSN=SAUNA
//     DD DISP=SHR,
//     DSN=JACUZZI
//BEDROOM DD DISP=SHR,
//     DSN=NICE.BED.WITH.CLEAN.SHEETS
//STEREO  DD DISP=SHR,
//     DSN=MUSIC.OF.YOUR.CHOICE
// PEND
//RUN4IT  EXEC JOGGER
```

```
//STEP1.DALE  DD DISP=SHR,
//   DSN=DALE.OF.YOUR.CHOICE
//STEP1.CHRIS DD DISP=SHR,
//   DSN=CHRIS.OF.YOUR.CHOICE
//STEP1.SWIM  DD DISP=SHR,
//   DSN=DIP.IN.THE.LAKE
//STEP2.BEDROOM DD DISP=SHR,
//   DSN=BEDROOM.OF.YOUR.CHOICE
//STEP2.STEREO DD DISP=SHR,
//   DSN=SOFT.RELAXING.MUSIC
//STEP2.VIDEO DD DISP=SHR,
//   DSN=SOME.AMUSING.VIDEO
```

Obviously one has tremendous opportunity to misstep by spelling a ddname incorrectly, so exercise the usual sensible caution. About spelling, I mean.

Consider the above example for another minute yet. Suppose you like the JOGGER procedure well enough, except for the BATH in STEP2, and you object to the BATH statement in the following rather complex way.

You like the SHOWER and you like the SAUNA, but you do not care for the JACUZZI at all. You want to keep the SHOWER and SAUNA as they are, replace the JACUZZI with a data set named WARM.HOT.TUB, and add another data set named TURKISH.TOWEL at the end. The JCL will look like this:

```
//SMITH5C6 JOB 1,SMITH,MSGCLASS=X
//JOGGER PROC
//STEP1 EXEC PGM=JOG
//DALE   DD DISP=SHR,
//   DSN=OVER.HILL.OVER.DALE
//LAKESIDE DD DISP=SHR,
//   DSN=TRAIL.WINDS.BY.THE.LAKE
//TRAIL   DD DISP=SHR,
// DSN=JOGGING.TRAIL.OF.YOUR.CHOICE
//STEP2 EXEC PGM=REST
```

```
//BATH   DD DISP=SHR,
//     DSN=SHOWER
//     DD DISP=SHR,
//     DSN=SAUNA
//     DD DISP=SHR,
//     DSN=JACUZZI
//BEDROOM DD DISP=SHR,
// DSN=NICE.BED.WITH.CLEAN.SHEETS
//STEREO DD DISP=SHR,
//   DSN=MUSIC.OF.YOUR.CHOICE
// PEND
//RUN4IT EXEC JOGGER
//STEP1.DALE  DD DISP=SHR,
//   DSN=DALE.OF.YOUR.CHOICE
//STEP1.CHRIS DD DISP=SHR,
//   DSN=CHRIS.OF.YOUR.CHOICE
//STEP1.SWIM  DD DISP=SHR,
//   DSN=DIP.IN.THE.LAKE
//STEP2.BATH  DD
//         DD
//         DD DISP=SHR,
//   DSN=WARM.HOT.TUB
//         DD DISP=SHR,
//   DSN=TURKISH.TOWEL
//STEP2.BEDROOM DD DISP=SHR,
// DSN=BEDROOM.OF.YOUR.CHOICE
//STEP2.STEREO DD DISP=SHR,
//   DSN=SOFT.RELAXING.MUSIC
//STEP2.VIDEO DD DISP=SHR,
//   DSN=SOME.AMUSING.VIDEO
```

How does the above work? For the first two DD cards on your override for STEP2.BATH you leave the operands area blank.

This tells MVS to keep whatever it found inside the original procedure for those first two cards.

On your third DD card for the STEP2.BATH override you specify the data set WARM.HOT.TUB, causing MVS to replace the reference to JACUZZI in the procedure with your override, that is, with the WARM.HOT.TUB data set.

On your fourth DD card for the STEP2.BATH concatenation you specify TURKISH.TOWEL and this is added to the other three.

Looks funny, but it works.

MERGING DCB PARAMETERS

We have not quite exhausted the discussion of overriding and adding DD statements. We still have the topic of merging DCB parameters. Consider the following example:

```
//SMITH5C7 JOB 1,SMITH,MSGCLASS=X
//JOGGER PROC
//STEP1 EXEC PGM=JOG
//TRAIL DD DISP=SHR,
// DSN=SOME.NICE.JOGGING.TRAIL
//STEP2 EXEC PGM=REST
//SHOWER DD DISP=SHR,
// DSN=COLD.SHOWER,DCB=(LRECL=80,
// RECFM=FB,
// BLKSIZE=23440,DSORG=PS)
// PEND
//RUN4IT EXEC JOGGER
//STEP2.SHOWER DD DISP=SHR,
// DSN=METEOR.SHOWER,
// DCB=LRECL=10
```

What happens?

The data set METEOR.SHOWER is used rather than the data set COLD.SHOWER, but the DCB parameters are merged. Any DCB subparameters specified on the overriding DD statement override what was specified within the PROC. For items that are not included within the

DCB on the overriding DD statement, the values within the PROC are used. This process, applied to the above example, nets you the following composite DCB:

DCB=(LRECL=10,RECFM=FB,BLKSIZE=23440,DSORG=PS)

SPECIFYING NON-JCL IN A PROCEDURE

One last thing to know about procedures. You cannot have non-JCL statements within a procedure.

For example, suppose you have the following JCL that you often run, and you want to turn it into a procedure:

```
//SMITH5C8 JOB 1,SMITH,MSGCLASS=X
//STEP1 EXEC PGM=PIRANHA
//FOOD DD *
 OMELETTE
 SOUFFLE
 QUICHE
/*
```

The procedure will look like this:

```
//PIRANHA PROC
//STEP1   EXEC PGM=PIRANHA
//FOOD    DD DDNAME=SYSIN
```

And, once you have put it in a procedure library, you will execute it like this:

```
//SMITH5C9 JOB 1,SMITH,MSGCLASS=X
// EXEC PIRANHA
 OMELETTE
 SOUFFLE
 QUICHE
```

The system will generate a //SYSIN DD * statement when it sees your first non-JCL line (OMELETTE). The SYSIN data will be used for the FOOD DD statement, because the FOOD DD statement within the PROC specifies DDNAME=SYSIN.

If that isn't good enough for you, then you need to put the three input lines (OMELETTE, SOUFFLE, and QUICHE) into a data set and point the FOOD DD statement within the PROC at the data set. For example, if you call the data set EGG.DATA, then the PROC will look like this:

```
//PIRANHA PROC
//STEP1  EXEC PGM=PIRANHA
//FOOD DD  DISP=OLD,DSN=EGG.DATA
```

What else do you want to know about procedures?

Using IEFRDER

Right, we promised you we'd talk about that IEFRDER special DD statement.

For this you need to know that there is another way to execute a procedure besides using an EXEC statement.

An operator can execute a procedure from the MVS operator console by the use of the START command.

For example, if the operators wanted to run the PIRANHA procedure (it seems unlikely) they could type the following command on the operator console:

```
START PIRANHA
```

When PIRANHA is started in this way, without a JOB statement obviously, it is called a STARTED TASK.

So, suppose the operators wanted to point PIRANHA to some particular set of data for the FOOD DD statement?

As it stands, they couldn't do it.

But you could modify the procedure to look like this:

```
//PIRANHA PROC
//STEP1  EXEC PGM=PIRANHA
//FOOD   DD DDNAME=IEFRDER
```

And now the operators could do this:

```
START PIRANHA,DSN=EGG.DATA
```

The system would fabricate, out of the ether, a DD statement having the ddname IEFRDER and containing the parameter DSN=EGG.DATA as supplied by the operator.

Wow. And that is why you ought not to have symbolic parameters with names such as DSN, even though it is not, strictly speaking, prohibited. It can lead to unexpected and awkward results.

Notice the obvious: You cannot say DDNAME=SYSIN and also say DDNAME=IEFRDER on the same DD statement. You have to choose. Which ends up meaning that any particular procedure has a bias in its design. It is basically intended to be used by programmers via the EXEC statement, or by the operators via the START command.

Okay, you understand procedures.

Chapter 13

ENHANCEMENTS TO JCL
AVAILABLE IN MVS/ESA

JCLLIB

The JCLLIB statement resembles the JOBLIB DD statement in spirit.

JOBLIB lets you obtain programs from private program libraries rather than from the default MVS system libraries.

JCLLIB lets you obtain JCL from private JCL libraries rather than the system default procedure libraries.

Same basic idea, except that it's JCL instead of programs.

Like JOBLIB, JCLLIB comes after the JOB statement but before the first EXEC statement in your JCL.

Note that JCLLIB is available only with MVS/ESA Version 4 or higher.

Notice that a JCLLIB statement is not a DD statement. It has the operation field JCLLIB.

The general syntax is:

```
//ANY JCLLIB ORDER=(SMITH.PRIVATE.JCLLIB,
//  SMITH.SECOND.JCLLIB,
//  SMITH.PROCLIB,
//  ANY.OTHER.JCL.LIBRARY)
```

Or, in its simpler form:

```
//  JCLLIB ORDER=SMITH.PRIVATE.JCLLIB
```

Why did they not make it a DD statement, with JCLLIB as the ddname? Why did they not use DSN for the keyword rather than ORDER? Beats me.

Anyway, you can now allocate a JCLLIB library for yourself and put your procedures into it for testing, rather than testing them as instream PROCs. Well, if you have ESA Version 4 you can. Make sure you allocate your JCLLIB data set with LRECL=80 and RECFM=FB and that it's a library (you give it some directory blocks to make it a library).

INCLUDE

Now the INCLUDE statement.

The INCLUDE statement includes a block of JCL statements from your JCLLIB. This block of JCL statements could be just a couple of DD statements. It is not, in other words, a PROC. INCLUDE just includes any old bunch of JCL you like, except that you are not allowed to INCLUDE another JOB statement.

The syntax is:

```
//ANYNAME  INCLUDE  MEMBER=ANYJCL
```

or, more simply:

```
//  INCLUDE  MEMBER=ANYJCL
```

Can you put an INCLUDE statement inside a PROC? Yes.
So this sort of PROC is valid:

```
//DOGSHOW PROC WINNER=CHIHUAUA
//DOGSHOW EXEC PGM=IEFBR14,
//     PARM=&WINNER
//  INCLUDE MEMBER=&WINNER
```

and it is executed like this:

```
//SMITH6A1 JOB 1,SMITH,MSGCLASS=X
// JCLLIB ORDER=SMITH.JCLLIB
//ROUND1 EXEC DOGSHOW
//REMATCH EXEC DOGSHOW,
//    WINNER=PEKINESE
```

What's the point? Consider.
Suppose SMITH.JCLLIB(CHIHUAUA) looks like this:

```
//CHIHUAUA DD DISP=SHR,
//    DSN=SMITH.CHIHUAUA.TUESDAY.DATA
//      DD DISP=SHR,
//    DSN=SMITH.CHIHUAUA.FEBRUARY.DATA
//      DD DISP=SHR,
//    DSN=SMITH.CHIHUAUA.JUNE1970.DATA
//.     DD DISP=SHR,
//    DSN=SMITH.CHIHUAUA.APRIL.DATA
//      DD DISP=SHR,
//    DSN=SMITH.CHIHUAUA.YEAR2001.DATA
```

Whereas SMITH.JCLLIB(PEKINESE) looks like this:

```
//PEKINESE DD DISP=SHR,
//    DSN=SMITH.PEKINESE.LASTYEAR.DATA
//      DD DISP=SHR,
//    DSN=SMITH.PEKINESE.THISYEAR.DATA
```

and JONES.JCLLIB(CHIHUAUA) looks like this:

```
//CHIHUAUA DD DISP=SHR,
//    DSN=JONES.CHIHUAUA.JANUARY.DATA
//      DD DISP=SHR,
//    DSN=JONES.CHIHUAUA.FEBRUARY.DATA
```

So, what was the point? To allow somebody to include a set of DD statements from a library rather than supplying them as overriding DD statements or added DD statements.

When you EXEC the DOGSHOW procedure in job SMITH6A1 above, it turns out the same as if you had done this:

```
//SMITH6A2 JOB 1,SMITH,MSGCLASS=X
//* RESTATEMENT OF SMITH6A1
//DOGSHOW PROC WINNER=CHIHUAUA
//DOGSHOW EXEC PGM=IEFBR14,
//    PARM=&WINNER
//    PEND
//ROUND1 EXEC DOGSHOW
//CHIHUAUA DD DISP=SHR,
//    DSN=SMITH.CHIHUAUA.TUESDAY.DATA
//    DD DISP=SHR,
//    DSN=SMITH.CHIHUAUA.FEBRUARY.DATA
//    DD DISP=SHR,
//    DSN=SMITH.CHIHUAUA.JUNE1970.DATA
//    DD DISP=SHR,
//    DSN=SMITH.CHIHUAUA.APRIL.DATA
//    DD DISP=SHR,
//    DSN=SMITH.CHIHUAUA.YEAR2001.DATA
//REMATCH EXEC DOGSHOW,WINNER=PEKINESE
//PEKINESE DD DISP=SHR,
//    DSN=SMITH.PEKINESE.LASTYEAR.DATA
//    DD DISP=SHR,
//    DSN=SMITH.PEKINESE.THISYEAR.DATA
```

Many other such gyrations are possible with the INCLUDE statement, as you can imagine.

SET

The SET statement (you guessed it, available only with Version 4 and higher of MVS/ESA) allows you to explicitly set the value of a symbolic parameter.

So you could reset the value of a symbolic parameter to something different right in the middle of a PROC if you wished to do so.

Moreover, you can, with the advent of SET, have symbolic parameters without PROCs.

You can run a job like this, if you should wish to do so (Why not, I just did):

```
//SMITH6B1 JOB 1,SMITH,MSGCLASS=X
//*
// SET DOG=BLACK
//*
//OKAY EXEC PGM=IEFBR14,PARM=&DOG
```

You know it works because, among the many messages in your output JCL listing, you see messages like these:

```
IEFC653I      SUBSTITUTION      JCL      -
       PGM=IEFBR14,PARM=BLACK
IEF142I SMITH6B1 OKAY - STEP WAS EXECUTED -
       COND CODE 0000
```

You might imagine that the SET statement will prove useful in conjunction with the IF-THEN-ELSE-ENDIF construction, but you would be mistaken if you made such a conjecture. It is not. The MVS JCL converter/ interpreter program always acts upon the SET statement, regardless of whether or not the SET statement appears within an IF or an ELSE. There are also certain other statements that the converter/ interpreter always processes regardless of their position within an IF; these include INCLUDE, PROC and PEND, and some other statements such as the lone // that signifies the end of a job. SET is a member of this set.

IF THEN ELSE ENDIF

This is the long-awaited replacement for the widely disliked COND parameter.

Hooray.

Available only as of MVS/ESA Version 4 naturally.

It looks basically like this:

```
//SMITH6C1 JOB 1,SMITH,MSGCLASS=X
//FIRST EXEC PGM=PIRANHA
//FOOD  DD  DISP=SHR,
//    DSN=SMITH.IMPORTED.MUSHROOM.DATA
//  IF  (RC = 0) THEN
//GOOD  EXEC PGM=PSAMPLE,PARM='/GOODJOB'
//BETTER EXEC PGM=PSAMPLE,
//     PARM='/GOODJOB'
//BEST  EXEC PGM=PSAMPLE,PARM='/GOODJOB'
//  ELSE
//BAD2  EXEC PGM=PSAMPLE,PARM='/BADJOB'
//WORSE EXEC PGM=PSAMPLE,PARM='/BADJOB'
//  ENDIF
//BYTHEWAY EXEC PGM=IEFBR14
```

Big improvement over COND, wouldn't you say? I thought you would. We think it is too.

In the above example, the step named FIRST will execute the program PIRANHA first.

The program PIRANHA will set some condition code when it finishes, presumably 0 if the data on the FOOD file was good, and 8 if the data was bad.

Following the execution of the FIRST step, the IF statement will test the condition code (return code). If the return code is equal to zero (RC = 0) then the following EXEC statements, named GOOD, BETTER, and BEST, will run.

Otherwise they will be skipped.

In that case, the ELSE statement will take effect, and the steps named BAD2 and WORSE will run instead.

The ENDIF statement terminates the group of statements controlled by the IF-THEN-ELSE-ENDIF.

Any statements subsequent to the ENDIF will execute the same as they would if the IF-THEN-ELSE-ENDIF had never been there. In our example, the step named BYTHEWAY will execute, regardless of the return code from FIRST.

Be aware of the following points:

The ELSE is optional, but the ENDIF is required.

You are not supposed to place any of the following JCL statements within an IF-THEN-ELSE-ENDIF group:

- JOB statement
- JCLLIB statement
- JOBCAT or STEPCAT DD statements

The following statements are not subject to IF-THEN-ELSE-ENDIF testing, that is, they will be processed all the same whether or not they happen to occur within an IF-THEN-ELSE-ENDIF group:

- PROC and PEND
- INCLUDE
- SET
- //*
- //
- /*
- JES2 and JES3 statements (we haven't explained these yet)
- JCL operator commands

There is an optional name field on the IF, the ELSE, and the ENDIF statements. It follows the same rules as step names and ddnames, with the additional restriction that, if used, it should be unique. You can have two steps in your job both named STEP1, but you should not have two IF statements with the name IFONLY.

If you specify COND on an EXEC statement within an IF block, both the IF and the COND are evaluated and used.

What tests can you specify for return codes besides = or EQ for equal? Anything from following list—you can use either the 2-letter abbreviation shown or the equivalent symbol (for example, you can use the abbreviation EQ or an equals sign, whichever you prefer).

> EQ   meaning Equal
>> or you can use an equals sign =
>
> NE   meaning Not Equal
>> or use the PL/I Not sign followed by an equals sign
>
> GE   meaning Greater Than Or Equal To
>> or use the mathematical symbols >=
>
> GT   meaning Greater Than
>> or use the mathematical symbol >
>
> NG   meaning Not Greater Than
>> or use the Not-sign followed by the greater-than symbol
>
> LE   meaning Less Than Or Equal To
>> or use the less-than sign followed by an equal sign <=
>
> LT   meaning Less Than
>> or use the less-than sign <
>
> NL   meaning Not Less Than
>> or use the Not-sign followed by the less-than sign
>
> NOT   meaning Not
>> or use the PL/I symbol for Not
>> (it looks like a hyphen bent down at the end)
>
> AND   meaning And
>> or use the PL/I symbol for And (an ampersand)
>
> OR   meaning Or
>> or use the PL/I symbol for Or (a vertical bar)

What are the IF syntax equivalents of qualified stepnames? Qualified stepnames. Example:

```
// IF (STEP1.LKED.RC LT  8) THEN
```

What are the IF syntax equivalents of COND=EVEN and COND=ONLY?

ABEND=TRUE and ABEND=FALSE

ABEND=TRUE can be abbreviated simply ABEND. ABEND=FALSE can be phrased as NOT ABEND. Hence you can have statements such as this, to test for a bad result from the prior step STEP1:

```
// IF (STEP1.ABEND OR STEP1.RC GT 0) THEN
```

Notice that GT in the above example means Greater Than, and is used instead of a greater than symbol if you prefer it.

And wait, there's more.

You can test for a particular abend code.

The following IF tests for an 0C4 abend in the prior step named STEP1:

```
// IF (STEP1.ABENDCC = S0C4) THEN
```

The following IF tests for a B37, D37, or E37 having happened in a prior step named STEP1:

```
// IF (STEP1.ABENDCC = SB37
// OR STEP1.ABENDCC = SD37
// OR STEP1.ABENDCC = SE37) THEN
```

The following example makes execution of STEP2 dependent on an abend 0C4 having happened in STEP1, and makes STEP3 dependent on an abend B37, D37, or E37 having happened in STEP1, while STEP4 is dependent on STEP3 having completed with a zero return code, and STEP5 is contingent on no abend having happened at any point:

```
//SMITH6C2 JOB 1,SMITH,MSGCLASS=X
//*
//STEP1 EXEC PGM=DODGY
//LIBRARY DD DISP=SHR,DSN=SMITH.LIBRARY
//*
```

```
// IF  (STEP1.ABENDCC = S0C4) THEN
//STEP2  EXEC PGM=PSAMPLE,
//     PARM='/ARRAY OUT OF BOUNDS'
// ENDIF
//*
// IF  (STEP1.ABENDCC = SB37
// OR STEP1.ABENDCC = SD37
// OR STEP1.ABENDCC = SE37) THEN
//STEP3  EXEC COMPRESS,D='SMITH.LIBRARY'
// ENDIF
//*
// IF  (STEP3.RC = 0) THEN
//STEP4  EXEC PGM=DODGY
//LIBRARY DD DISP=SHR,DSN=SMITH.LIBRARY
// ENDIF
//*
// IF (NOT ABEND) THEN
//STEP5  EXEC PGM=PSAMPLE,
//     PARM='/ALL SYSTEMS GO'
// ENDIF
```

So there you have it, the magnificent and long awaited replacement for the COND parameter.

It is pretty nice actually.

Chapter 14

THE JOB STATEMENT

The JOB statement comes at the beginning of your JCL deck and identifies your JOB as a separate set of work. It should contain information identifying the owner of the work, the class of work to be done, and so on. Most of the fields on the JOB statement have defaults. The default values vary from one installation to another. For your own particular case, you will probably have to ask someone at your site to find out the local conventions. The following general discussion gives you an overall view.

THE JOB NAME

The JOB statement must have a name, called the jobname.

The jobname is very like the ddname and the step name, except that the jobname is always required. The JOB name must be from 1 to 8 characters. There is no space between the // and the name but there must be at least one space between the name and the word JOB and one space after the word JOB. The name may consist of a combination of uppercase letters, numbers, and the national characters, except that the name must start with a letter or national character. Same rules as for ddnames, step names, and so on. In addition, some installations require you to use your TSO userid as the first part of the job name.

There is also a restriction that you may not use the national characters if you are using AL tapes. You must confine your job name to only letters and numbers in that case. A restriction you will have to live with somehow.

The name should be unique from your own point of view. MVS will not get upset if you submit a few jobs each called DALEJOB1.

Note, however:

If you submit multiple jobs with the same name, only one of them will run at a time. MVS will not allow two jobs of the same name to run at the same time.

If you want to speak to the operator about your job DALEJOB1, and you have seven of them, the operator will not necessarily know which one you are talking about.

By the way, speaking to the operators is frowned on in some computer departments. The computer operations management often wants the operators to keep the computers working at maximum efficiency rather than speaking to programmers. Management often have these funny ideas.

There are two positional parameters on the JOB statement. The first is used to contain accounting information. The second is used for the programmers name.

Both of these may be optional at any given company, or they might be required. Depends how the systems programmers have set up the system.

Accounting Information

Most installations will require some type of accounting information. In fact MVS will allow up to 142 characters of accounting information. It is likely that you will need some accounting information, although at some companies it will not be required.

It is generally used for billing or for keeping track of how much computer time your project is using.

The required accounting information may be a special account code that is shared by your project team, or it may be an individual code given to you. The code will probably not have any apparent relationship to anything else.

Not only will you be given the code but you will also be given any other special requirements that your installation may have for the accounting information field. As this can change from company to company, you more or less have to ask someone, probably your immediate manager.

The format could be quite strange.

Ordinarily you will need to enclose it within single quote marks (apostrophes) if it contains any hyphens, commas, or other odd characters. Sometimes parentheses are sufficient.

Programmer Name Field

One thing you won't have to ask anyone is your name. We can be certain you have that. The name parameter is the second positional parameter of the JOB statement.

At many companies the name field is optional.

Certainly it need not contain your name. You can put more or less any string of characters you wish in the name field. However, you may be expected to use your name. It might be used for delivering sysouts.

If sysout listings are not delivered, however, you can probably put some other identifying string in the programmer name field. Something like 'PSAMPLE AUGUST 3RD' or whatever you find helpful, as long as you keep it down to 20 characters in length.

If you look at the following JOB statement you will find both accounting information and the programmer name field:

```
//DALEJOB1   JOB   '4852,B3',DALE
```

The accounting number contains two components. The first is the account code and the second happens to be the room number where the programmer is located.

In fact that type of accounting information is fairly typical of what is commonly used.

You will also notice the two components are included in single quotation marks. That way MVS will treat them all as the first position parameter. Parentheses are usually sufficient if you prefer parentheses.

The second positional parameter is the name information. You want to change the name to your own. When Chris was here there was only one Chris in room B3.

You replaced Chris, and kept the JOB statement.

But let's suppose your name is Dale and there are two other Dales in room B3 with you. You can put your full name within those single quotation marks as long as you do not exceed 20 characters including the spaces. Let's see what the JOB statement looks like now:

//DALEJOB1   JOB   '4852,B3','DALE PATEL'

The second Dale has a different problem, being named Dale O'Neill. As you remember, and I am sure you do remember, you can put two single quotation marks adjacent to each other and only end up with one. Let's look at another JOB statement:

//DALEJOB2   JOB   '4852,B3','DALE O''NEILL'

Just for the sake of completeness, let's look at the JOB statement for Dale Tronniclourifinnetski. This name cannot be used on its own as it has 21 letters, and will not fit within the limit of 20. Dale does not wish parts of this proud family name taken out to suit the requirements of the JOB statement, and has come up with this as a solution:

//DALEJOB3   JOB   '4852,B3','DALE T'

If you have a name that exceeds 20 characters, then you should spend a little time thinking how you want your name to look on the JOB statement. Of course, you don't really have to put your name in the name field - the computer doesn't know the difference - you can put any string of text up to 20 characters long.

As a point of interest, the full stop (period, dot, point) does not count as a special character when it appears within the programmer name field. Hence the following JOB statement is valid as it stands:

//SUZUKI7A   JOB   (1,B4),
// D.T.SUZUKI,MSGCLASS=X

There are default values for all the parameters on the JOB statement other than the accounting information and the programmer name field. These defaults may well suit your requirements, and the default values may well be different from installation to installation. Let's have a look in more detail at some common parameters you may use.

NOTIFY

The NOTIFY parameter tells MVS to send a message to a TSO terminal as soon as the JOB completes. You simply provide the TSO userid and MVS takes care of the rest. You will probably want to specify your own userid but there is no reason you can't use a different one if you have some good business reason for creating a nuisance. The NOTIFY parameter on the JOB statement looks like this:

```
//SMITH7N1   JOB   (5842,S7),'MOI',NOTIFY=JONES
```

MSGCLASS

The MSGCLASS parameter is used to tell MVS where you want the JCL part of your listing to be printed.

The values are the same as SYSOUT values.

MSGCLASS=X usually means you will look at your listing under TSO, MSGCLASS=A usually means it will be printed on a printer, and so on.

The MSGCLASS parameter is particularly useful as it provides you with the ability to refer back to it in the various DD SYSOUT=* statements. I know you remember from earlier reading that when you code the SYSOUT= parameter on a DD statement you can use a variety of letters or numbers, or you can use the *. If you use the * you are saying you want the same output class used as is specified on the MSGCLASS parameter. If you build the JCL carefully you won't have to use override cards or other techniques for this function.

In the following example two SYSOUT files refer to the MSGCLASS parameter in the JOB statement. You can use this technique for many more DD statements than two.

```
//MYJOB    JOB    (9977,W4),
//  'MYSELF',MSGCLASS=A
//PRINT EXEC PGM=IEBGENER
//SYSIN DD DUMMY
//SYSPRINT DD SYSOUT=*
//SYSUT2 DD SYSOUT=*
//SYSUT1 DD *
     by changing the job card
     i can print this anywhere
     i want.
     the power is awesome
/*
```

Along with the MSGCLASS parameter we find the MSGLEVEL parameter. While they are closely related, they are independent of each other. You can use one or the other or both or neither.

MSGLEVEL

The MSGLEVEL parameter tell MVS how much of the job log to print. The job log is a fancy name for the JCL and the messages that are associated with it. Basically it is the stuff that appears at the top of your job listing that perhaps you never wanted to look at before. I say before, because by now you are getting pretty good at this JCL stuff.

MSGLEVEL has two positional sub-parameters. The first is used to specify how much JCL you want to print, while the second is used to specify the type of messages you want to print.

Let's look at the second parameter first. There are two possible values, the numbers 0 and 1. The value 1 is used to print the JCL, JES, operator, and SMS messages. The value 0 is used to print only the JCL messages; however, if the job abnormally terminates the other messages will print as well.

Now back to the first parameter. It has three values. Not surprisingly they are the numbers 0, 1, and 2. The value 0 is used to print only the JOB statement. The value 2 is used to print the JCL statements and the JES control statements. The value 1 does everything that is in 2 but also includes any cataloged procedures and the replacement of symbolic parameters in those procedures. There are several combinations of coding the MSGLEVEL parameter but the one you should use is in the following example. It gets you everything:

```
//GOODJOB JOB (5842,H1),'SAMPLE',
//      MSGLEVEL=(1,1)
```

You will often see the following used instead, which gets you nothing:

```
//BADJOB  JOB (5842,H1),
//      'SAMPLE',MSGLEVEL=(0,0)
```

You should now be familiar enough with JCL to be able to understand many of the things that are printed on the job log. Sometimes reading the job log may not seem to be the most exciting thing to do, but it usually helps in problem resolution; leaving you free to do something more interesting after the problems are resolved.

JOB STATEMENT PARAMETERS THAT CONTROL PROCESSING

CLASS

The CLASS parameter describes the general resource requirements of your job.

Each installation will have its own list of available job classes and related resources.

The rules for these are usually enforced by MVS, if the systems programmers have instructed MVS to enforce them. At some places the systems programmers will rely on voluntary compliance with the rules. In that case, if you don't follow the rules, you should not be surprised if the operator cancels your job.

The job classes are the letters and numbers. We can have 36 classes. That does not mean that all 36 will be used. Let's look at an example of job classes in an imaginary company:

CLASS	REQUIREMENT
0 to 9	Production
A	Test that takes less 30 seconds
B	Test that uses computer tapes
C	Test that takes up to 15 minutes
D	Test that takes more than 15 minutes
E	Test that requires operator responses

Suppose that your MVS system is set up in such a way that only one or two CLASS=A jobs can run at once. In that case, if you submit a JOB that will run for an hour and you use CLASS=A then your co-workers will wonder why their jobs are not running. In the hour that your JOB is running at least 120 other jobs could have run. So, even if the systems programmers have not gone to the trouble to make MVS enforce the rules, and even if the operators don't cancel your job, and even if you are not a big fan of law and order, still, be a good neighbor and use the correct job class. That way you will have the weight of righteous indignation behind you when you complain about somebody else running a job for 5 hours in class A.

REGION

The REGION parameter tells MVS how much virtual storage (memory) your job will need.

Similar to REGION on the EXEC statement.

The value you use on the JOB statement, if you use it, should be the amount of storage required by the step that uses the most storage. If you have coded the REGION parameter on the EXEC statements, then the value on the JOB statement will be used instead. It is coded the same way as on the EXEC statements.

You probably do not need to use the REGION parameter because the default value is usually large enough to satisfy most needs.

Usually the REGION parameter is used to increase the amount of storage over the default value. But you may sometime want to decrease the amount of storage. It really doesn't matter, the REGION parameter is coded the same way.

Suppose the default REGION value is 8 Megabytes (REGION =8M) and you have a program that grabs the remainder of the region for a working area. Your program insists on initializing all the working areas before it actually starts working. If you have determined that the whole program needs, say 1/2 a megabyte, then the extra 7.5 megabytes are being initialized unnecessarily. Depending on how Job Classes are set up at your installation, you might be able to run in a better Job Class if you specify a small region. Here are the JOB statements before and after the change in the REGION parameter:

```
//DALEJOB1 JOB (5842,C9),'DEFAULT REGION',
//     CLASS=C
//MYJOB2 JOB (5842,C9),'REGION SPECIFIED',
//  CLASS=A,REGION=512K
```

Note that on some MVS systems specifying REGION=0 has the same effect as specifying the maximum available region.

TIME

The TIME parameter on the JOB statement is coded the same way as it is on the EXEC statement. However, it does not replace the value used on any individual EXEC statements. Instead it specifies a total time for the entire job.

The general format of the TIME parameter is the same as on the EXEC statement : TIME=(minutes,seconds) or TIME=(minutes) or TIME=(,seconds) or, for endless time, TIME=NOLIMIT, or for slightly less than endless, TIME=MAXIMUM.

TIME=1440 is an older form used in place of TIME=NOLIMIT (because there are 1440 minutes in a 24-hour day). Similarly you will sometimes see TIME=1439. This last form is used to keep time recording active; time recording is suspended with TIME=1440. So TIME=1439 is the older form for TIME=MAXIMUM. Finally, on some systems TIME=0 means the same as TIME=NOLIMIT. On other systems, it means zero. The IBM manual recommends against using TIME=0 on the JOB statement. It says the results are unpredictable.

Suppose you have a JOB with three steps. The total JOB is to use no more than 5 minutes execution time and each step is to use no more than 2 minutes execution time. In the following example the final step may not even get to use its two minutes, depending on how long the previous steps take.

```
//MYJOB3 JOB (5842,C9),'WATCH THIS',
//    CLASS=C,TIME=5
//STEP1 EXEC PGM=PROGRAM1,TIME=2
//*    THIS STEP WILL USE
//*    1 MINUTE 55 SECONDS
//*
//STEP2 EXEC PGM=PROGRAM2,TIME=2
//*    THIS STEP WILL ALSO USE
//*    1 MINUTE 55 SECONDS
//*
//STEP3 EXEC PGM=PROGRAM3,TIME=2
//*    THIS STEP ONLY HAS
//*    1 MINUTE 10 SECONDS AVAILABLE
```

If you had coded the final step with TIME=(,30) it naturally would only have 30 seconds and not the 70 seconds remaining. Of course you could have coded the JOB statement with TIME=7 and avoided the situation, but then I would not have an example.

There is one other thing you might want to know about the TIME parameter, and this holds whether it is coded in the JOB or EXEC statements. The timing is not very accurate. The system will convert your time into a number of units. A unit is 1.048576 seconds, that sounds pretty accurate. But 30 seconds gets converted to 29 units which is 30.408704 seconds. Again you say that is close enough. But the system does not check the time constantly, it only looks at the time every 10.5 seconds. In this case the system might have looked at the execution time used by this step if it finds, say 30.2 seconds, you get another 10.5 seconds.

If you think of MVS as something that is meant to assist you in getting your work done, and not as a police officer ready to catch any minor infraction of the rules, then you will not have any difficulty coping with the fact that the TIME parameter is not terribly accurate.

The moral of this is if you want to boil an egg you would be better off with an egg timer than the TIME parameter.

RESTART: How to get things started..... Again

Suppose you have a JOB that was running but for some reason was not able to complete. Let's say there was a power failure, because I know your program would not have a bug which would cause it to abend. Anyway, this was a very long JOB with 15 steps, and the power failed during step 12. It would be a pity to have to run the first 11 steps again just to get back to where things were when the power failed.

Enter the RESTART parameter.

The RESTART parameter has a form that is of particular interest to us. It is called the 'deferred step restart'. This is a curious use of the word deferred in that the RESTART parameter actually gives you an opportunity to nominate the step that will be the first to be executed, thereby skipping over the steps that precede the step nominated. The default value naturally is to have the JOB start at the first step.

In the example I proposed earlier the first 11 steps completed successfully and the power was lost while the 12th step was executing. Let us suppose, for the purposes of this example, that such uninspired stepnames as STEP1, STEP2, etc were used. We want to start at the 12th step which has been called (you guessed it) STEP12. The JOB statement would look something like this:

```
//SMITH7R1 JOB (5842,C9),
//    'POWER FAIL RECOVERY',
//    CLASS=C,RESTART=STEP12
```

The job would begin executing at STEP12.

So you now know how to code the RESTART parameter. But things are not quite as simple as that.

This job will restart successfully only if the JCL has been constructed correctly.

It is possible to have JCL that will work correctly as long as it is executed in its entirety.

Suppose STEP12 needs a file that was created in STEP9 but was created as a temporary file and passed to subsequent steps.

When the JOB statement specifies STEP12 as the first step to be executed, MVS assumes that everything required by STEP12 will still be available.

In the case of our example, the temporary data set created in STEP9 will have disappeared in the way that temporary data sets do, and the restarted job will fail.

Passed files are not the only thing that can go wrong. Backward references can cause restart problems as well.

You remember backward references. Referbacks. Don't use referbacks in JCL that will be a candidate for RESTART processing. When a job is restarted somewhere in the middle, there won't be any first part of the job for the referbacks to refer back to.

One more thing to be aware of. If a step has a COND parameter that refers to a step that was bypassed during the restart then that condition test will be ignored. In our example, if STEP13 is not to execute in the event of STEP11 having a condition of 7 or greater, then the test will not be made. Remember the COND only lasts for the duration of a JOB. In our example where the JOB is restarted at STEP12, STEP11 is no longer part of the JOB.

Finally, if the JOB uses generation data sets, sometimes known as GDG's, the restart can get really complicated. If the JOB uses GDG's then be very careful. See the section on GDG's.

The RESTART parameter may be coded several ways, but we are only interested in two forms. In the first instance you use the 'stepname' and in the second case you use the 'stepname.procstepname' form.

First example. The JOB statement in this example causes the job to start from DANCING, skipping DINNER and MOVIES:

```
//SMITH7R2 1,'TEST JOB RESTART',
//     MSGCLASS=X,RESTART=DANCING
//DINNER EXEC PGM=DINNER
//MOVIES EXEC PGM=MOVIES
//DANCING EXEC PGM=DANCING
//BEDTIME EXEC PGM=BEDTIME
```

Second example.

The JOB statement in this example causes the job to start from the MIDDLE step of the SNOWMAN procedure executed in BUILD:

```
//SMITH7R3 JOB 1,FLAKE,MSGCLASS=X,
//     RESTART=BUILD.MIDDLE
//SNOWFALL PROC
//FLAKEY  EXEC PGM=IEFBR14
// PEND
//SNOWMAN PROC NAME=FROSTY
//BOTTOM  EXEC PGM=PSAMPLE,
//     PARM='&NAME.  THE SNOWMAN'
//MIDDLE  EXEC PGM=IEFBR14
//HEAD    EXEC PGM=IEFBR14
// PEND
//SNOWFALL EXEC SNOWFALL
//BUILD   EXEC SNOWMAN
```

Obviously you would only want to start from the MIDDLE step of the BUILD of SNOWMAN if, previously, you had run the SNOWFALL step and the BOTTOM step of the BUILD of SNOWMAN. And that shows why they call the parameter RESTART rather than START.

SOME PARAMETERS THAT ARE USED LESS OFTEN

There are several parameters that are only available with certain versions of MVS such as MVS/ESA or RACF subsystem. There are others parameters that are generally available, but you may not ever use them. We'll cover some of these briefly now.

PERFORM

You remember from the CLASS parameter something about the scheduling of work through MVS.

The MVS systems programmers generally set up the system in such a way that jobs in different classes are automatically associated with certain performance groups, that is, some have higher priority than others when several want to use the CPU or some other resource at the same time. Usually long-running jobs are given lower priority than quick small jobs.

The systems programmers make up big complicated specifications stating which performance characteristics (priorities) will be associated with which performance groups, and which performance groups will be associated with which job classes. Each particular type of work is assigned to some particular performance group. These groups are assigned numbers, called performance group numbers, in much the same arbitrary way as classes are assigned.

PERFORM is short for performance group number. Sometimes abbreviated PGN on various reports and displays.

The PERFORM parameter overrides the default performance group. If it is used, it is generally used to improve the performance of a particular job because it is important that it run quickly on some particular occasion. The payroll is late, say. If your installation expects the PERFORM parameter to be used, you will be told what numeric value to use. Don't think that high numbers are necessarily better than low numbers or vice versa. The numbers are arbitrary, like the classes.

Example of coding the PERFORM parameter on the JOB statement:

```
//SMITH7P1 JOB (4816,A5),'SMITH',
//       CLASS=C,PERFORM=17
```

When the job gets into execution, as they say, it will be controlled according to the locally defined rules for performance group 17, whatever they may be. Also note that the performance characteristics might change from time to time as operational requirements change. Example: Suppose arbitrarily that PERFORM=17 used to be a special performance group that made a job run at a high priority. Too many people found out about it and started using it without authorization. This slowed down other work on the system. So the systems programmers might now change PERFORM=17 to be a special low priority group. I've seen it happen.

ADDRSPC

One of the main features of MVS is the efficient use of processor storage (memory). If a program occupies 800K of storage, it may only be using 60K at any one time. If another program is running at the same time and it needs some memory, MVS will save the unused 740K on what is called virtual memory, that is, MVS will page the unused pages out to disk. As the program progresses through its execution MVS will keep track of which parts of memory are required at any one time, and make the required memory available in real storage (real memory) as needed.

You can see that if ten programs similar to the one described were running at the same time they would need 10 x 800K of storage, or 8000K of storage. But in fact they probably really only need 10 x 60K or 600K. This is quite a neat thing to do, because you can see that you can fit the working parts of 10 programs in less than the total area required for one program. While it does not take much time for MVS to maneuver these programs about, it does take some. Too long in fact for some special kinds of programs, particularly those that are very sensitive to timing considerations.

MVS assigns memory to a program in a block that is called an address space. If you need to make sure that a particular program runs in real memory, rather than virtual memory, you can code ADDRSPC=REAL on the JOB statement. If ADDRSPC=REAL is coded you should also code the REGION parameter because the default region size is far too large for real memory.

ADDRSPC is also a parameter on the EXEC statement. If your job has more than one step and not all steps require real memory, you might be better off to code ADDRSPC on the EXEC of the programs that require it. No sense in giving the whole job real memory when only one step requires it. On the other hand, coding ADDRSPC on the JOB statement may have scheduling advantages. Check with your local systems programmers before you use this. Many MVS systems do not allow for it at all. Some allow only 64K for it, and so on.

TYPRUN

There is an interesting parameter that you can put on the JOB statement that will prevent MVS from executing your job altogether, or at least for a little while. Why would you want to do that, you ask? Well, one of the values you can code on the JOB statement is TYPRUN=SCAN. This asks MVS to check your JCL for syntax errors. It is similar to compiling a program and looking at the error messages before executing the program. Anyway it is pretty fast, and you can check your JCL for SOME types of errors this way.

It is often important to prevent a job from executing too early. By using TYPRUN=HOLD you can ask MVS to hold a job until the operator releases it.

Example. Suppose you have two jobs, one that creates a file and another that reads the file. You do not want the job that reads the file to run before the file has been created. You code the following type of JCL:

Job 1:

```
//MAKEFILE JOB (8542,S7),
// 'MY NAME',CLASS=A
// EXEC PGM=IEFBR14
//D DD DISP=(NEW,CATLG),
// UNIT=SYSDA,
// SPACE=(CYL,(1)),
// DSN=CLAUDE.MONET,
// DCB=(LRECL=80,RECFM=FB,
// BLKSIZE=23440,DSORG=PS)
```

Job 2, with TYPRUN=HOLD:

```
//READFILE JOB (5842,S7),'ME AGAIN',
// CLASS=A,TYPRUN=HOLD
// EXEC PGM=WHATEVER
//INPUT DD DISP=OLD,DSN=CLAUDE.MONET
```

The job MAKEFILE will run in its turn, everything else being equal. However the job READFILE will wait until the operator releases it. How the operator knows to release the job is not really of interest at this point, let's assume you and the operator had lunch together and came to some agreement. Be that as it may, the job READFILE was prevented from running until the job MAKEFILE finished its work.

The last variation of interest is TYPRUN=JCLHOLD. Let's suppose your job uses a cataloged procedure, or it will when the procedure gets added to the cataloged procedure library. If you code TYPRUN=JCLHOLD then MVS will not even look for the cataloged procedure until the job is released. Of course you still have the problem of the operator knowing when to release the job. You may even have to have lunch with the systems programmer who looks after the cataloged procedures library.

COND

You remember the discussion on the COND parameter in the chapter on the EXEC statement. Well, the COND parameter may be coded on the JOB statement as well, either in addition to or instead of the COND on the EXEC statement. If COND is coded on the JOB statement then MVS will supplement the EXEC statement COND with the JOB statement COND. Both sets of COND tests will be made.

The main difference between them is if the COND on the JOB statement is found to be true, then the entire JOB terminates, bypassing all of the rest of the steps.

RACF PARAMETERS USER - GROUP - PASSWORD

Many installations have some type of security system which is meant to prevent access to sensitive information or to the computer itself. There is an IBM subsystem called RACF (Resource Access Control Facility). There are other subsystem products available from other suppliers which are similar to IBM's RACF.

A subsystem bears the same relationship to a system as a subparameter bears to a parameter. Hence you will sometimes hear RACF called a security system, and you will sometimes hear it called a subsystem. The distinction is not too important.

If RACF is installed on your system there may well be default values which will allow you to do some basic work, or the default may allow you to do work associated with the TSO USERID you have been assigned. There is no way of knowing what the default values are from one installation to another. They are customized very individually at each company.

Because RACF is a product of IBM, a few RACF parameters are available on the JOB statement. The non-IBM security systems generally allow you to use these same parameters, and the processing of them is then intercepted by the non-IBM security subsystem.

The security parameters available on the JOB statement are GROUP, USER, and PASSWORD. The parameters may be optional in certain situations, depending on the way the security system has been set up. Usually none are required. However, if either the PASSWORD or GROUP parameter is coded then USER must also be coded.

The USER parameter is used to identify the person who is submitting the JOB, or the person to whom the job belongs. If you submit your own job you use your own USERID on the USER parameter.

However, if I asked you to submit one of my jobs for me you would use my USERID on the USER parameter. The point would either be to allow the job to have access to data sets that I was authorized to use but you were not authorized to use, or else to prevent the job from using data sets that you were authorized to use but I was not.

The GROUP parameter is associated with the USER parameter. Each USER is associated with a default GROUP. The group can be thought of as a set of RACF security rules to be applied to the job. If for some reason you have alternate sets of security rules, then you specify the GROUP parameter. For example, perhaps you do some work for the payroll department and other work for accounting. You want your accounting jobs to run with a different set of security rules than your payroll department jobs. If you are set up to use two groups, named ACCOUNTS and PAYROLL, and your userid is SMITH, they you can use job statements like these:

```
//PAYROLL1 JOB 1,SMITH,
//      GROUP=PAYROLL,USER=SMITH ... etc.
```

```
//ACCOUNT1 JOB 1,SMITH,
//      GROUP=ACCOUNTS,USER=SMITH ... etc.
```

PASSWORD is another security parameter on the JOB statement.

For some curious reason whenever PASSWORD is coded on the JOB statement it must be on the first line (the first card). The PASSWORD must not be put on the continuation portions of the JOB statement. Strange but true.

In the example where you are submitting a job on behalf on someone else it seems reasonable to require the password. The PASSWORD parameter can also be used to change the password, in which case the old password is coded first and the new password follows.

Example: the JOB statement asks that the password be changed from ABCDE to VWXYZ for USERID MYNAME.

```
//DALE JOB 6688,ME,PASSWORD=(ABCDE,VWXYZ),
//      USER=MYNAME
```

Example: the JOB statement provides RACF authorization to use a different USER, GROUP, and PASSWORD than the default:

```
//YOUR JOB (4852,F3),YOU,PASSWORD=VWXYZ,
//      USER=MYNAME,GROUP=MYGROUP
```

SECTION 4.

ADVANCED JCL

Chapter 15

A JOURNEY THROUGH MVS WITH A JOB

Let's follow the journey of your JOB through MVS. No matter where your JOB was created, whether it was in a TSO session, or some other subsystem that allows you to work at a terminal and create JOBs for MVS to do, the JOB must get into MVS somewhere or another. You may even have a JOB in the form of real punched cards that you picked up at a museum somewhere. No matter, the JOB must actually be given to MVS. MVS gets JOBs through a program called a READER. The first READER programs were used to read real punched cards from card reading machines. The READER programs were modified slightly to read card images from anywhere. They could read card images from computer tapes, or disk files, or even real cards. They still do much the same thing as they have done for decades.

The READER program is part of the MVS system, and it would not be unusual for several READERs to be operating concurrently. The READERs are generally started automatically by MVS, but a computer operator may stop and start READERs in order to provide a bit of human control to the activity of MVS. Obviously if all the READERs are stopped MVS will not be able to get any new JOBs into the system. The operator may actually do this if there is a requirement to prevent new work from getting into the system. In any event the READER is the first component of MVS that will see your JOB.

The JCL of a JOB must start with a JOB card, however the end of the JCL can be determined by one of three events. One is the presence of an 'end of job' card, which has only a // in columns 1 and 2 with the rest of the card blank. A second method of finding the end of the JCL for a JOB is for the READER to find another JOB card. The third way to determine the end of the JCL is if the READER program cannot find any more cards to read

If the reader finds any input card data following either a DD * or a DD DATA card it will store those card images on a DASD file and save that data until the JOB is executed, at which time the card images will be given to the program one at a time as the program requires them. The remainder of the JCL is saved until it is required at JOB 'execution' time. The JOB has now entered a queue and will wait its turn to be run by MVS.

If your JOB uses a cataloged PROCEDURE, a copy of the procedure is taken at this time and stored with your JCL. If the procedure is changed (by some systems programmer) between the time your JOB is read and the time is run, then your JOB will use the old version of the procedure.

There are a number of 'INPUT QUEUES' maintained by MVS. The queue your job has been put into is determined by the JOB CLASS. You remember you put a CLASS= parameter on the JOB card. If you did not put a CLASS= parameter on the JOB card the system has a default class which is assigned. The operator has the ability to transfer your JOB from one queue to another, but generally the operator will not do that.

It is important to enter the correct CLASS on your JOB card as the operators are likely to cancel your job if you violate the rules. For example you use the CLASS that is reserved for JOBs that will complete in less than 30 seconds and do not require any operator action; however your JOB needs a tape and asks the operator to answer a question. Your JOB is now preventing well behaved JOBs from being run while the operator looks for your tape. Your JOB will be cancelled by the operator, unless you happen to be the Chief Executive of the company or the head of the computer department.

Your JOB is securely in the correct QUEUE and working its way towards the time when it will actually be executed. It will eventually be selected by another program called an 'INITIATOR.' Your JCL will be extensively processed by the INITIATOR. Most of your JCL statements are in fact instructions to the INITIATOR program.

The INITIATOR program is another integral part of MVS. There will most certainly be a number of copies of the INITIATOR program running. Each copy of the INITIATOR program that is running will look at one or more input QUEUEs. If you are using a JOB CLASS that is looked at by more than one INITIATOR then your JOB will be run by MVS much sooner. In any event an INITIATOR program has selected your JOB to be run.

The INITIATOR must be able to locate your program to load it into main memory, it will use the instructions you gave it with the STEPLIB and JOBLIB statements, if you did not specify any STEPLIB or JOBLIB statements then MVS will look in it's own libraries. If the program cannot be located in any of the libraries then the STEP will terminate with a system error code such as S80A.

The INITIATOR will do several other important functions for you. It will make the connections between the various old files that your program will need. You may remember that the READER stored the card images that were located after any DD * or DD DATA statements, the INITIATOR fill find the location of those card images, your program must still read them though.

The INITIATOR will ensure that any file that you do not want to SHARE (because you did not code DISP=SHR) is not made available to any other JOB in the system. If you are quite happy to share all your files, but some other JOB has started prior to your JOB and the other JOB does not allow sharing of a file you need, then your JOB will have to wait for the other JOB to complete. If the other JOB is a very long running JOB then your JOB will have a very long wait.

The INITIATOR will also allocate the DASD and tape drives your JOB STEP will need. This will ensure that the drive is available when you need it. Even if you code DEFER in your UNIT parameter the drive is still allocated, the only thing that is deferred is mounting the tape on the drive. Mounting is a new word for you in this context, it is the word used to describe the process the operator follows when loading a tape.

Another important thing the INITIATOR does is to allocate the SPACE you requested for your NEW DASD files. The INITIATOR will only get the initial primary space, so if you have requested secondary space it may not be there when you need it. So you should try to get your primary space allocation correct the first time.

After all that has been done, the INITIATOR starts your program. The first instruction in your program that is meant to execute will be given control. Your program can now process quite happily until it reaches normal completion, or until it reaches an abnormal termination (ABTERM) or abnormal end (ABEND). No matter what happens, when your program is done the INITIATOR takes charge again.

The INITIATOR starts to tidy up after the program completes. You remember your JOB is comprised of one or more STEPs, each STEP is a program. Once the step is complete many of the resources used in the step will be made available to the released to the system again.

If the step did not terminate normally, any files that were opened will be closed on your behalf by the INITIATOR. If the program you were using was not a 'tidy' program and did not close the files it used then those files will be closed by the INITIATOR for you. I know any program YOU would write will close all the files properly, and not expect the INITIATOR to do the work for you. It is not only a bad practice to leave this kind of thing to the INITIATOR, but you may not get the results you want. Remember the INITIATOR is trying to tidy things up for itself, not for you. Imagine if someone decided to tidy your disk for you, you may never find anything again.

If you had a card image file, remember the DD* or DD DATA statements, that card image file will be deleted. The space it used will be returned to MVS.

Any tapes that you used can now be removed from the tape drive and the tape drives will be returned to MVS, unless you specified RETAIN in the VOLUME command in which case the tape will remain on the tape drive.

If you were using DASD files, any files that are to be deleted because you specified DELETE in the DISP parameter (or the default was DELETE) then those files will be deleted. Any space that can be released from a DASD file because you specified RLSE in the SPACE command will now be released.

Any files that are to be cataloged or uncataloged will now have those actions done. If a file was located with the catalog, and you specified DELETE in the DISP command the file will now be uncataloged. However if the file was located because you specified the UNIT and VOLUME information in the DD statement, the cataloged entry will not be removed simply by specifying DELETE in the DISP command.

Once the INITIATOR has tidied up at the end of a STEP, it checks to see if there is another STEP to run in the JOB. If there is, that STEP will now be started. This process will continue until all the STEPs are done. When the last STEP has terminated, the INITIATOR tidies up anything that may be left over. For example, any files that have been PASSed via the DISP command will be taken care of now. For example , suppose the first STEP creates a DASD file with a DISP=(NEW,PASS), the second STEP specifies DISP=(OLD,PASS) for the same file. No other STEPs in the JOB refer to the file at all. At the end of the JOB the INITIATOR will delete the file. This is not an unreasonable thing to do. If the file were required, you should have said KEEP.

If you had coded RETAIN in the VOLUME command and the volume is still on the drive, the INITIATOR will remove that RETAIN attribute in order to allow another JOB to use the drive.

Once the INITIATOR has tidied up all the little odds and ends, it can look at the QUEUE to see if there is another JOB ready to start.

You now know the reason one of the most powerful programs is IEFBR14. This is a one instruction program that has as its one and only instruction an exit command. As soon as the program start, it finishes. But it does provide you with the ability to create DASD files, delete DASD files, change entries in the CATALOG, and do all sorts of other neat things. It does all this because it allows the INITIATOR to get on with the work it does best. Please note the IEFBR14 will always provide a return code of zero.

Here is an example. Suppose you have a program that you have to run a number of times. Each time the program runs it creates an output file. Now you are really only interested in keeping the output file from the very final run of the program. You can use IEFBR14 to delete the file BEFORE your program runs.

```
//MYJOB JOB (1234,4FTY),
//      'JOB FOR ME',CLASS=7
//*   THE FIRST STEP IS AN IEFBR14
//*   TO DELETE MY FILES.—MY FILES
//*   ARE ALWAYS CATALOGED.
//DELETE1 EXEC PGM=IEFBR14
//A      DD DSN=MY.FILE.ONE,
//      DISP=(OLD,DELETE)
//*   THATS ALL THERE IS TO IT. THE
//*   CATALOG WILL FIND THE FILE
//*   WHEN THE STEP STARTS. THE FILE
//*   WILL BE DELETED AT THE END.
//PROGRAM EXEC PGM=PROGRAM1
//STEPLIB DD DSN=MY.LOADLIB,DISP=SHR
//OUTPUT DD DSN=MY.FILE.ONE,
// DISP=(NEW,CATLG),
//      UNIT=SYSDA,
//      SPACE=(TRK,(5,1,1))
//INPUT DD *
my input file happens to be card
images this is only an example
of the card images i could go on
and fill up lots of pages of the
book with this kind of stuff but
you get the idea
/*
//REPORT DD SYSOUT=A
//
```

Chapter 16

JOB SCHEDULING

You have finally reached that time when the set of computer programs you have been developing has finished the development phase, and it has been thoroughly tested.

That magical time when you can look forward to a relaxing early evening away from work. Maybe meet a few friends you haven't been able to see for a while. Maybe even see some members of your family while they are still awake.

You are quite satisfied with all the hard work you have done, and you should be. By the way, let me add my own congratulations for a job well done.

Now it is up to the operations people to run the programs. They won't have any difficulty. After all, they push work through the computers all the time.

And this is such a simple system. With only four jobs to run daily. Three jobs weekly, including the one that must be run at 7:45 AM on Mondays. Two jobs get run on the first working day of the month. One gets run every fourth Friday for the Accounting Department. Then there are the annual, semi-annual, and quarterly jobs. Of course there are also the jobs that run with a special parameter whenever there happen to be two full moons in the calendar month. Etc., etc.

Maybe the system is not as simple as you thought. Remember, this system has been a part of you. You know its every requirement.

Now you suddenly panic! Will the operators look after your system as well as you have? Are they capable?

Maybe you should continue looking after it for a bit longer. No, that is not possible. The boss has already told you about your next project. You will be needed for that.

You now understand the look of anguish on your parents' faces the time you announced you were leaving home.

Never fear. Just as you survived without your parents, your system will survive without you.

Just as your parents gave you advice, you will have to advise the operators. You will tell them how to take care of your system.

Because operators are often on shift work, you won't see all of them. So you must write everything down.

Every operations department has a scheduling system of some kind. Some are very sophisticated software systems that blend into MVS so well that you hardly know about them. Others are manually controlled. No matter which is being used, the work for a developer is much the same.

The relationship of each job to any other job will have to be defined. For example, you can hardly run the job to print the payroll before the job that calculates the payroll has been completed successfully.

The sequence of running the jobs must be specified. That won't be very difficult for you to do. But any unusual job sequences must also be specified. And the reasons for the unusual sequences should be clearly defined.

Even knowing when a job has completed successfully can some-times be a problem. Obviously if a job abends it was not successful. But return codes, you remember that wonderful COND parameter which tests them, are sometimes an indication of the success of a job. For example a Return Code of 5 may be alright in one job but not in another. There is no way for the operators to know unless you tell them.

Unfortunately there is no such thing as inter job condition code testing in JCL. Somehow the success of a job has to be checked before the next job in the sequence can start.

In a manual system, the JCLLOG must be inspected. Remember the MSGLEVEL parameter on the JOB statement?

Any unusual conditions must be checked out. If everything looks alright, no abends and all return codes are zero, then the next job can be started.

You can make the task of inspecting all the step return codes easier by making the following step the very last step in each job.

//ALLDONE EXEC PGM=IEFBR14,COND=(0,NE)

or:

```
// IF ( RC = 0 AND ABEND = FALSE ) THEN
//ALLDONE EXEC PGM=IEFBR14
// ENDIF
```

If any previous step abended or had a return code that did not happen to be zero then the IEFBR14 will not execute. Now the only return code that will need to be inspected by the operators is the return code from the step ALLDONE.

Naturally this example will not work if some step can produce a return code other than zero and be considered to have completed successfully. In that case you will have to have a more complex COND or IF-THEN-ELSE-ENDIF.

Once all the requirements to run the system have been recorded, including the starting time for certain jobs, then the system can be handed over to operations.

AUTOMATED JOB SCHEDULERS

Many installations are using automated scheduling systems. These systems all operate pretty much the same way. They have the ability to check the results of one or more jobs. If everything agrees with the rules then the next job will be submitted to MVS.

How does that work?

The JOBLOG has to be inspected. The job card may have to change to use a certain MSGCLASS. The automated scheduler will read that special MSGCLASS and look for certain JOBNAMEs.

Any conditions that have been achieved can be checked off on the list of rules.

If a JOB cannot be checked off automatically because it does not conform to some rule or another, then a real live human operator type person will receive an appropriate message. The operator will then decide on the course of action. These automated schedulers regularly review the list of rules to determine if any new jobs can be submitted to MVS from its list of submittable jobs. The submittable jobs are maintained on a special library.

Did I mention that one of the rules can be to submit a job to MVS at a particular time of day? This facility can be very handy to ensure an 'online' system is available even for users that happen to be in a different time zone.

It would not be unusual to have to make changes to the JCL to have a job qualify for working with an automated scheduling system. Changing the MSGCLASS on the JOB statement is only one of the changes that might be required. It really depends on the scheduling system being used. You will have to talk this over with the operations staff at your site.

If you have planned everything well, your programs should be put safely into production with their supporting JCL, and you should be able to go on to your next project without looking back.

Chapter 17

UTILITIES, COMPILERS, AND OTHER HANDY PROGRAMS

The word utility is short for the phrase "utility programs", which means "useful programs" in the sense that the programs are of fairly general usefulness. The utility programs generally are used to manipulate data sets or to give you information about data sets.

Utility programs provide a way for you to have batch jobs perform tasks that you normally do at a terminal using TSO/ISPF; tasks such as copying files. Sitting at a terminal copying files seems easy, but if you have a lot of files that need to be copied you might see the merit of doing it with a batch job.

You have already been introduced to IEBGENER and IEBCOPY, which are programs of this type. There are a lot more. We will talk briefly about a few of them in this chapter.

IEBCOPY

You are already familiar with IEBCOPY from other chapters. Here we will review it briefly, and show some more of its capabilities.

IEBCOPY, as you recall, is a program you use only with libraries. Thus we will now discuss libraries again, in a little more detail than in earlier chapters.

Libraries, you recall, are data sets that have members.

A library is also known as a Partitioned Data Set, or PDS.

Libraries are used extensively under MVS.

Load modules—programs in executable form—must reside in libraries in order to be executable. When you want to execute a load module, the name of the data set that contains the load module can be specified on the STEPLIB or JOBLIB statement. The program to be executed, that is, the specific member of the library, is named in the PGM parameter of the EXEC statement.

You have probably noticed that TSO/SPF is oriented towards the use of libraries for program source.

MVS itself also uses libraries extensively; for example, JCL procedures are kept in PROCLIBs (PROCedure LIBraries) and parameters are kept in PARMLIBs (PARaMeter LIBraries).

A PDS requires a bit of description to understand it. A PDS may only reside on disk. A PDS is a single file but behaves a little bit like an entire disk.

A disk has a list of the files that are held on the disk at any one time. That list is called a VTOC, or 'Volume Table Of Contents.' A very large number of files can be held on the disk, and the files may have any of several file structures. There may be VSAM files, flat files, Data Bases, Partitioned Data Sets, or other special file structures.

A PDS may be used to hold a number of other files, but the other files are in reality treated as small flat files. A PDS has an area of its SPACE set aside at the beginning to hold a Directory of these flat files. Each of the small flat files is known as a member of the PDS.

The Directory will contain the names of the members that are currently contained in the PDS. If a member is added to the PDS an entry goes into the Directory. The entry contains the name of the member and a pointer to the location of the member. New members are added in the available space after the end of the last of the existing members. When a member is replaced, it is not re-written in the same place. The new version is written at the end, as if it were a new member, and the directory is updated to point to the new location of the member.

Similarly, if some records are added to a member that is already in the PDS, the new records are not tacked onto the end of the existing member. The entire member is copied to the next available space after all the other members, the new records are added onto the end of it there, and then the Directory is updated to point to the new location of the member.

It is possible to update the data in a member right where it is, but this is not the usual method. For example, you can use PL/I as follows to update in place a member consisting of one 80-byte record:

```
DECLARE CARD FILE RECORD
 UPDATE SEQL ENV(FB BLKSIZE(80));
DECLARE ACE CHARACTER(80);
OPEN FILE(CARD);
READ FILE(CARD) INTO(ACE);
ACE = '**** NEW DATA ****';
REWRITE FILE(CARD) FROM(ACE);
CLOSE FILE(CARD);
```

Let us return to our discussion of the usual method, however, which involves relocating the modified member at the end of all the other existing members in the PDS.

If a member is deleted from the PDS, the appropriate member name is removed from the Directory of the PDS. It has been known for novices to use JCL to try to delete a member of a PDS by coding DELETE in the DISP parameter of the DD statement. You and I know better than to do that. We know that particular action will delete the entire PDS because the DISP parameter is for the full data set, not a single member.

The deleting and updating of members in a PDS leaves gaps in the middle.

This is what happens.

Imagine a PDS has three members called A, B, and C, with A at the beginning of the PDS, B immediately after it, and C just after B.

Now suppose we delete member B. We have member A at the beginning, an unused area where member B was, and finally member C.

Now we add some records to member A. The new, bigger version of member A will be rewritten after member C. This leaves a larger unused area at the beginning. Any new member, or a member that is being replaced, will be placed after the last member on the PDS.

'After a time, with some members being changed and others being deleted, the PDS will have several gaps of unused space scattered throughout the file. The unused space is not considered to be available space, just unused. This is not very efficient, and eventually the amount of available space at the end of the PDS will not be sufficient to hold even a small member. At this point you need to compress the PDS to reclaim all of the unused space.

BACKING UP, RESTORING, AND COMPRESSING A PDS

Most MVS operations departments have a schedule for compressing libraries, that is, for reorganizing the PDS files to make unused space available once again. Note that this is not necessary for a PDSE data set. If you have a PDS that suffers from the problem I just described, ask the operations people if they can put your PDS on their schedule.

If you prefer to do the job yourself (it's quicker that way), the following example shows how to do it. The first step will take a backup copy of your PDS. This is only a precaution. The point of taking a backup is this: The compress could fail partway through, after the library is partially compressed. For example, this might happen if the job ran out of time or if there were a power failure. In such a case the library would be left mangled, unusable, trashed. Hence the truly cautious person precedes every compress with a backup. It is a good policy anyway to take periodic backup copies of your PDS. The second step in the following example compresses the PDS.

```
//SMITH8A1 JOB 1,SMITH,MSGCLASS=X
//STEP1  EXEC PGM=IEBCOPY
//SYSPRINT DD SYSOUT=*
//SYSUT1  DD DSN=MY.PDS,
//     DISP=OLD
//SYSUT2  DD DSN=MY.SAVED.PDS,
//     DISP=OLD,UNIT=TAPE,
//     VOL=SER=MYTAPE
//SYSIN   DD DUMMY
```

```
//STEP2  EXEC PGM=IEBCOPY,
//    COND=(0,NE,STEP1)
//SYSPRINT DD SYSOUT=*
//SYSUT1  DD DSN=MY.PDS,DISP=OLD
//SYSUT2  DD DSN=MY.PDS,DISP=OLD
//SYSIN  DD DUMMY
```

Step 2 in the above example has the COND parameter specified in such a way that the second step will execute only if the first step, the backup of the PDS, was successful. If through some remote possibility the PDS is lost, you have a backup of it on tape and can recreate it easily. Naturally any updates to the PDS that were done after the backup was created will be lost, but if you did the backup and the compress all in one step, as in the example above, then there will not be any intervening updates.

To restore the damaged PDS, you would first delete or rename the damaged version, and then recreate it as follows:

```
//STEP1  EXEC PGM=IEBCOPY
//SYSPRINT DD SYSOUT=*
//SYSUT1  DD DSN=MY.SAVED.PDS,
//    DISP=OLD,UNIT=TAPE,
//    VOL=SER=MYTAPE
//SYSUT2  DD DSN=MY.PDS,
//    DISP=(NEW,CATLG),
//    UNIT=SYSDA,
//    VOL=SER=MYDISK,
//    SPACE=(CYL,(10,,64))
//SYSIN  DD DUMMY
```

ALIAS NAMES

One member can actually be known by more than one name. The extra name is put into the Directory of the PDS and is called an Alias. So a single member can be referred to by its real name or its alias. This may be helpful in some situations, but it requires extra planning. See the discussion of alias names in Chapter 4 under Library Member Names.

PARTIAL AND FULL COPYING OF A PDS (LIBRARY)

Say you were asked to start work on modifying a set of programs that are currently in production. Naturally you are not going to change the actual production versions of the programs; you are going to take a copy of the programs. You are going to copy members from one PDS to another. You can do this using IEBCOPY.

The program IEBCOPY does not insist that you use specific DDNAMEs for the files you are copying. It does require a SYSPRINT DD statement to print messages. A simple copy of one entire PDS to another would look like this:

```
//COPY EXEC PGM=IEBCOPY
//SYSPRINT DD SYSOUT=*
//I DD DSN=MY.SOURCE.LIBRARY,
//   DISP=SHR
//O DD DISP=(,CATLG),
// DSN=MY.NEW.SOURCE.LIBRARY.FOR.TESTING,
// UNIT=SYSDA,SPACE=(CYL,(2,,64)
//SYSIN DD *
   COPY  OUTDD=O,INDD=I
```

As a result of this IEBCOPY, each member in one PDS is copied to the other. The new PDS will not have any embedded unused space. The COPY statement allows the DDNAMEs to be anything. For brevity this example uses I for input and O for output.

IEBCOPY will accept a continuation of the COPY statement without the usual requirement of a comma as the last character on a line. Note, however, that the OUTDD keyword must appear on the first line if the statement is continued. If you try to put INDD on the first line and OUTDD on the second, the OUTDD will be considered missing. This appears to be just a quirk with no obvious underlying meaning.

IEBCOPY will even allow the use of abbreviations for 'COPY', 'INDD', and 'OUTDD', so the statement could have looked like this and done the job required:

C O=O,I=I

If there happened to be two source libraries which needed to be copied to the new PDS, the IEBCOPY might look like this:

```
//COPY EXEC PGM=IEBCOPY
//SYSPRINT DD SYSOUT=*
//I1  DD DSN=MY.SOURCE.LIBRARY,DISP=SHR
//I2  DD DISP=SHR,
//    DSN=MY.OTHER.SOURCE.LIBRARY
//O DD DISP=(,CATLG),
//  DSN=MY.NEW.SOURCE.LIBRARY.FOR.TESTING,
//  UNIT=SYSDA,SPACE=(CYL,(2,,64)
//SYSIN DD *
   COPY  OUTDD=O
      INDD=I1
      INDD=I2
```

In this case all the members from the input file I1 are copied to the output file O, and then the members from input file I2 are copied to the output file O. However everything from I2 might not get copied to O. If a name is in the Directory of O and is also in the Directory of I2 then that name will not be used for the copy operation as shown above.

Suppose the PDS into which you are copying already has a member named J. If the PDS from which you are copying also has a member named J, then J will not be copied when the COPY statement is coded as shown in the above example.

If the member J on the input PDS happens to have an Alias name of K, then the copy will take place and the member will be named K in the output PDS. (The use of any Alias, in a PDS as in life, can cause confusion. Use them if you must, but don't be surprised if they lead to such confusion occasionally.)

If you want members of the output PDS to be replaced by the members of the same name from the input PDS, you can tell IEBCOPY by specifying R for REPLACE, as follows:

```
            COPY  OUTDD=O,
                  INDD=I1
                  INDD=((I2,R))
```

Now any member from I2 will be copied to the output PDS even if the name already exists on the PDS. The members from I1 will only be copied if the names do not exist on the output PDS.

The format of the second INDD assignment is slightly different than the first. The R indicates the replace function is to be used for any similarly named members on the output PDS. The parentheses are important, without the parentheses IEBCOPY would look for another input PDS with a DDNAME of R.

IEBCOPY is very flexible in allowing the way the INDD parameter is coded. You may put several input PDS DDNAMEs on a single INDD assignment. Some of the PDSs might have the replace option, others might not. For the benefit of readability you should use the format as in the previous example, that is, put each input PDS on a separate INDD line, and if the replace option is required for a full input PDS use the R parameter as shown in double parentheses.

A complete input PDS will be eligible to be copied unless the INDD assignment is followed immediately with instructions to either EXCLUDE or SELECT certain members.

In the following example all of the members from I1 will be copied to O, with the exception of any member that has a name that is the same as the name of an existing member of the output PDS. The situation for PDS I2 is different. With the exception of the members that are in the EX-CLUDE list, all members in I2 will be copied to the output PDS.

```
COPY  OUTDD=O
   INDD=I1
   INDD=((I2,R))
   EXCLUDE MEMBERS=(PROGRAM7,PROGRAM9,PROGRAM3)
```

The abbreviations E and M may be used for EXCLUDE and MEM-
BER, and several EXCLUDE statements may appear one after another
and will be treated as continuations. The previous example would work
the same way if it happened to be coded as follows:

```
C  O=O
   I=I1
   I=((I2,R))
   E M=PROGRAM7
   E M=PROGRAM9
   E M=PROGRAM3
```

Very often only certain members need to be copied. The members to
be copied are identified through the SELECT statement, which may be
abbreviated as S. The SELECT statement may have several members
listed using the MEMBER parameter, which may be abbreviated as M.

Several SELECT statements may appear in succession and will be
treated as a continuation of the first. This is the format you should generally prefer, for ease of readability, as will become apparent shortly.

In the next example the member PROGRAM1 will be copied if that
name is not already in use in the output PDS.

The member PROG5 will be copied and replace any pre-existing
member of the same name.

The member PROG4 will be copied and given the new name PRO-
GRAM6 on the output PDS, but only if the name PROGRAM6 is not
already in use.

And finally the member PROG2 will be copied and given the new
name PROG8 and replace any member with the same name.

```
C  O=O
   I=I
S M=PROG1
S M=(PROG5,,R)
S M=(PROG4,PROG6)
S M=(PROG2,PROG8,R)
```

All the above member parameters could have been put on one SELECT statement and IEBCOPY would unravel all the levels of parentheses, member names, new names, and replace indicators. The form that follows would do the same as the one above, but it is a lot less readable. Have some sympathy for anyone who might have to look at your IEBCOPY.

S M=(PROG1,(PROG5,,R),(PROG4,PROG6),(PROG2,PROG8,R))

In summary, then, the major rules of IEBCOPY and how you are likely to use them are as follows.

IEBCOPY will be used to copy members to an output PDS from one or more other input PDSs.

The COPY statement will specify the name of the output PDS DDNAME.

An input PDS is specified on an INDD assignment. All the members in the input PDS are eligible to be copied unless the INDD assignment is followed by an EXCLUDE or SELECT statement.

A member of the output PDS will not be replaced unless the R parameter is coded as the second subparameter of the INDD assignment or as the third subparameter of the SELECT statement.

SELECT and EXCLUDE may not be used at the same time for the same INDD assignment.

For readability you should only put one member on each EXCLUDE or SELECT statement.

EXCLUDE and SELECT statements that occur consecutively are treated as continuations of the first in the sequence.

The SELECT statement may be used to give a new name to the member in the output PDS when it is copied.

Reblocking a load library

A PDS should normally use a block size that will allow the maximum amount of information to be kept on a track. However, different types of disks have different track capacities. If a PDS has been in use on a 3380 and has a BLKSIZE of 23470, that is very efficient. The BLKSIZE will need to be changed, though, if the PDS is ever relocated to a model 3330 disk, where the track size, and hence the maximum block size, is only 13030. (The maximum block size for a 3350 disk is 19069. 3330, 3350, 2314, and 2311 are old models of disk that are no longer manufactured, but there are still some old ones in use.)

The idea is that various models of disk can have different track sizes. Consequently you may have received a copy of a load library that has a ridiculously small block size, and you may, reasonably enough, want to change it; or you might be installing some software in a small out-of-luck country that has become so desperately impoverished, or so cut off from the civilized world by U.N. sanctions, that the government has resorted to buying old 3330 disk drives on the junkyard spare parts black market; or a new model of disk drive might be introduced tomorrow.

Reblocking a load library requires some special attention. Each member of the load library was created with the Linkage Editor program. The Linkage Editor puts special control information into the load module. IEBCOPY has an instruction that will rebuild that special information when the load module is copied to another device type.

The instruction is called COPYMOD and it is coded similarly to the COPY statement. There is an additional parameter available, MAXBLK, which may be used to limit the block size to less than the default for the disk type being copied to.

Why would you want to limit the block size? Good question.

The default block size for any device is the maximum size of the track or 32760, whichever is smaller. The 3380 has a track size of 47476, so if the default of 32760 were used only one block would fit on a track.

In the first example, a member will be copied from a 3330 to a 3350 device.

```
//STEP1  EXEC PGM=IEBCOPY
//SYSPRINT DD SYSOUT=*
//I   DD DSN=MY.SMALL.DISK.PDS,
//    DISP=SHR,UNIT=3330,
//    VOL=SER=DISK01,
//    DCB=BLKSIZE=13030
//O   DD DSN=MY.BIGGER.DISK.PDS,
//    DISP=SHR,UNIT=3350,
//    VOL=SER=DISK01,
//    DCB=BLKSIZE=19069
//SYSIN DD *
 COPYMOD OUTDD=O,INDD=I
 SELECT MEMBER=((PROGRAM1,,R))
 /*
```

In the next example the complete library on a 3380 will be copied to a 3350.

```
//STEP1  EXEC PGM=IEBCOPY
//SYSPRINT DD SYSOUT=*
//I   DD DSN=MY.BIGGEST.DISK.PDS,
//    DISP=SHR,UNIT=3380,
//    VOL=SER=DISK03,
//    DCB=BLKSIZE=23470
//O   DD DSN=MY.BIGGER.DISK.PDS,
//    DISP=SHR,UNIT=3350,
//    VOL=SER=DISK01,
//    DCB=BLKSIZE=19069
//SYSIN DD *
 COPYMOD OUTDD=O,INDD=I
 /*
```

In the final example, an unloaded version of a PDS exists on tape. The PDS will be loaded to a 3380.

```
//STEP1  EXEC PGM=IEBCOPY
//SYSPRINT DD SYSOUT=*
//O  DD DSN=MY.NEW.DISK.PDS,
//    DISP=(,CATLG),UNIT=3380,
//    SPACE=(CYL,(10,5,30)),
//    VOL⁻SER=DISK03,DCB=BLKSIZE=23470
//T  DD DSN=MY.UNLOADED.PDS,
//    DISP=OLD,UNIT=TAPE,
//    VOL=SER=TAPE01
//SYSIN DD *
    COPYMOD OUTDD=O,INDD=T,MAXBLK=23470
/*
```

There are certain attributes that may be specified when a load module is processed by the Linkage Editor that will restrict IEBCOPY in reblocking that load module. One example is the NE option, which means the load module is 'not editable.' Barring these rare occurrences, however, you ought to be able to reblock load modules happily ever after using the above examples as guides.

ISRSUPC—SPF COMPARE AND SUPER SEARCH IN JCL

If you use SPF in TSO, you have probably noticed the nice utilities available as options 3.12 through 3.14, that is, as selections 12 to 14 on the menu for option 3:

12 SUPERC   - Compare data sets
14 SEARCH-FOR - Search data sets for strings of data

You can accomplish both of these functions through JCL by executing the same program—ISRSUPC—in a batch job. This is particularly useful if you have a lot of searches and comparisons to do, especially if they are all going to have to be done again from time to time with new data.

Our first example compares the member named VERSION2 with

327

the member named VERSION1 in the library SMITH.MEMO.TEXT
and produces a list of the differences it finds, line by line. The output
listing comes out on the ddname OUTDD. The DD statements OLDDD
and NEWDD point to the two files to be compared. In this case we
point to two separate members of one library, but you could just as
easily point to different data sets. The JCL to accomplish the first
example:

```
//SMITH8B1 JOB 1,COMPARE,
//    CLASS=I,MSGCLASS=X
//COMPARE EXEC PGM=ISRSUPC,
//    PARM=(DELTAL,LINECMP)
//OLDDD DD DISP=SHR,
//    DSN=SMITH.MEMO.TEXT(VERSION1)
//NEWDD DD DISP=SHR,
//    DSN=SMITH.MEMO.TEXT(VERSION2)
//OUTDD DD SYSOUT=*
```

Suppose that the member named VERSION1 is composed entirely of
the following two lines from Shakespeare:

OUT, OUT,
BRIEF CANDLE

and the member named VERSION2 is composed entirely of these two
lines from Shakespeare:

OUT, OUT,
DAMNED SPOT

The output from job SMITH8B1 will contain the following lines:

I - BRIEF CANDLE
D - DAMNED SPOT

The I in this stands for insert, and the D stands for delete. In other words, ISRSUPC is telling you that the line "DAMNED SPOT" was inserted and the line "BRIEF CANDLE" deleted.

If you ran the above job and it failed with an 806 abend, this means that MVS could not find the program ISRSUPC. If you do in fact have ISPF on your system, then you should add a STEPLIB DD statement to help MVS find ISRSUPC. The STEPLIB you need to use might look like this:

```
//STEPLIB DD DISP=SHR,
//    DSN=ISR.V3R3M0.ISRLPA
```

Note the naming convention. V3R3M0 means Version 3, Release 3, Modification level 0. The next software upgrade to ISPF will thus use different dataset names..

You should be able to find out exactly what STEPLIB you need to use, if any, by going into SPF option 3.13, extended compare, selecting any two arbitrary data sets to compare, specifying batch compare rather than online, and specifying YES you do want to edit the JCL. You will then be shown the JCL that is generated. If it contains a STEPLIB or JOBLIB, note the name of the data set. Use that data set in all your JCL that executes ISRSUPC.

Next example. If you used a STEPLIB in the above example, you should use the same STEPLIB here as well. The following example will search through the entire library SMITH.MEMO.TEXT and list every line that contains the word OUT:

```
//SMITH8B2 JOB 1,SEARCH,
//    CLASS=I,MSGCLASS=X
//SEARCH EXEC PGM=ISRSUPC,
//    PARM=(SRCHCMP,'ANYC')
//OUTDD   DD SYSOUT=*
//SYSIN   DD *
 SRCHFOR 'OUT'
//NEWDD   DD DISP=SHR,
//    DSN=SMITH.MEMO.TEXT
```

You could have searched for some longer string rather than the word OUT. You could have gone looking for the phrase 'BRIEF CANDLE' for example. Just enclose the string you want to find within apostrophes on the SRCHFOR statement in the SYSIN you give to ISRSUPC.

Assuming that the data set SMITH.MEMO.TEXT contains only the two members VERSION1 and VERSION2, as shown already, a listing will be produced with the following information.

```
VERSION1
    1 OUT,OUT
VERSION2
    1 OUT,OUT
```

What is this telling us?

That the string OUT was found in the member VERSION1 and also in the member VERSION2. The lines where it was found are shown on the listing, in this case on line 1 for each member.

As you can see, using ISRSUPC in JCL can save you a lot of time relative to searching through big data sets at your TSO terminal, and such comparisons might occasionally be useful to include within procedures or other sets of JCL that run regularly. For example, you could make a comparison of the old and new program source statements a regular part of your procedure for installing new versions of programs.

There are various options you can specify on SYSIN to ISRSUPC. If you are comparing two data sets, and you want to change the columns that are used in the comparison, you can specify CMPCOLM. The following example compares two data sets as in our first example, but it specifies columns 1 through 80 for the comparison:

```
//SMITH8B3 JOB 1,COMPARE,
//    CLASS=I,MSGCLASS=X
//COMPARE EXEC PGM=ISRSUPC,
//    PARM=(DELTAL,LINECMP)
//OLDDD  DD  DISP=SHR,
//    DSN=SMITH.MEMO.TEXT(VERSION1)
```

```
//NEWDD  DD  DISP=SHR,
//     DSN=SMITH.MEMO.TEXT(VERSION2)
//OUTDD  DD  SYSOUT=*
//SYSIN  DD  *
CMPCOLM 1:80
/*
```

If you want to find out many more options you can specify, go into the TSO SPF 3.13 extended compare menu and read the HELP text available from there (type the word HELP on the command line and press the enter key).

IDCAMS AND VSAM

IDCAMS is the program that deals with VSAM data sets. It is used to create them, delete them, rename them, alter them, copy them, print them, and so on.

You recall that VSAM data sets are not usually created and deleted by JCL, although now they can be, if you are using SMS (System Managed Storage) (You probably are). The easiest way you can create a VSAM data set via JCL is to use the LIKE parameter to model your new VSAM data set after some existing VSAM data set. For an Indexed VSAM data set, both the DATA and INDEX components will be created. When VSAM data sets are deleted by specifying DISP=(OLD,DELETE), both the DATA and INDEX components are deleted. You can also create a VSAM data set via JCL with SMS by specifying a DATACLASS that is tailor-made to the type of VSAM file you want to create, or by specifying a new data set name in a format automatically associated with a DATACLASS so defined. Before you can do those things, though, you need to know how those things are defined. They are set up by the MVS Systems Support group at your installation, and they are different from one installation to another. Kind of like UNIT class. Odds are none of the defaults suit your specific purpose most of the time.

In most cases, people still use IDCAMS to create and delete VSAM data sets.

Besides dealing with VSAM files, IDCAMS can perform some useful functions for ordinary, non-VSAM data sets, such as printing, and even printing a hex dump should you have need of such a thing.

Let's start with a totally trivial example, just to introduce you to IDCAMS. The following example prints SMITH.MEMO.TEXT(VERSION1) in both hexadecimal and character format, sort of like a dump:

```
//SMITH8C1 JOB 1,COMPARE,MSGCLASS=X
//PRINT EXEC PGM=IDCAMS
//SYSPRINT DD SYSOUT=*
 PRINT    -
 INDATASET(SMITH.MEMO.TEXT(VERSION1))
```

INDATASET can be abbreviated IDS if you prefer.

The main use of the above example is that you get to see what the data looks like in hexadecimal, which can be handy for finding bad data characters that don't correspond to anything printable. The ordinary-looking letters off on the right hand side of the listing are the EBCDIC (normal) equivalent of the hexadecimal codes on the left. For example, hexadecimal 40D6E4E3 corresponds to a blank followed by the word OUT. Hex 40 is a blank space. Hex D6 is the letter O, E4 is U, and E3 is T. Right, Okay, fine, but now you want to do something, maybe create a new VSAM file.

For that matter, you may even wonder what a VSAM file exactly is. Perhaps you find that you have to use VSAM files a lot, and you've noticed that they don't follow the same rules as other data sets.

Let's talk about VSAM, then.

IDCAMS History and relationship to Databases

Data bases are almost always VSAM files. This is true for most IMS data bases, for DB2 data bases, and for most other data base types.

In fact VSAM was developed for data bases.

How are data bases different from other data sets?

The critical difference is that you usually read or write one individual specific data base record at a time, or some specifically selected set of records, rather than processing all of the records in the file.

For example, your company might have a customer data base that contains one unique record for each customer. If you want to make an enquiry about any one particular customer's account, you don't want to search through a large flat file to find the record in question. You want to select that one particular record quickly.

How to go about this has been a big question ever since the question first presented itself.

If you think about it offhand, you might imagine you could have a big library with each customer record represented as a separate member. This turns out to be an exceptionally bad idea, however. For one thing, each member name is limited to eight characters in length. For another, the response time is slow. Various other ideas have been tried.

At length IBM invented VSAM to address the problem.

With a VSAM file, you can have keys of any length up to the currently allowable maximum, which is always much more than eight. On the MVS/ESA Version 4 system we are using here the maximum length allowable for a VSAM key is 255.

The key of a record in a VSAM file plays the same role as the name of a member of a library: It provides a unique identity for the particular chunk of data to which it refers.

Thus you can set up a VSAM file with a 20-digit account number as the key, and then write a program that reads, writes, and replaces individual records by specifying the account number each time, in much the same way that a person using TSO edits individual members of a library by specifying the member name.

Just as you can have alias names for members of libraries, you can have alternate keys for VSAM files. In the case of a VSAM file, if you want to have an alternate key, you must set up a second VSAM file. This second VSAM file is called an alternate index. You can have complicated sets of VSAM files with more than one alternate index.

IBM has gone to a lot of work to make VSAM response time pretty quick.

333

IMS data bases, DB2 data bases, and most other data base methods use VSAM files.

IMS seems to be the quickest.

DB2 is a relational data base system: you retrieve not necessarily individual records, but groups of records in table format, like what you would get with a spread sheet. DB2 is newer than IMS, and trendier. DB2 tables are manipulated using SQL, the same language used with Oracle. (SQL can be pronounced sequel.)

There are many other competing data base products on the market from non-IBM sources. You can also have plain VSAM files that you use as data bases without any fancy data base method superimposed.

VSAM files contain control information interspersed with the data, and the data within the VSAM file is not necessarily arranged in the order you would expect it to be, so a VSAM file can look a bit strange to the eye. It is arranged that way to make it more efficient.

You cannot manipulate these rather strange files with ordinary text editors such as SPF option 2. There are some products on the market which will allow you to manipulate VSAM data; most notably a product called File-Aid, available from CompuWare; they have a special version for IMS data bases and another special version for DB2 data bases.

When IBM invented VSAM, IBM created a special program to be used for setting up and manipulating VSAM files. That program is IDCAMS. It will do other things also. For example, it will print files, as you saw above. But its basic reason for being is to set up, manipulate and manage VSAM files.

Now let's talk about how you go about using it to do that.

DEFINING VSAM STRUCTURES USING DEFINE CLUSTER

The JCL should be identical to what you used above.

The control statements you give to IDCAMS on SYSIN will of course be different.

Creating a new VSAM file is also called defining the VSAM file. Often one deletes a VSAM file and then creates it again all in the same set of SYSIN statements. This process is called delete-defining the file.

When you define a VSAM file, you supply on SYSIN all of the same type of information you would supply in JCL if you were creating a non-VSAM file. The syntax is different, and the names of the parameters are different; some of the parameters are only approximate equivalents of their JCL counterparts; some JCL parameters have no IDCAMS counterparts, and some IDCAMS parameters have no JCL counterparts; still, the general idea is the same.

So this is a good place to point out that you can use the MODEL parameter in IDCAMS to similar effect as the LIKE parameter in JCL. (This is what people did before the LIKE parameter was invented.) So, before showing you a lot of individual parameters, here is an example of the IDCAMS statement you would use to copy the attributes of some existing VSAM file:

DEFINE CLUSTER (NAME('new.vsam.file') -
MODEL('some.other.vsam.file'))

If some existing VSAM file is almost, but not quite, what you want, you can use MODEL and specify only the additional parameters you want to change. For example:

DEFINE CLUSTER (NAME('new.vsam.file') -
MODEL('some.other.vsam.file') -
CYLINDERS(20))

You can probably guess the meaning of CYLINDERS(20), but you will probably want explanations for some of the other parameters. We will try to cover these by analogy to JCL parameters.

Control Interval Size, for example, is the VSAM counterpart of block size, but there are some differences. Within a VSAM file parts of each block are used for control information rather than for storing your data. Hence a VSAM file is larger than its flat file counterpart, and a VSAM control interval is not a multiple of the record length. A VSAM control interval must be either 256, 1024, 2048, 4096, 8192, or 16384 bytes in size. (Each of these numbers is double the preceding number.) The consideration for speedy performance is the same here as with block size: A bigger control interval

335

means fewer I/O operations if you are processing the entire file sequentially, and this means faster response time on sequential processing. Note, however, that if you are reading and writing small records at random in a large VSAM file, then the bigger block size (control interval size) may not get you any performance improvement over a smaller size. Control interval size is abbreviated CISZ, pronounced See eye size.

The approximate equivalents of some of the basic VSAM parameters and JCL parameters is as follows:

VSAM parameter	*abbreviation*	*analogous JCL*
CONTROLINTERVALSIZE	CISZ or CNVSZ	BLKSIZE
RECORDSIZE	RECSZ	LRECL
SHAREOPTIONS	SHR	DISP
TRACKS	TRK	SPACE
CYLINDERS	CYL	SPACE
RECORDS	REC	SPACE
KILOBYTES	KB	SPACE
MEGABYTES	MB	SPACE
NONINDEXED	NIXD	DSORG=PS
NAME		DSN
VOLUMES		VOL=SER=
TO		EXPDT
FOR		RETPD

Let's consider the parameter NONINDEXED first.

A non-indexed VSAM file resembles an ordinary flat file in that the records are stored sequentially, one after the next, like cards in a deck. A non-indexed file has no keys. It is known also as an ESDS, for Entry Sequenced Data Set.

The opposite of NONINDEXED is INDEXED. LINEAR, NUMBERED, and RELATIVE RECORD are other possibilities. Since most VSAM files are INDEXED we will concentrate our discussion on that type.

If you want a really thorough description of VSAM, see one of the IBM manuals on Access Method Services—IBM manuals change their order numbers from time to time, and sometimes even change their titles, so you may have to search for the right one. The AMS in IDCAMS stands for Access Method Services, a name that hasn't changed in quite a long time.

The identifying characteristic of an indexed file is that an indexed file has keys.

A VSAM file with keys is also called a Key Sequenced Data Set, or KSDS.

You can read through an indexed VSAM file from top to bottom, retrieving all of the records sequentially. You might write a program that will run once a month to generate bills for all of the customers in the data base, for example. More often you will want your programs to retrieve individual records by key; to access a particular customer record, for example.

If a VSAM file is INDEXED it will be composed of two entirely separate parts, an INDEX component and a DATA component.

The DATA component is where the records are actually kept.

The INDEX component performs a function something like that of the directory of a library. It points to the records in the DATA component. When you attempt to read a record from a VSAM file, MVS first checks the INDEX component to find out approximately where in the DATA component that specific record is stored. Then MVS reads the DATA component to obtain the actual record.

Ordinarily you will set up your DATA and INDEX components as separate data sets.

You will therefore specify three names when you define the VSAM file.

You will specify the name of the file itself. In the ordinary case, the file itself is also called the cluster. Setting up an ordinary VSAM file, then, is also called defining a VSAM cluster.

You will specify the data set name for the DATA component.

Also you will specify the data set name of the INDEX component.

That makes three names altogether. Note that the name of the cluster appears in the catalog, but it does not represent an actual data set. The catalog entry for the cluster just contains a lot of information about the cluster, and a reference to the two actual data sets: The data component and the index component are the actual data sets that exist on disk.

It is a good idea to keep some logic to the names. For example, if your VSAM file is to be called SMITH.CUSTOMER.DATABASE then you might name the DATA component SMITH.CUSTOMER.DATABASE.DATA and you might—you guessed it—name the INDEX component SMITH.CUSTOMER.DATABASE.INDEX (which brings us to the NAME parameter).

You specify the names you have chosen with the NAME parameter.

At this point you are ready to see the skeletal form of the command you will give to IDCAMS to define your file. The following simplified example does not contain sufficient information to define the VSAM file completely, but first just consider the basic structure:

```
    DEFINE CLUSTER ( NAME(SMITH.CUSTOMER.DATABASE)    -
            INDEXED           -
            UNIQUE            ) -
     DATA  ( NAME(SMITH.CUSTOMER.DATABASE.DATA) ) -
     INDEX ( NAME(SMITH.CUSTOMER.DATABASE.INDEX) )
```

The hyphens in the above are continuation characters. The three lines shown are all part of the one DEFINE command. The last line does not end with a hyphen because it is not continued.

Observe the placement of the parentheses.

All parameters applicable to the CLUSTER as a whole are enclosed within one set of parentheses.

After that, all parameters applicable to the DATA component are enclosed within a demarcating set of parentheses.

Then all parameters applicable to the INDEX component are separately enclosed within their own demarcating set of parentheses.

It is not necessary to use any particular columns. The above example is aligned purely for readability.

Think of the word UNIQUE in the above command as meaning something like ordinary or normal. The opposite of UNIQUE is SUBALLOCATE. Suballocation is a strange arrangement that lets several separate VSAM files reside in the same data set. Don't even think about it.

The command shown above would not be sufficient to get your file defined for you, of course. We need to flesh it out with some more parameters. You could, of course, use the MODEL parameter already shown. But besides that.

Let's say that you want your file to have a 20-character customer account number as the key. Let us further assume that the 20-byte key appears in the first 20 columns of each customer record. IDCAMS thinks of the first column of each record as 0 rather than 1, so we tell IDCAMS that the key is 20 bytes long, starting in column 0:

```
DEFINE CLUSTER ( NAME(SMITH.CUSTOMER.DATABASE)    -
     INDEXED  UNIQUE KEYS(20 0)          ) -
     DATA   ( NAME(SMITH.CUSTOMER.DATABASE.DATA) ) -
     INDEX  ( NAME(SMITH.CUSTOMER.DATABASE.INDEX) ) )
```

We need yet more parameters, of course, before the DEFINE will actually work.

We will need to specify how big the VSAM file is going to be and where it is going to reside.

Let's say that your customer records are 500 bytes long, that is, the file would be LRECL=500 if it were an ordinary file. Let us further assume that you will have 25,000 such records in the file. You decide to let VSAM calculate the space for you.

339

You tell IDCAMS to put the DATA component on volume DISK01 and to put the INDEX component on volume DISK02. Response time is speedier when you put the two components on separate volumes. Your DEFINE now looks like this:

```
DEFINE CLUSTER ( NAME(SMITH.CUSTOMER.DATABASE)    -
        INDEXED        -
        UNIQUE         -
        KEYS(20 0)     -
        RECORDSIZE(500)        -
        RECORDS(25000)         ) -
    DATA  ( NAME(SMITH.CUSTOMER.DATABASE.DATA) -
        VOLUME(DISK01)         ) -
    INDEX ( NAME(SMITH.CUSTOMER.DATABASE.INDEX) -
        VOLUME(DISK02)         )
```

Although the above arrangement gives you faster response time on average, the systems and operations staffs tend to be against it because it makes backup and restore operations more difficult and possibly even unreliable. It basically means that they have to back up the two disks at the same time to make sure the backup copies of the two components form a matched set. Because of this objection, in most cases you will probably end up putting both components on the same disk volume as follows:

```
DEFINE CLUSTER ( NAME(SMITH.CUSTOMER.DATABASE)    -
        INDEXED        -
        UNIQUE         -
        KEYS(20 0)     -
        VOLUME(DISK01)         -
        RECORDSIZE(500)        -
        RECORDS(25000)         ) -
    DATA  ( NAME(SMITH.CUSTOMER.DATABASE.DATA) ) -
    INDEX ( NAME(SMITH.CUSTOMER.DATABASE.INDEX))
```

Your most basic VSAM DEFINE is now complete. You can actually submit the following job and define a VSAM file for yourself, provided you change the volume from DISK02 to some acceptable volume you actually have available, and provided also that you change the three NAME values and the JOB statement. The basic VSAM define:

```
//SMITH8C2 JOB 2,DEFINE.DATABASE,MSGCLASS=X
//CUSTOMER EXEC PGM=IDCAMS
//SYSPRINT DD SYSOUT=*
DEFINE CLUSTER ( NAME(SMITH.CUSTOMER.DATABASE)  -
        INDEXED          -
        UNIQUE           -
        KEYS(20 0)       -
        VOLUME(DISK01)       -
        RECORDSIZE(500)      -
        RECORDS(25000)        ) -
    DATA        -
    ( NAME(SMITH.CUSTOMER.DATABASE.DATA) ) -
    INDEX       -
    ( NAME(SMITH.CUSTOMER.DATABASE.INDEX))
```

There are numerous other parameters that you have not specified in your VSAM DEFINE above. Most of these are not too interesting or important, and you can safely accept the defaults. There are a few of them that you might want to specify, however. SHAREOPTIONS is the first of these.

The SHAREOPTIONS parameter controls whether a VSAM file will be shareable between different jobs that are running at the same time. This is a function that would be performed by the DISP parameter at execution time for ordinary files; but for a VSAM file, the shareability is a permanent attribute of the file itself.

There are two subparameters of SHAREOPTIONS. The second subparameter has to do with sharing the file between two different MVS systems, a practice which is not advisable in any case. The second subparameter can be either 3 or 4, and is usually set to 3. The first subparameter can be 1, 2, 3, or 4.

The meanings of the usual values for SHAREOPTIONS are these:
SHAREOPTIONS(1,3) means that any number of jobs may simultaneously read the file, as long as none of them attempts to update it. If any job tries to update the file, that job must have exclusive use of the file; other jobs will be locked out.

SHAREOPTIONS(2,3) means that any number of jobs may simultaneously read the file, AND one of them may update it without locking out the others.

SHAREOPTIONS(3,3) means that any number of jobs may simultaneously update the file, and if you wipe out each other's changes or mess up the file it's your own tough luck.

SHAREOPTIONS(4,3) means the same as (3,3) except that each job's data buffers are refreshed for each request. But it is still your own hard luck if you mangle the file.

Notice that IMS counts as one single job, and CICS also counts as one single job. Thus, if you have defined your file with SHAREOPTIONS(2,3) and it is allocated to IMS or to CICS, then all of the users of that IMS or that CICS will be able to update the file in their turn; you can rely on IMS or CICS to handle the queuing.

A batch job, however, will not be able to obtain exclusive use of the file while it is allocated to CICS or IMS.

Vocabulary item: Batch window.

The batch window is the period of time when IMS or CICS is down and during which batch jobs can get exclusive use of the VSAM files that are ordinarily allocated to IMS or CICS. Most IMS data bases and DB2 data bases, in fact most data bases in general, are really VSAM files. Thus the time when IMS or CICS is down is the time when ordinary jobs can have the data bases all to themselves. If you know what time IMS or CICS is brought down in the evening, and what time it is brought up in the morning, then you know the size of your batch window. Or you can just estimate it roughly as "too small". In fact in some companies it is zero; the online systems are never brought down at all if it is possible to avoid doing so. Banks with online cash machines often fall into this group.

How can a batch job update a data base at all in such an environment?

If you are dealing with IMS, the batch job must run as a BMP (Batch Message Processor) (as opposed to running in DLI mode). When a batch job runs in BMP mode, IMS handles the queuing, just as if the batch job were another IMS terminal user.

It is also possible for the operators to issue commands that stop any transactions that might use some particular data base, and then de-allocate that data base from the online system (IMS or CICS) for a while. This is obviously an inconvenience for the ordinary users of the online system, since they will not be able to use those transactions for the duration of the interruption.

All of which goes to explain why you may be discouraged from writing batch jobs that use online data bases.

Thus it is that, especially on test systems, people often define their VSAM files with SHAREOPTIONS(3,3) and take their chances. If you do this, don't be too surprised if your data base starts to have I/O errors and you have to delete it and define it all over again.

FREESPACE is the other parameter you ought to know. Abbreviated FSPC. If you say you want anything other than (0,0) you are saying that you want part of your data base left empty.

Why, you may ask, would you want to leave part of your data base empty?

Let's talk about it.

As you know, a control interval is loosely equivalent to a physical block. A control area is a group of control intervals.

The first subparameter of FREESPACE (the first number within the parentheses) states what percentage of each control interval is to be left empty. The second subparameter (the second number) specifies what percentage of each control area is to be left empty.

Okay.

As you perhaps do not know, but will quickly come to realize if you work with VSAM files, there are two modes in which you can put records into a VSAM file.

The first mode happens when the VSAM file is empty. Hence it is called initial load mode. The idea is that you may have an enormous flat file someplace containing all of the records that you want to put into your VSAM file. You will then run one long-running job to load all of those records into the file.

As likely as not you will have no such initial load file. In this case you will load one dummy record into the VSAM file. You will do this because, if you do not do it, your programs will not be able to insert records. This is true because the other mode, called insert mode, can only be used with VSAM files that already have something in them.

An empty VSAM file is loaded with an initial load.

Thereafter records are inserted in insert mode.

You see the difference.

(I didn't design the system, I'm just telling you about how it works.)

Suppose, though, that you did have an enormous flat file with, say, one record for each customer; and you wanted to load all of those records, representing your existing customers, into your VSAM file initially. Thereafter new customers would be added with programs using insert mode in small volumes, a few each day.

If you are using the customer account number as the key, and the customer account numbers are ascending numbers, this example isn't going to be very convincing, so let's assume that you use the customer's initials as the first three characters of the account number.

New customers will have various unpredictable names.

So, what you might want to do is this: You might want to leave some empty space in each block so there would be room for new customers to fit in the same block adjacent to old customers with adjacent customer numbers.

That is what FREESPACE allows you to do.

Why do you want to make sure there is room for new customer records to be stored in the same block with the old ones to which they are logically adjacent?

If there is no room available, then you will get what is called a CI (control interval) split; or, the same thing but worse, a CA (control area) split. This means that the system will take the existing block (or group of blocks) and break it in half, putting half of the records into each of the new blocks (for a CI split) or groups of blocks (for a CA split). After it does that, there will be plenty of room. The only problem with it is that it is time consuming and involves lots of I/Os. That means that it will slow down response time for whoever happens to be the unlucky person doing the update that triggers the split.

What you can do is this: Define the VSAM file initially with FREESPACE(50,50) and then do the large initial load. After it is complete, execute IDCAMS again and use ALTER to change the FREESPACE to 0. Something like this:

```
//SMITH8C3 JOB 3,DEFINE.DATABASE,MSGCLASS=X
//CUSTOMER EXEC PGM=IDCAMS
//SYSPRINT DD SYSOUT=*
DELETE (SMITH.CUSTOMER.DATABASE) PURGE CLUSTER
SET LASTCC = 0
SET MAXCC = 0
DEFINE CLUSTER          -
    ( NAME(SMITH.CUSTOMER.DATABASE)       -
    INDEXED   UNIQUE KEYS(20 0)           -
        VOLUME(DISK01)          -
        FREESPACE(50,50)        -
        RECORDSIZE(500)         -
        RECORDS(25000)          ) -
    DATA      -
    ( NAME(SMITH.CUSTOMER.DATABASE.DATA) )-
    INDEX            -
    ( NAME(SMITH.CUSTOMER.DATABASE.INDEX))

//SMITH8C4 JOB 4,LOAD.DATABASE,MSGCLASS=X
//LOAD    EXEC PGM=IDCAMS
//BIGFILE DD DISP=OLD,
```

```
//      DSN=SMITH.BIG.CUSTOMER.FILE
//SYSPRINT DD SYSOUT=*
REPRO  INFILE(BIGFILE)-
    OUTDATASET(SMITH.CUSTOMER.DATABASE)

//SMITH8C5 JOB 5,ALTER.DATABASE,MSGCLASS=X
//ALTER   EXEC PGM=IDCAMS
//SYSPRINT DD SYSOUT=*
ALTER  SMITH.CUSTOMER.DATABASE -
    FREESPACE(0,0)
```

The job that does the DEFINE for the VSAM file above first does a delete. Then it sets the condition code to zero. That way, if the file already exists, it will be deleted before being redefined; if it does not exist, the bad return code from the failed delete will not show up as a bad condition code in the JCL.

The job that loads the file above uses the REPRO command when executing IDCAMS. You can use REPRO to copy non-VSAM files also if you like. REPRO is a general purpose copier, similar to IEBGENER.

If you are not doing a large initial load, that is, if your initial load consists of loading one dummy record, then there is probably no reason not to accept the default value of FREESPACE(0,0) when you define your VSAM file in the first place.

One final note about FREESPACE. If you let IDCAMS decide how many tracks or cylinders to allocate for your data set, that is, if you specify the RECORDS parameter to tell IDCAMS how many records you want and let IDCAMS figure out how much SPACE that really is, then note: IDCAMS does not take into consideration the FREESPACE when doing the figuring. Thus, in the above example, your file would run out of space if you specified FREESPACE(50,50) and then loaded more than half of your estimated 25000 records in the initial load.

So much for FREESPACE.

The other VSAM parameters are not very interesting. You can omit them and accept the defaults safely. If the local customs at your company include specifying parameters such as IMBED and REPLICATE, feel free to adopt the local convention whatever it is.

One last parameter.

Suppose that you want a simple way to define a VSAM cluster without coding all those parameters and values and things. You want it to look exactly like some other VSAM file. Easily done: you use the MODEL parameter. You can define a VSAM file named SMITH.FOTOCOPY with the same parameters and values as the VSAM file named BIG.OFFICIAL.VSAM.FILE as follows:

```
DEFINE CLUSTER ( NAME(SMITH.FOTOCOPY) -
           MODEL(BIG.OFFICIAL.VSAM.FILE) )
```

Often you will want to override just one or two parameters when using MODEL. Typically you will want to put your file on a different disk volume and give it a smaller space allocation. In that case the syntax is this:

```
DEFINE CLUSTER ( NAME('SMITH.FOTOCOPY') -
           MODEL(BIG.OFFICIAL.VSAM.FILE) -
           VOLUME(TEST01) CYLINDERS(4) )
```

One minor problem with using the MODEL parameter is that the system will make up the names for your actual DATA and INDEX components. Names like SMITH.WOM7STIT.G5R6EAAA.W0RBTTIT.IZ0DTTIT, that sort of thing.

COPYING VSAM FILES

VSAM files can be copied to other VSAM files with the REPRO statement. This also works for copying non-VSAM files to non-VSAM files, and, more importantly, for copying non-VSAM files to VSAM files. The one thing you should remember is that the output VSAM file should be empty in order to use REPRO to populate it.

Example of copying one VSAM file to another:

```
// EXEC PGM=IDCAMS
//SYSPRINT DD SYSOUT=*
//IN  DD DISP=SHR,
//   DSN=SOME.OLD.VSAM.FILE
//OUT DD DISP=SHR,
//   DSN=MY.NEW.VSAM.FILE
//SYSIN DD *
     REPRO   INFILE(IN)   OUTFILE(OUT)
```

In the above example, the words IN and OUT are made-up ddnames. You can make up other ddnames if you prefer.

Instead of using INFILE and OUTFILE, referring to ddnames, you can use INDATASET and OUTDATASET to copy data sets without DD statements. These parameters are abbreviated IDS and ODS. You can also mix and match, specifying INFILE with OUTDATASET and so on. Examples:

```
//  EXEC PGM=IDCAMS
//SYSPRINT DD SYSOUT=*
//IN  DD DISP=SHR,
//   DSN=SOME.OLD.VSAM.FILE
//SYSIN DD *
  REPRO INFILE(IN)     -
          OUTDATASET(MY.NEW.VSAM.FILE)
```

```
//  EXEC PGM=IDCAMS
//SYSPRINT DD SYSOUT=*
//SYSIN DD *
  REPRO INDATASET(SOME.OLD.FILE)    -
          ODS(MY.NEW.FILE)
```

Example of copying VSAM files to output flat files :

```
//JOB2  JOB 2,CLASS=D,MSGCLASS=X
//UNLOAD  EXEC PGM=IDCAMS
```

```
//SYSPRINT DD SYSOUT=*
//IN1  DD DISP=OLD,
//    DSN=SOME.EXISTING.KSDS1
//OUT1 DD DISP=(,CATLG),
//    DSN=MY.UNLOADOF.KSDS1,
//    DCB=(RECFM=U,
//    BLKSIZE=32760,DSORG=PS),
//    SPACE=(CYL,(10,50),RLSE),
//    UNIT=SYSDA
//INKSDS2 DD DISP=OLD,
//    DSN=SOME.EXISTING.KSDS2
//FLATOUT2 DD DISP=(,CATLG),
//    DSN=MY.UNLOADOF.KSDS2,
//    DCB=(RECFM=U,
//    BLKSIZE=32760,DSORG=PS),
//    SPACE=(CYL,(10,50),RLSE),
//    UNIT=SYSDA
//SYSIN DD *
   REPRO  INFILE(IN1)  OUTFILE(OUT1)
   REPRO INFILE(INKSDS2) OUTFILE(FLATOUT2)
```

Example of copying an input flat file to an output VSAM file. This example uses instream input, that is, DD * input. It's not convenient to use an instream file if your data records are shorter or longer than the instream file, which is usually 80 bytes (card image). But, just for example:

```
//JOB3  JOB 3,CLASS=D,MSGCLASS=X
//THREE EXEC PGM=IDCAMS
//SYSPRINT DD SYSOUT=*
//IN  DD  *
record 1
record 2
etc etc
/*
//SYSIN DD *
```

REPRO INFILE(IN)   -
    OUTDATASET(MY.NEW.VSAM.FILE)

Example of delete-defining two VSAM files and then copying two
input flat files into the VSAM files. Note this example uses the same two
flat files that were created in JOB2 above.

```
//JOB4  JOB 4,CLASS=D,MSGCLASS=X
//JOBNAME  JOB 1,CLASS=D,MSGCLASS=X
//RELOAD  EXEC PGM=IDCAMS
//SYSPRINT DD SYSOUT=*
//IN1 DD DISP=OLD,
//  DSN=MY.UNLOADOF.KSDS1
//IN2 DD DISP=OLD,
//  DSN=MY.UNLOADOF.KSDS2
//SYSIN DD *
 DELETE    -
  'MY.NEWCOPY.OF.KSDS1'  CLUSTER  PURGE
 DELETE    -
  'MY.NEWCOPY.OF.KSDS2' CLUSTER PURGE
 SET MAXCC=0
 DEF  CL  (NAME('MY.NEWCOPY.OF.KSDS1')  -
  MODEL('SOME.EXISTING.KSDS1'))
 DEF CL (NAME('MY.NEWCOPY.OF.KSDS2') -
  MODEL('SOME.EXISTING.KSDS2'))
 REPRO INFILE(IN1)  -
  ODS('MY.NEWCOPY.OF.KSDS1')
 REPRO INFILE(IN2)  -
  ODS('MY.NEWCOPY.OF.KSDS2')
```

There are other things you can do with IDCAMS as well. You can
define Generation Data Groups (GDGs) and so forth. Generation Data
Groups are discussed, with examples, in Chapter 20. If you want to do
any of the other things not described here, consult the IBM manual
on IDCAMS. You really ought to have a good set of IBM manuals at

hand someplace. If they are not available, request that they be ordered. They are quite inexpensive and extremely useful. At many companies these manuals are available online from TSO. They are generally accessed with some simple option like READ or READMVS or some variant. If it isn't on the menu, ask around. If they are not available online, then try to order them. Order the JCL manuals too, for that matter. There are a lot of obscure parameters we do not cover in the present book due to lack of space and a desire not to bore the reader beyond all reasonable limits. Get a Utilities manual too while you're at it. And a set of manuals on COBOL, PL/I, or whatever language you're using. These things are well worth having around. If the manuals are not available online, and your company will not buy them, then decide which one will be most useful, buy it for yourself by ordering directly from IBM and paying money, and then keep it locked in your desk (you need a lockable desk to get this to work); then make a show of looking up useful things when the others are stumped about them; and if anyone asks to borrow your manual or even to look at it, refuse to let them see it until the company agrees to buy more manuals.

COMPILERS AND THE LINKAGE EDITOR

A compiler translates your program source statements, which make sense to you, into computer machine language zeroes and ones, which make sense to the computer. This collection of zeroes and ones is called machine language or object code.

The compiler is itself a program. The PL/I compiler (IEL0AA) is a different program than the LE PL/I compiler (IEL1AA) and the old COBOL compiler (IKFCBL00). The old COBOL compiler (IKFCBL00) is a different program than the COBOL 2 compiler (IGYCRCTL) and the MVS/COBOL (LE) compiler.

The compiler program reads your program source statements as its input data. It reads these from the ddname SYSIN.

For most compilers you may include special compiler instructions along with your program on SYSIN. For example, if you are programming in PL/I you can include the instructions (SUBRG): and (STRG): just before your PROC statement, to tell the PL/I compiler to create the compiled program in such a way that an error message will occur if your program refers to an array subscript that is outside the bounds of its array, or a part of a string that is outside the length of that string.

Besides whatever compiler instructions you include with your program source statements on SYSIN, you may also specify special compiler instructions in the PARM parameter on the EXEC statement. For example, if you are programming in PL/I, you can include GOSTMT in the PARM string to tell the PL/I compiler to include the actual program statement number in the error message whenever the program abends, rather than just telling you the hexadecimal memory address. These special compiler instructions are called compiler options.

When the PL/I or COBOL compiler has translated your program source statements into machine readable instructions, it writes the result as an output file. Most compilers write the output to the ddname SYSLIN. The output is called object code, an object deck or an object module.

The output of the compiler is still not quite executable. Some more manipulations need to be done by another program, the Linkage Editor. The Linkage Editor (another program, named IEWL or HEWL) reads its input from the ddname SYSLIN. This DD statement should refer to the same data set that was produced as output from the compiler (usually also on ddname SYSLIN). Thus the Linkage Editor reads as input whatever was written by the compiler as output.

In addition to reading the output from the compiler, the Linkage Editor can also read specific instructions you give it on SYSLIN together with the output from the compiler.

Generally you will compile a program by executing a JCL procedure that contains a step with an EXEC statement for the compiler, followed by another step that executes the Linkage Editor. The Linkage Editor step usually has the step name LKED. The SYSLIN DD statement in the Link Edit step in the procedure will be a concatenation of the SYSLIN output from the compiler and a DDNAME=SYSIN reference. This lets you supply your own Linkage Editor instructions on LKED.SYSIN if you wish to do so.

In addition to reading control statements from SYSIN (SYSLIN), the Linkage Editor can also obtain information from the PARM on the EXEC statement. Normally the PARM will be specified on both the compile and the Link Edit step within the procedure you are using, and you will override these to specify additional options. Since the PARM you specify will override the PARM within the PROC, be sure that in addition to your added options you also specify any options that are already specified in the PARM within the PROC (unless you are deliberately eliminating them).

The Linkage Editor can include called subroutines as part of the output load module. These it usually includes from SYSLIB. Thus, if your program calls an external subroutine called JDATE, and if you want this subroutine to become part of the load module for your program, then the library containing the load module named JDATE should be mentioned in SYSLIB when you invoke the Linkage Editor. You can use any ddname of your choice rather than SYSLIB, but if you do so, you must explicitly code Linkage Editor control statements, e.g., INCLUDE SYSLIB(JDATE).

In addition to the subroutines that your program calls by explicit reference, other subroutines are included to perform standard functions such as OPEN, CLOSE, READ, WRITE, and so on.

Subroutines which are called by your program, but which the Linkage Editor does not include in the load module, are called unresolved external references. These are not necessarily a problem, as they may be resolved at execution time if the language you are using automatically loads routines on an as needed basis. In such cases you should have NCAL specified in the PARM to the Linkage Editor to prevent the load module from being marked NOT EXECUTABLE.

There are several such things you might want to be able to tell the compilers and the Linkage Editor to do for you. The purpose of the present section is to acquaint you briefly with some of the more likely ones.

For example, you might want to tell them whether your program is to be reentrant and reusable, whether it is to use 31-bit addressing, whether it is to have APF authorization, and so on.

Well, you say, you might, if you had a clue what I was talking about. Right. Well. Let's talk about reentrancy first then.

Re-Entrancy, Reusability

Suppose you have a load module of your program sitting in memory someplace, and it does something that online users want to do. Updates a customer's account or something. Now suppose two or more people sitting in front of terminals happen to want to use the load module at the same time; to update different accounts, say. What happens? Depends.

If the variables and I/O areas that the program uses are part of the load module itself, then only one person can use the load module at a time. Such a load module is called self-modifying.

Suppose a concrete case. The program has a variable called IB, for intermediate balance. One user runs the program, and in the course of the program's calculations the value of IB changes from an initial value of zero to some other amount - say zero minus a payment that was just made. The program then updates the customer file with the new information. The variable IB within your load module now contains the changed value. If a second user comes along and tries to use the same copy of the load module that is already in memory, IB will not have an initial value of zero anymore. IB will have whatever value was left over by the last user, and the result of the calculation will be wrong.

In such a case, a new copy of the load module needs to be brought in from disk for each new user. This is not a very efficient solution if the program is used a lot.

What can be done? The program can begin by setting all of its variables equal to zero, blank spaces, or whatever initial values are appropriate. Now a second user will be able to use the same copy of the load module that is already in memory. Such a load module is said to be serially reusable. This is abbreviated REUS, or occasionally RU.

This is still not quite satisfactory because it means that the second user has to wait until the first user is finished. In a large online system with hundreds of users, this still causes noticeable delays.

So, what more can be done? The program can be made reentrant, meaning that everyone can use the same copy of the load module at the same time. How can this be achieved? The variables must all reside in areas outside the load module rather than within it. In PL/I terms, the variables must be AUTOMATIC rather than STATIC.

How does this work? The translated program ends up doing GETMAINs. (Main in this context means main storage, or memory.) This means that each user of the program gets a separate area of memory to use for the variables. The part of memory where the load module itself resides remains unchanged. Now each user will have a separate copy of the variable IB which will be obtained when that user starts executing the program and released when the user finishes. Provided the program assigns appropriate initial values to all of its variables, things will work well. This is the speediest solution. Reentrant is abbreviated RENT, or occasionally RN.

Now, how does the online system know whether your load module is self-modifying or reusable or reentrant?

When the Linkage Editor produces a load module, it marks the load module as reusable, reentrant, or neither. The online system generally relies on this information.

How does the Linkage Editor decide how to mark the load module? It goes by what you tell it in the PARM (e.g., RENT and REUS mean reentrant and reusable), and by what the compiler has noted in the translated program on SYSLIN (if you have not told the compiler to make the program reentrant, it will generally tell the Linkage Editor not to do so) and finally by the attributes of any included subroutines (if your load module is altogether reentrant except that it calls one little external subroutine that is not reentrant, and if that subroutine is link-edited together into the final load module, then the load module will not be reentrant.)

Thus your instructions to the compiler must match your instructions to the Linkage Editor.

Note a trap here. If your program is actually self-modifying, but you somehow manage to get the Linkage Editor to mark it as reentrant, what will happen? Sporadic failures when it is used. Why sporadic? Why not every time after the first time the program is executed? Because the system will not keep the load module in memory for long if it is not actually being used. The system will allocate the memory to something else, and then bring in a fresh copy of the program when somebody actually wants to execute it. If it is a program that is not executed very often, this can result in a problem that shows itself only occasionally—in the rare event that two people happen to use it at the same time. An exception to this occurs if the people who set up the online system make your program RESIDENT or PRE-LOADED. In this case the same copy is used over and over regardless, and the failure should be solid rather than sporadic.

Not all compilers are capable of generating reentrant code. The current versions of the PL/I compiler and the COBOL 2 compiler are able to do this, however.

To instruct the COBOL 2 compiler to generate reentrant code, you need to specify RENT as one of the options in the PARM string that you pass to the compiler. If you specify RENT you should also specify RES, which causes most of the COBOL 2 routines to be left out of the final load module, rather than being included as part of it. This means they will be found separately at the time the program actually executes. Besides specifying RENT and RES in the PARM to the COBOL 2 compiler, you need to specify RENT as one of the options in the PARM string you pass to the Linkage Editor.

To instruct the PL/I compiler to generate reentrant code, you need to ensure that your program does not have any STATIC variables that it modifies as described for IB above. Best is to have all variables default to AUTO-MATIC rather than STATIC. Additionally you should specify REENTRANT as one of the options in the OPTIONS on the PROC statement, for example:

FASTJOB:PROC OPTIONS(MAIN,REENTRANT);

Besides specifying REENTRANT in the compiler options, you need to specify RENT as one of the options in the PARM string you pass to the Linkage Editor.

Notice that if a program written in one language calls subroutines written in a different language, it is often the case that the resulting load modules cannot be marked reentrant, due to difficulties with the inter-language interface routines. Basically they don't trust each other, that is, neither language trusts that routines generated by the other compiler are really reentrant.

So much for reentrancy and reusability.

ADDRESSING MODE (AMODE), RESIDENCY MODE (RMODE), AND SO ON

Now you may as well know about 31-bit addressing, that is, AMODE and RMODE.

AMODE means addressing mode. RMODE means residency mode.

Each can be 31, meaning 31-bit addressing is used, or 24, meaning 24-bit addressing is used, or ANY, meaning either way is okay.

As you recall from Chapter 1, every address in memory has an address, and one word is used to refer to the address. Since one word is four bytes long and each byte is 8 bits, the 24-bit addresses use only 3 bytes of the word. An entire byte is leftover. The new modern 31-bit addresses use all of the word except one bit. (8 times 4 is 32. Minus one bit gives 31.) Hence bigger addresses are possible with 31-bit addressing, meaning that your program can refer to more memory. This is an improvement. Consequently people everywhere are tending to convert their programs from the older 24-bit mode to the newer 31-bit mode. You may get caught up in this, so you may as well be acquainted with the ideas involved.

Residency mode (RMODE) means the type of memory where your program will reside. If your program is able to reside in 31-bit memory, that means that it can be loaded into areas of memory with addresses over 16 Megabytes. (24 bit addresses go up to 16 Meg. 31-bit addresses go up to 2 Gigabytes.)

Addressing mode (AMODE) means the type of addresses your program is capable of using for referring to areas of memory outside of itself. For example, if your program is a subroutine, and your subroutine is called from another program, and that other program passes the subroutine a parameter with a 31-bit address, then your program may or may not be able to handle the situation. If it cannot, it is using 24-bit addressing mode. Obviously it is better if subroutines have AMODE equal to ANY, that is, if they can handle either type of address.

Generally the newest versions of the COBOL and PL/I compilers are capable of generating code that can operate with 31-bit addresses as well as 24-bit addresses. To convert to 31-bit addressing for these programs is generally a straightforward process of recompiling and re-Link-Editing the programs, specifying AMODE(ANY) and RMODE(ANY) in the PARM string that is passed to the Linkage Editor. However, if the programs call subroutines that use only 24-bit addressing mode, then they cannot be converted in this way. First the subroutines have to be converted. After that is done the main programs can be converted successfully. If your programs need to call subroutines written in other languages that do not support 31-bit addressing, then those programs cannot be converted to 31-bit addressing.

So much for AMODE and RMODE.

APF Authorization

APF authorization is the other thing you might want to use.

APF stands for Authorized Program Facility.

Certain functions need to be APF authorized. These are programs that are allowed to do things that might present some security risk from the MVS point of view.

Note that this is entirely different from RACF security.

For example, programs that bypass password protection (most full-disk backup programs) require APF authorization. APF authorization is required for any program that has its own highly efficient I/O routines; for example again, most full-disk backup programs. There are other miscellaneous situations that cause a program to require APF authorization.

If you happen to acquire a program that requires APF authorization, it must be placed in a load library that is on the APF list, and it should be Link-Edited with AC(1) in the PARM to the Linkage Editor.

Note also that you must not concatenate the load library together on STEPLIB or JOBLIB with any non-APF-authorized libraries. If you do so, you will lose authorization.

There are other various things you can communicate to the Linkage Editor through the PARM. LIST says you want a listing. XREF says you want a cross reference listing. There are other options that are not of very great general interest. If you want a more complete list of the possible things you can request from the Linkage Editor, consult the IBM Linkage Editor Reference Manual. Think of this activity as similar to looking up a word in the unabridged dictionary.

IKJEFTO1: Executing TSO commands in a batch Job

If you use TSO a lot, you might have come to the point where you rely on familiar TSO commands and want to be able to issue these TSO commands from a batch Job. You might, for example, want to execute a CLIST you have, or send yourself a message with the TSO SEND command. It is easy to execute TSO in batch. An example follows.

```
//SMITH8E0 JOB  1,TSO.EXAMPLE,
//     MSGCLASS=X
//TSO EXEC PGM=IKJEFT01,
//       DYNAMNBR=20
//SYSPROC DD DSN=SMITH.CLIST,
//     DISP=SHR
//     DD DSN=OTHER.CLIST,
//     DISP=SHR
//SYSLBL  DD DSN=SYS1.BRODCAST,
//     DISP=SHR
//SYSTSPRT DD SYSOUT=*
//SYSTSIN DD DDNAME=SYSIN
  LISTDS 'SMITH.LOADLIB' S H M
  SEND 'YOUR BATCH LISTPDS +
  IS DONE ',U(SMITH),LOGON
```

What happens in the above example? The program IKJEFT01 is

executed. IKJEFT01 is TSO. Be sure to include a large DYNAMNBR on the EXEC statement, because TSO uses dynamic allocation a lot.

TSO looks at the DD statement for SYSPROC to find any CLISTs you try to execute. Point it to your own CLIST library plus any general purpose CLIST libraries your group uses.

If you use the SEND command, include the SYSLBL DD statement pointing to SYS1.BRODCAST, where TSO messages are kept.

TSO writes its output messages to SYSTSPRT. SYSTSPRT is the TSO counterpart of SYSPRINT.

TSO reads its input messages from SYSTSIN. SYSTSIN is the TSO counterpart of SYSIN.

In the above example, the input on SYSTSIN tells TSO to list the names of the members of the data set 'SMITH.LOADLIB' and then to send a message to TSO user SMITH. You can adapt this to execute any TSO commands you wish, with the exception that you cannot execute full-screen processors such as SPF.

Notice that one of the DD DYNAM statements implied by the DYNAMNBR will be used by the LISTDS command. This is not obvious just from looking at the JCL, but it means that DYNAMNBR actually is required on the EXEC statement (unless your place has a default for it that will cover your needs).

If you want the output from your TSO commands to be placed in a data set rather than being written to SYSOUT, you can change the above JCL so that the SYSTSPRT DD statement points to a disk data set rather than to SYSOUT.

That's all there is to it.

A few examples of handy things you can do with batch TSO:

Example 1 - Delete a member of a library:

```
//SMITH8E1 JOB  1,TSO.EXAMPLE,
//    MSGCLASS=X
//STEP1   EXEC PGM=IKJEFT01,
//    DYNAMNBR=20
//SYSTSPRT DD SYSOUT=*
//SYSTSIN DD *
```

```
    DELETE 'SMITH.SOURCE.LIBRARY(VERSION1)'
/*
```

Example 2 - Delete an entire data set:

```
//SMITH8E2 JOB  1,TSO.EXAMPLE,
//      MSGCLASS=X
//STEP1  EXEC PGM=IKJEFT01,
//      DYNAMNBR=20
//SYSTSPRT DD SYSOUT=*
//SYSTSIN DD *
    DELETE 'SMITH.UNNEEDED.DATASET'
/*
```

Example 3 - You are not sure whether or not the data set named
SMITH.UNLOADED.DATA already exists. You execute a TSO step to
delete it prior to executing the step that normally creates it. If the data set
exists, it will be deleted in the first step and then recreated in the second
step. If it does not exist, the DELETE command will fail, but the next step
will still run and create the data set:

```
//SMITH8E3 JOB  1,TSO.EXAMPLE,MSGCLASS=X
//STEP1  EXEC PGM=IKJEFT01,DYNAMNBR=20
//SYSTSPRT DD SYSOUT=*
//SYSTSIN DD *
    DELETE 'SMITH.UNLOADED.DATA'
//STEP2  EXEC UNLOAD or whatever you use
//DFSURGU1 DD DISP=(NEW,CATLG),
//      DSN=SMITH.UNLOADED.DATA,
//      UNIT=SYSDA,
//      SPACE=(CYL,(15,45),RLSE)
```

Example 4 - Rename a member of a library:

```
//SMITH8E4 JOB  1,TSO.EXAMPLE,MSGCLASS=X
```

```
//STEP1   EXEC PGM=IKJEFT01,DYNAMNBR=20
//SYSTSPRT DD SYSOUT=*
//SYSTSIN DD *
 RENAME -
 'SMITH.SOURCE.LIBRARY(VERSION1)'-
   (VERSION2)
/*
```

Example 5 - Rename an entire data set:

```
//SMITH8E5 JOB  1,TSO.EXAMPLE,MSGCLASS=X
//STEP1   EXEC PGM=IKJEFT01,DYNAMNBR=20
//SYSTSPRT DD SYSOUT=*
//SYSTSIN DD *
 RENAME 'SMITH.SOURCE.LIBRARY'-
   'SMITH.OLD.LIBRARY'
/*
```

Example 6 - Send detailed messages to yourself about the progress of a batch job:

```
//SMITH8E6 JOB  1,BIG.JOB,
//     MSGCLASS=X,TIME=20
//STEP1 EXEC PGM=LONGTIME
//IN   DD  DISP=SHR,
//   DSN=BIG.INPUT.FILE
//OUT  DD  DISP=SHR,
//   DSN=BIG.OUTPUT.FILE
//*
//ABEND EXEC PGM=IKJEFT01,
//   DYNAMNBR=20,COND=(ONLY)
//SYSLBL  DD DSN=SYS1.BRODCAST,
//    DISP=SHR
//SYSTSPRT DD SYSOUT=*
//SYSTSIN DD *
```

```
  SEND   'STEP1 OF JOB SMITH8E5 +
  ABENDED ',U(SMITH),LOGON
/*
//CC0  EXEC PGM=IKJEFT01,
//    DYNAMNBR=20,COND=(0,NE,STEP1)
//SYSLBL  DD DSN=SYS1.BRODCAST,
//     DISP=SHR
//SYSTSPRT DD SYSOUT=*
//SYSTSIN DD *
  SEND 'STEP1 OF JOB SMITH8E5+
  DONE, CC=0 ',U(SMITH),LOGON
//GT0  EXEC PGM=IKJEFT01,
//    DYNAMNBR=20,COND=(0,GT,STEP1)
//SYSLBL  DD DSN=SYS1.BRODCAST,
//    DISP=SHR
//SYSTSPRT DD SYSOUT=*
//SYSTSIN DD *
  SEND 'STEP1 OF JOB SMITH8E5 HAD+
  NONZERO CC ',U(SMITH),LOGON
//*
//STEP2 EXEC PGM=NEXTPGM
//IN  DD  DISP=SHR,
//    DSN=BIG.OUTPUT.FILE
```

SORT

For some reason, it seems that the records in files are often arranged in some sequence other than what we need them to be. The easiest way to rearrange the sequence is to put the file through a 'sort' program.

There are a number of SORT programs available from IBM and other suppliers. There is almost certainly one in every MVS installation. No matter which one is available at the installation where you work, the basic functions are requested in much the same way. The non-IBM suppliers generally use the same format as used by the IBM-supplied SORT program. The examples in this section will be based on the IBM program

DFSORT, but if you are using a non-IBM SORT program, these examples will probably work exactly the same way.

What are the basic functions?

You must tell the SORT program where the input file is. That is done with a straightforward JCL DD statement for the ddname SORTIN.

You must also tell the SORT program where to put the output file after the records have been rearranged. That is done with a JCL DD statement for the ddname SORTOUT.

You need to tell the SORT program how to rearrange the records, that is, into what order you want them rearranged. This information is communicated to the SORT program with control statements you supply in SYSIN.

The ddname SYSOUT is used by the SORT program to print messages (the way most utility programs use SYSPRINT).

Here is a simple example of sorting a file in ascending sequence by the contents of the first five bytes of the record:

```
//SORTTHIS EXEC PGM=SORT
//SYSOUT  DD SYSOUT=*
//SORTIN  DD DISP=OLD,
//   DSN=MY.HIGGELDY.PIGGELDY.FILE
//SORTOUT  DD DISP=(,CATLG),
//   DSN=MY.NEAT.AND.ORDERLY.FILE,
//   UNIT=SYSDA,SPACE=(CYL,(3,2))
//SYSIN DD *
   SORT   FIELDS=(1,5,CH,A)
/*
```

Most versions of SORT will attempt to complete all the sorting in memory, which makes sorting extremely fast. If a large file needs to be sorted, the SORT program will require some external storage as an additional work space. The SORT program can be installed by your systems programmers in such a way that these external areas are automatically created.

If the external areas are not created automatically, you can provide the external work areas by putting in some extra DD statements. Not surprisingly they have the ddnames SORTWK01, SORTWK02, SORTWK03 and so on, and are called sort work areas.

The sort work areas should be on disk and will only be required for the duration of the step doing the sorting. An example could look as simple as this:

```
//SORTWK01 DD UNIT=SYSDA,SPACE=(CYL,5)
//SORTWK02 DD UNIT=SYSDA,SPACE=(CYL,5)
//SORTWK03 DD UNIT=SYSDA,SPACE=(CYL,5)
```

Most installations have a cataloged procedure called SORT. If a generalized procedure of this sort is being used the sort work area DD statements may or may not be included in the procedure. In any case you will certainly need to specify the SORTIN and SORTOUT DD statements, and the SORT control statement(s) on SYSIN.

Let's analyze the SORT control statement that was used above:

```
SORT   FIELDS=(1,5,CH,A)
```

The SORT program is told that it should SORT, rather than do something else. It is then told to sort a 'FIELD' which starts in position 1 of the record and is 5 bytes in length. The field is to be treated as character type data (CH) and is to be sorted into ascending (A) sequence. In other words, it will be sorted into alphabetical order based on the first five letters of each record.

Vocabulary item. The word "field" has traditionally been used to define a unit of information, that is, a string of adjacent bytes, which will be handled automatically by an information processing machine. Those machines are computers and their predecessors.

The next example is more complex. A file is going to be sorted by three fields.

The file to be sorted contains information about customers.

The required sequence will put all the records for each sales representative together.

The salesperson number is a two byte binary number in positions 1 and 2 of the record. There can be more than one record with the same salesperson number. This is because each salesperson can have more than one customer.

So, within the group of records for each salesperson, the customers for each salesperson will be sorted by customer name. The customer name is 20 characters long starting in position 21.

Finally, the date the customer made a payment will be sorted in descending sequence. The date is in Julian date format of YYDDD and is kept in packed decimal starting in position 10 for 3 bytes.

Have a close look at the example SORT control card in the following JCL and compare it to the field descriptions just given.

```
//SORT EXEC PGM=SORT
//SYSOUT  DD SYSOUT=*
//SORTIN  DD DISP=OLD,
//   DSN=MY.SALES.RECORDS
//SORTOUT DD DISP=OLD,
//   DSN=MY.SALES.RECORDS
//SORTWK01 DD UNIT=SYSDA,
//   SPACE=(CYL,2)
//SORTWK02 DD UNIT=SYSDA,
//   SPACE=(CYL,2)
//SORTWK03 DD UNIT=SYSDA,
//   SPACE=(CYL,2)
//SYSIN DD *
    SORT    FIELDS=(1,2,BI,A,21,20,CH,A,10,3,PD,D)
/*
```

That is not very readable, is it? SORT does allow statements to be continued. You simply finish one line with a comma and start the next line between positions 2 and 71. The same statement is a bit more readable this way:

```
    SORT    FIELDS=(1,2,BI,A,
            21,20,CH,A,
```

10,3,PD,D)

Did you spot the fact that SORTIN and SORTOUT were the same file? The SORT program allows you to do that because the complete SORTIN file is read and rearranged before the SORTOUT is written. Nevertheless, it's a bad idea, because you can destroy your input file if the job happens to fail with the output only partially complete (if there is a power failure, for example, or the job runs over its time limit).

Before we move on from the SORT FIELDS let's look again at how the SORT FIELDS are used. You must specify the first byte of a field from the beginning of the record. Next you specify the length of the field in bytes. The type of field that is being sorted, CH for character, BI for binary, PD for packed decimal. Lastly you specify the sorting sequence, A for ascending or D for descending.

If the file you are sorting happens to be contain variable length records, there will be (as you remember from the discussion of RECFM=VB) an extra four bytes at the beginning of each record. This four byte area contains the record length.

The SORT program makes absolutely no assumptions about the four bytes at the beginning of the varying length record. The control statements must be adjusted to allow for them. If a file were to be sorted on the first 10 positions of a record, the fixed length record would have a control statement like this:

SORT FIELDS=(1,10,CH,A)

while the variable length record would have this:

SORT FIELDS=(5,10,CH,A)

As you see, when you are sorting varying length records the starting position has to be increased by four to allow for the record length bytes at the beginning.

The SORT program is both versatile and efficient. It is possible to make a sequence of work more efficient by using some of the fancier features of the SORT program.

Imagine you have to read of file of 15,000 records and select certain records to be sorted. Imagine further that you expect 10,000 of the records to be of interest to you, but that the other 5,000 are not significant for this particular problem. You are expected to produce a file of the 10,000 selected records in a different format for another user.

The method that may come to mind immediately is to write a program that will read the file and copy the required records to a new format output file, then sort the smaller file.

The number of records to be read and written in this example is 45,000. That is made up as 15,000 reads for the selection program, 10,000 writes for the selection program, 10,000 reads for the sort input, and 10,000 writes for the sort output.

Using a special facility of the SORT program it is possible to do the whole thing with far fewer reads and writes and still get the desired result without writing a program. Sound intriguing, doesn't it? Read on.

The SORT program will allow you to select or reject records from the input file to be included in the sorted output file. That is, after a record is read the record will be accepted depending on rules that you put into an INCLUDE statement. Conversely, you could use an OMIT statement to specify rules for rejecting records.

Suppose we know that the records to be sorted must contain the letters 'XRB' in positions 117 to 119, and we are only interested in records where the numeric value in one specific field is greater that the numeric value in another specific field. The two numeric fields happen to be six bytes in length and are both packed decimal. The field that must be higher starts in position 365 and the lower field starts in 570. We can use the following INCLUDE statement:

```
INCLUDE COND=(365,6,PD,
       GT,
       570,6,PD,
       AND,
       117,3,CH,EQ,C'XRB')
```

The OMIT statement for the same conditions would look like this:

```
OMIT COND=(365,6,PD,
       LE,
       570,6,PD,
       AND,
       117,3,CH,NE,C'XRB')
```

The INCLUDE and OMIT statements can use nested condition tests. It is always recommended that nesting should use parentheses for clarity. The connectors between each test are AND and OR.

The operators between the comparitors in any condition test are:

- EQ   Equal to
- NE   Not equal to
- GT   Greater than
- LT   Less than
- GE   Greater than or equal to
- LE   Less than or equal to

Now suppose that you want to produce an output file where the reformatted file needs only a few fields from the original input file. SORT to the rescue again. This time the fields that are required are specified in the OUTREC statement.

In the tradition of the SORT parameters, the OUTREC will look like another string of numbers. Not surprising, because it is a string of numbers. The numbers represent the starting position and length of the required fields from the input record. The field will be placed in the next available position in the output record. Any other value can also be put into the output record.

In the following example the word 'SELECTED ' will be put in the record in the first 9 positions. Positions 10 to 24 will receive the fields that were in the INCLUDE statement. After that the fields that were in the SORT statement will be placed in positions 25 to 49.

```
//SORT EXEC PGM=SORT
```

```
//SYSOUT DD SYSOUT=*
//SORTIN DD DSN=MY.SALES.RECORDS,
//    DISP=OLD
//SORTOUT DD DISP=(,CATLG),
//    DSN=MY.SELECTED.SALES.RECORDS,
//    UNIT=SYSDA,SPACE=(CYL,2),
//    DCB=(RECFM=FB,LRECL=49,
//    BLKSIZE=23716)
 INCLUDE COND=(365,6,PD,
        GT,
        570,6,PD,
        AND,
        117,3,CH,EQ,C'XRB')
 SORT FIELDS=(5,2,BI,A,
        25,20,CH,A,
        14,3,PD,D)
 OUTREC FIELDS=(C'SELECTED ',
        17,3,
        365,6,
        570,6,
        5,2,
        25,20,
        14,3)
```

The SORTIN has an LRECL of 1847. The SORTOUT will be much shorter. Therefore the LRECL needs to be coded on the DD statement. You will notice that the BLKSIZE also has to be specified in the DCB for the SORTOUT file, and that is a multiple of the new LRECL.

While the above example will work, it is not very efficient. You see that we have just sorted 10,000 records of 1847 bytes in length when we could have sorted 10,000 records of only 49 bytes in length. When the OUTREC control statement is used the records are reformatted after they have been sorted, just before they are is written to the output file.

There is an INREC control statement which works just the same way except that the record is reformatted before it is sorted rather than after.

While it is more efficient, the SORT control statement will have to be changed because the fields have actually moved to different locations in the new record. The same example with the INREC control statement would look like this:

```
//SORT EXEC PGM=SORT
//SYSOUT DD SYSOUT=*
//SORTIN DD DSN=MY.SALES.RECORDS,
//    DISP=OLD
//SORTOUT DD DISP=(,CATLG),
//    DSN=MY.SELECTED.SALES.RECORDS,
//    UNIT=SYSDA,SPACE=(CYL,2),
//    DCB=(RECFM=FB,LRECL=49,
//    BLKSIZE=23716)
//SYSIN DD *
 INCLUDE COND=(365,6,PD,
        GT,
        570,6,PD,
        AND,
        117,3,CH,EQ,C'XRB')
 INREC FIELDS=(C'SELECTED ',
        17,3,
        365,6,
        570,6,
        5,2,
        25,20,
        14,3)
 SORT FIELDS=(25,2,BI,A,
        27,20,CH,A,
        46,3,PD,D)
 /*
```

The SORT function of the SORT program operates several phases. We have looked at the input phase which uses the SELECT, OMIT, and INREC statements; the sort phase which uses the SORT statement, and

371

the output phase which uses the OUTREC statement. There is one more control statement worth looking at before we move on. It is the SUM statement.

At the end of the sort phase, if two or more records have been sorted together because they have the same values in the sort control fields, then those records can be amalgamated with the SUM statement. For example if a file was sorted by some part or item number and each record has a field of units sold, it would be possible to ask the SORT program to amalgamate the records together so that only one record would be written to the output file. That record would contain the SUM of the units sold. The control statements would look like this:

```
SORT FIELDS=(25,2,BI,A,
      27,20,CH,A,
      46,3,PD,D)
SUM FIELDS=(130,8,PD)
```

If there were more than one field which needed to be accumulated, then you would continue defining the extra fields within the parentheses. The usual formula for defining fields to the SORT program apply, that is, the offset from the beginning of the record, the length of the field, and the type of field.

There are some restrictions however. A field that is a sort control field may not be involved in an accumulation operation. All the fields must be in the first 4092 bytes of the record. There are only four types of fields that may be accumulated; they are packed decimal which is defined as PD and has a maximum length of 16 bytes; zoned decimal which is defined as ZD and has a maximum length of 18 bytes; unsigned binary which is defined as BI and has a length of 2, 4, or 8; and signed binary which is defined as FI and has a length of 2, 4, or 8.

It is only the fields that have been defined in the SUM statement that are amalgamated into the record that is written as output. If there is other vital information that you need on the records that are not written as output, then you should not use the SUM statement.

If the accumulated new value for the field involved in the SUM operation is larger than the field can hold, then the SORT program will not proceed with the accumulation. The SORT program will write more than one record to the output file with the same values in the sort control fields.

Warning: If a field involved in an accumulation contains non-decimal data, and you have specified that it contains decimal data (PD), then the SORT program may abend with a completion code of 0C7.

The SUM statement may also be used if no accumulation is to be done, that is, it may be used to eliminate duplicate records. You can code SUM=NONE to specify that only one record with a specific sort control key will be written to the output file. That is to say, there will not be any duplicates.

The following example takes an input data set consisting of 80-byte records and produces an output file with all duplicate records eliminated:

```
//SORT EXEC PGM=SORT
//SYSOUT  DD SYSOUT=*
//SORTIN  DD DSN=SMITH.CARDS.DATA,
//      DISP=OLD
//SORTOUT DD DSN=SMITH.NEW.CARDDATA,
//      DISP=(,CATLG),
//      UNIT=SYSDA,SPACE=(CYL,(8,5))
//SYSIN DD *
SORT FIELDS=(1,80,CH,A)
RECORD TYPE=F,LENGTH=(80)
SUM FIELDS=NONE
END
/*
```

The SORT program can also be used to take two or more files that are already in the desired final sequence and MERGE them together.

```
//SORT  EXEC PGM=SORT
//SYSOUT  DD SYSOUT=*
```

```
//SORTIN01 DD DISP=OLD,
//    DSN=MY.SALES.RECORDS.CHICAGO
//SORTIN02 DD DISP=OLD,
//    DSN=MY.SALES.RECORDS.BERLIN
//SORTIN03 DD DSN=MY.SALES.RECORDS.PARIS,
//    DISP=OLD
//SORTOUT DD DISP=(,CATLG),
// DSN=MY.SALES.RECORDS.ALL.OVER,
//    UNIT=SYSDA,SPACE=(CYL,(8,5))
//SYSIN DD *
  MERGE FIELDS=(25,2,BI,A,
          27,20,CH,A,
          46,3,PD,D)
/*
```

The INCLUDE or OMIT statement as well as the INREC and OUTREC statements can be used with the MERGE statement in order to produce the required output file.

The SORT program is so efficient that it is often used to replace IEBGENER for making an exact copy of a flat file. When DFSORT is installed, the systems programmer has the option of making this an automatic facility. However, there are other ways of doing the same thing.

If the program ICEGENER is specified on the EXEC statement, then DFSORT will be used. Or more correctly, DFSORT will determine if it can be used, if for some reason DFSORT cannot do the job then it will get IEBGENER to do the work. No matter which is actually used, the work will get done. The return codes are from the IEBGENER definition.

```
//WHODUNIT EXEC PGM=ICEGENER
//SYSIN DD DUMMY
//SYSPRINT DD SYSOUT=*
//SYSUT1 DD DSN=MY.INPUT.TO.GENER,
//    DISP=SHR
//SYSUT2 DD DSN=MY.OUTPUT.FROM.GENER,
//    DISP=(,CATLG),
//    UNIT=SYSDA,SPACE=(CYL,(3,3))
```

Incidentally, most versions of SORT, when used in this way, will actually allow you to print a VSAM file as if it were an ordinary flat file.

Another way of doing a copy using the SORT program is given in the following example. Notice the changes for three of the ddnames being used and the name of the program.

```
//WHODUNIT EXEC PGM=SORT
//SYSIN DD *
  OPTION COPY
//SYSOUT  DD SYSOUT=*
//SORTIN DD DSN=MY.INPUT.TO.GENER,
//    DISP=SHR
//SORTOUT DD DSN=MY.OUTPUT.FROM.GENER,
//    DISP=(,CATLG),
//    UNIT=SYSDA,SPACE=(CYL,(3,3))
```

The control statement uses OPTION COPY but you could have used either of the next two control statements to do the same thing

SORT FIELDS=COPY

Or

MERGE FIELDS=COPY

You may also use the INCLUDE or OMIT control statement in order to restrict what does get copied from the SORTIN file. The INREC and OUTREC control statements are also available in order to create a different record format which will be written to the SORTOUT file.

Whether you want to SORT, MERGE, or COPY files, the SORT program will work happily with flat files or VSAM files, fixed length files or variable length files. There are some restrictions though. You should still create your empty VSAM file with IDCAMS. If you are creating a VSAM file with keys, the sort parameters must put the file in the sequence of the key. If you are using variable length records all references to fields in the record must be in the part of the record that does not vary.

The SORT program allows you to 'stitch in' your own programs, or routines, through a facility it calls User Exits. There are several places where SORT will allow a user exit, but you will probably never want to use more than two. The two are called E15, which takes care of input to the sort, and E35, which takes care of output from the sort.

The idea is this.

Whenever the SORT program has an input record, or when the end of the input file is reached, the SORT program will call the E15 exit. The E15 exit routine can tell the SORT program to drop the record, accept the record, or even replace the record with a totally new record that the exit makes up and inserts.

Similarly, the E35 exit will be called by the SORT program whenever a record is ready to be written as output to the SORTOUT file, or when there are no more records to be written to the SORTOUT file. The E35 exit routine can tell the SORT program to drop the record, accept the record, or provide a totally new record to be written to the output file.

These routines can be written if the INCLUDE, OMIT, INREC, and OUTREC statements are not suitable for the problem. Information on how to write these routines can be found in the appropriate programming language manual such as PL/1 or COBOL. Or Assembler language, of course.

You now have all the information about the SORT program that you are ever likely to want.

DITTO

You may or may not have DITTO on your system. If you do have DITTO, this discussion will explain how to use it.

In the earliest days of the use of IBM 360 computers there were functions that were not particularly easy to use. JCL was one of them but there were also some utility programs that qualified for that distinction. To help remedy that situation many programmers wrote their own programs which overcame the problems of the less popular utilities. The programmers then proceeded to give these programs away to anyone who wanted them. That's right, give them away, free, gratis, and for nothing. Remember this was during the 1960's, which might explain it. Anyway DITTO was one of these programs, and it became very popular.

DITTO did not however have official IBM sanction. When new file structures like VSAM, or new disk and tape drives came along, DITTO was not immediately upgraded to support them.

The dedicated users of DITTO got together and told IBM that DITTO was good and it should be brought into the official product line. After a suitable period of considering the case, IBM announced a new product called MVS/DITTO, Product code 5665-370, and they even went to the trouble of saying the word DITTO was an acronym for Data Interfile Transfer, Testing, and Operations Utility. The down side of this is that DITTO is no longer free.

When DITTO operates in batch mode it will look for its instruction from the SYSIN DD * file, naturally you will remember to put a /* at the end. To operate in batch mode you must code a PARM on the EXEC statement. It might look like this.

```
//DITTO EXEC PGM=DITTO,
//     PARM='JOBSTREAM'
//SYSPRINT DD SYSOUT=*
//SYSIN DD *
$$DITTO XXX
$$DITTO EOJ
/*
```

In the British Isles you would say ££DITTO instead of $$DITTO in the DITTO input commands. The command in the above example will give you a list of all the DITTO functions, then finish.

DITTO can also operate in console mode. Console mode allows a TSO user or an operator at an operators console to have an interactive session with DITTO. If you allowed to use console mode in your installation, you should reply 'EOJ' to finish.

The same example in console mode would look like this:

XXX
EOJ

DITTO can be particularly useful when you are working with tape, and you are not sure what is on the tape. In the following example DITTO will produce a map of the tape A12345. We have been told that the tape is an ASCII tape.

```
//DITTO EXEC PGM=DITTO,
//    PARM='JOBSTREAM'
//SYSPRINT DD SYSOUT=*
//TAPEIN  DD DSN=DUMM1,DISP=OLD,
//     UNIT=TAPE,
//     VOL=SER=A12345,
//     LABEL=(1,BLP)
//SYSIN DD *
$$DITTO SET PRINTLEN=80,ASCII=YES
$$DITTO TMP INPUT=TAPEIN,NFILES=EOV
$$DITTO EOJ
/*
```

You will see that the tape is specified on the TAPEIN DD statement. By saying LABEL=(1,BLP) we are telling MVS not to check the tape labels for correctness. In this situation we may not be absolutely sure the tape label information is correct.

The first DITTO command tells DITTO to use only 80 positions for the print length, that will make the list easy to read on a terminal. The instruction ASCII=YES tells DITTO to convert ASCII characters to EBCDIC for printing purposes.

The second DITTO command tells DITTO to produce the short tape map for the tape on TAPEIN. We want a map for all files, that is the number of files to the end of volume, NFILES=EOV.

Lastly we tell DITTO that there is no more.

DITTO will produce a listing which shows the location of each tapemark, each label will be printed, and the number of blocks in each file will be shown.

378

The listing will look something like this:

ANSI VOL1 LABEL =

VOL1A12345
1—5—10—15—20—25—30—35—40

—45—50—55—60—65—70—75—80

HDR1 LABEL =

HDR1DATA.SET.NAME.IS A1234500010001
1—5—10—15—20—25—30—35—40

0093181
—45—50—55—60—65—70—75—80

HDR2 LABEL =

HDR2D0200000137
1—5—10—15—20—25—30—35—40

—45—50—55—60—65—70—75—80

* TAPE MARK
*   2353 DATA BLOCKS
* TAPE MARK

EOF1 LABEL =

EOF1DATA.SET.NAME.IS A1234500010001
1—5—10—15—20—25—30—35—40
0093181   002353
—45—50—55—60—65—70—75—80

EOF2 LABEL =

EOF2D0200000137
1—5—10—15—20—25—30—35—40

—45—50—55—60—65—70—75—80

* TAPE MARK
* TAPE MARK

From the listing we might be able to identify any problem we had with the tape. For example, the DSNAME we expected might have had a slightly different spelling from the name actually found on the tape. We might also discover that the file we thought was the second file on the tape is actually the third. The possibilities are endless.

Because the positions of tapemarks are also identified, you should always look for a tapemark that appears before the volume label. That is a sure sign that you should use the LTM value in the LABEL parameter, that is, LABEL=(1,LTM), where LTM means 'leading tape mark'. MVS standard label tapes do not have leading tape marks.

Vocabulary item. A tape mark is a unique bit pattern that is written on a tape. Tape marks are used to mark the boundaries between the various things that are written on tapes. The bit pattern is unique because it is one that cannot be written as data. You normally do not need to be aware of tape marks, but if something goes wrong, it is good to know where they should be and why they should be there.

For an ordinary standard label tape, the order is this: The first thing on the tape is the volume label, which is a single 80-character record that begins with VOL1 followed by the volume serial number of the tape. The volume label is followed by the header label for the first data set on the tape. The header label begins with HDR1 followed by the name of the data set. The header label is followed by a tape mark. Thus the VOL1 and HDR1 labels, taken together, constitute the first file of the tape when the tape is processed in Bypass-Label-Processing (,BLP) mode.

The first tape mark is followed by the first data set on the tape. The data set is followed by another tape mark.

Then comes the trailer label for the first data set. The trailer label tells how big the data set is, and contains some other information of that sort.

After the trailer label comes another tape mark, followed by the header label for the next data set if a next data set exists, and so on. After all of the data sets and labels on the tape, there are two tape marks together to signify the end of the tape.

Operators may initialize new tapes using DITTO.

Assume that the procedure that executes DITTO is named DITTO and it is set up with INTAPE as the ddname for the tape.

The operator first starts the DITTO procedure by entering the appropriate operator command:

    START DITTO

and then, for each tape to be initialized, the operator enters the following at the console:

    INT,INTAPE,volser

Where "volser" is replaced by the actual volume serial number to be assigned to the tape.

If the tape is an ASCII label tape the command is this:

    INT,INTAPE,volser,ASCII

I am making the assumption the DDNAME being used is INTAPE, obviously the command would be different for another DDNAME. The operator simply has to key in the volume serial number as required. DITTO will also take the command in sections and prompt the operator for the next response. It might look something like this

    INT
    ddname?

TAPEIN
serial?

A12345,ASCII

Because the last parameter of ASCII is optional, it is important to include it with the answer for the serial number. You get the idea. But as it is unlikely that you will be using console mode when you use DITTO, the remainder of the examples will be in batch mode.

DITTO is often used to print the contents of a tape. The basic commands are TP and TD with a few variations. The TP form will print the tape file in character format. The TD form will print the tape file in character and hex dump format. The following example will print the header and trailer labels in character format and the data file in character and hex dump format. Label information always uses character format so we don't really need a dump.

```
//DITTO EXEC PGM=DITTO,
//    PARM='JOBSTREAM'
//SYSPRINT DD SYSOUT=*
//TAPEIN DD DSN=DUMM1,
//    DISP=OLD,
//    UNIT=TAPE,
//    VOL=SER=A12345,
//    LABEL=(1,BLP)
//SYSIN DD *
$$DITTO SET PRINTLEN=80
$$DITTO TP INPUT=TAPEIN
$$DITTO TD INPUT=TAPEIN
$$DITTO TP INPUT=TAPEIN
$$DITTO EOJ
/*
```

DITTO will print the data as blocks and will not even attempt to isolate the logical records in the basic TP and TD formats. You can direct DITTO to print logical records with the appropriate variations of TP and

TD. These are the TPV, TPD, TDV, and TDD forms. The V indicates the records are variable length and DITTO will use the record descriptor word (RDW) at the front of each logical record. If the file is fixed length you can use the D suffix to tell DITTO to deblock the records for printing purposes. You must also tell DITTO how long an individual record is so it knows how it should deblock the records.

In the next example, we will print the first two files on the tape. The first file has variable length records, while the second has fixed length records of 147 bytes.

```
//DITTO EXEC PGM=DITTO,
//   PARM='JOBSTREAM'
//SYSPRINT DD SYSOUT=*
//TAPEIN DD DSN=DUMM1,
//   DISP=OLD,UNIT=TAPE,
//   VOL=SER=A12345,
//   LABEL=(1,BLP)
//SYSIN DD *
$$DITTO SET PRINTLEN=80
$$DITTO TP INPUT=TAPEIN
$$DITTO TDV INPUT=TAPEIN
$$DITTO TP INPUT=TAPEIN
$$DITTO TP INPUT=TAPEIN
$$DITTO TDD INPUT=TAPEIN,RECSIZE=147
$$DITTO TP INPUT=TAPEIN
$$DITTO EOJ
/*
```

If you do not want to print the full file you can add the NBLKS=nnn parameter to the TP and TD statements, when that number of blocks is printed DITTO will move on to the nest statement.

If you are using the D or V forms (deblock or variable) you can add the NLRECS=nnn parameter which tells ditto to print that number of logical records before moving on to the next statement.

In addition to that you can also tell DITTO to print a certain number of files with the NFILES=nnn parameter. You should remember that DITTO thinks of a file as any data that comes before a tapemark. That means the header and trailer labels that identify a file to MVS are in fact treated as files by DITTO. It might sound a bit confusing so let's look at an example. We have a tape that contains three files that MVS would look at by saying LABEL=1, LABEL=2, or LABEL 3 as appropriate. As far as DITTO is concerned the tape contains 9 files. Lets look at it a bit more closely.

```
hdr TM data TM tlr TM   hdr TM data TM tlr TM   hdr TM
    data TM tlr TM
< MVS DATA FILE 1 >< MVS DATA FILE 2 >< MVS
    DATA FILE 3 >
```

MVS will look at groups of header data and trailer as a single file, while DITTO will look at anything up to a tapemark as a single file.

Now lets print that imaginary tape with a single DITTO command. Happily we know the three files contain logical records of 80 bytes. Coincidentally MVS tape labels are 80 bytes as well. By the way, we only want to print the first 60 records on each file.

```
//DITTO EXEC PGM=DITTO,PARM='JOBSTREAM'
//SYSPRINT DD SYSOUT=*
//TAPEIN DD DSN=DUMM1,DISP=OLD,
//   UNIT=TAPE,VOL=SER=A12345,
//   LABEL=(1,BLP)
//SYSIN DD *
$$DITTO SET PRINTLEN=80
$$DITTO                              TDD
    INPUT=TAPEIN,RECSIZE=80,NLRECS=60,NFILES=9
$$DITTO EOJ
/*
```

DITTO can work with more than tapes. It can also work with VSAM files. However as you have already read the section on IDCAMS we will not spend too much time on the DITTO VSAM functions. Here is one where we want to print the first 200 records of a VSAM file in both character and HEX dump format:

```
//DITTO EXEC PGM=DITTO,PARM='JOBSTREAM'
//SYSPRINT DD SYSOUT=*
//VSAMIN DD DSN=MY.VSAM,DISP=OLD
//SYSIN DD *
$$DITTO SET PRINTLEN=80
$$DITTO VD INPUT=VSAMIN,NLRECS=200
$$DITTO EOJ
/*
```

Here is a example where we want to create a sequential (flat file) version of the VSAM file. A sequential version of a file is sometimes called a QSAM file, where QSAM stands for Queued Sequential Access Method. The command we will use is VQ, for VSAM to QSAM. In this example the QSAM version will be on tape, but it could easily go to disk by changing the UNIT parameter on the DD statement and also using a SPACE parameter.

```
//DITTO EXEC PGM=DITTO,
//   PARM='JOBSTREAM'
//SYSPRINT DD SYSOUT=*
//VSAMIN DD DSN=MY.VSAM,FILE,
//   DISP=OLD
//QSAMOUT DD DSN=MY.QSAM.FILE,
//   DISP=(,KEEP),UNIT=TAPE,
//   VOL=SER=B35786
//SYSIN DD *
$$DITTO SET PRINTLEN=80
$$DITTO VQ INPUT=VSAMIN,OUTPUT=QSAMOUT
$$DITTO EOJ
/*
```

DITTO is versatile in that it can work with tape or disk and just about any file organization. It can even work with cards. Naturally it can print, which makes it very useful for problem determination. It can even be used to search for a specific value on either tape or disk.

IEHPROGM

You will sometimes see the following sort of thing:

```
//STEP4    EXEC PGM=IEHPROGM
//SYSPRINT DD SYSOUT=*
//DD1      DD UNIT=3380,
//         VOL=SER=PROD03,DISP=OLD
//SYSIN    DD *
           SCRATCH MEMBER=PCAY552,    +
           DSNAME=ISD.YPGM.LLIB,      +
           VOL=3380=PROD03,PURGE
/*
```

If it happens to be part of some long standing and thus sacrosanct standard, you may be required to include it in your own JCL on occasion, so you may as well understand it.

IEHPROGM is used in the above example to delete the member named PCAY552 from the library ISD.YPGM.LLIB, which resides on the disk volume named PROD03. PROD03 is a model 3380 disk. In other words, this is a way of deleting a member from a library.

SCRATCH means delete. The operands may be specified in any order, and you will often see DSNAME specified before MEMBER. My recommendation is that you ought always to place the MEMBER parameter before the DSNAME parameter. This is because if you make a mistake in coding the operands and you have DSNAME specified prior to MEMBER, the result can be that the entire data set is deleted as a result of the MEMBER operand being ignored.

The following syntax rules apply to the coding of the SCRATCH statement in the SYSIN to IEHPROGM (and in the SYSIN to most of the other old-style utility programs):

- Operands are separated by commas.
  - There should be no intervening blanks between operands.
  - If all of the operands do not fit on one line, you continue the operands onto the next line by placing any non-blank character in column 72 of the incomplete statement and beginning the continuation precisely in column 16.

Of course you can delete a member of a library with a batch TSO session rather than using IEHPROGM. For example:

```
//SMITH8H2 JOB  1,TSO.EXAMPLE,MSGCLASS=X
//*
//STEP4   EXEC PGM=IKJEFT01,
//        DYNAMNBR=20
//SYSTSPRT DD SYSOUT=*
//OPTIONAL DD DISP=OLD,
//        DSN=ISD.YPGM.LLIB,
//        VOL=SER=PROD03,
//        UNIT=3380
//SYSTSIN DD *
  DELETE 'ISD.YPGM.LLIB(PCAY522)'
/*
```

IEBGENER

As you already know from earlier chapters, IEBGENER is a generalized copying program that reads the file designated by SYSUT1 and copies it to SYSUT2.

IEBGENER also allows you to perform simple editing of the data records while they are being copied.

For example, you might want to read an input data set with LRECL 94 and copy it to an output data set of LRECL 80, truncating the last 14 bytes.

Or you might prefer to cut out the first 14 bytes instead, or 7 bytes on each side, or a field in the middle someplace.

If you have read the section on SORT, you already know that you can include selected fields and eliminate others in the output records produced on SORTOUT.

You can do the same thing when executing IEBGENER.

The syntax is different, but the results are the same.

You remember the SYSIN statement that you always specified as DUMMY in earlier examples? Now you will supply control statements to IEBGENER on SYSIN to specify the editing you want.

Example: copy the data from an input data set with LRECL 94 to an output data set with LRECL 80, chopping off the last 14 bytes of each record:

```
//SMITH8I1 JOB 1,MSGCLASS=X
//*
//* COPY 94-BYTE INPUT RECORDS TO
//* 80-BYTE OUTPUT RECORDS DROPPING
//* THE LAST 14 BYTES OFF EACH
//* OUTPUT RECORD
//*
//STEP1   EXEC PGM=IEBGENER
//SYSPRINT DD SYSOUT=*
//SYSUT1  DD DISP=OLD,
//     DSN=SMITH.LRECL94.DATASET
//SYSUT2  DD DISP=OLD,
//     DSN=SMITH.LRECL80.DATASET
//SYSIN   DD *
        GENERATE    MAXFLDS=1
        RECORD   FIELD=(80)
/*
```

In the above example, the GENERATE statement tells IEBGENER that there will be, at the most, one FIELD parameter on the subsequent RECORD statement(s). The RECORD statement in the above example describes one output field that you want on your output records, and the length of that field is 80 bytes.

Example: copy the data from an input data set with LRECL 80 to an output data set with LRECL 72, dropping off the first 8 bytes from the beginning of each record:

```
//SMITH8I3 JOB 3,MSGCLASS=X
//*
//* COPY 80-BYTE INPUT RECORDS
//* TO 72-BYTE OUTPUT RECORDS,
//* DROPPING THE FIRST 8 BYTES
//*
//STEP1  EXEC PGM=IEBGENER
//SYSPRINT DD SYSOUT=*
//SYSUT1  DD DISP=OLD,
//     DSN=SMITH.LRECL80.DATASET
//SYSUT2  DD DISP=OLD,
//     DSN=SMITH.LRECL72.DATASET
//SYSIN   DD *
        GENERATE   MAXFLDS=2
        RECORD     FIELD=(72,9)
/*
```

In the example given as job SMITH8I3 above, the FIELD parameter on the RECORD statement contains 2 numbers. The first number, 72, is the length of the field in the output record. The second number, 9, is the starting position in the input record from which the data is to be copied. Thus the example will copy a field 72 bytes in length starting from position 9 of the input record. The data that was in position 9 on input will be in position 1 on output. The first 8 bytes from the input record will be dropped from the output record.

Next example:

Someone has shown you a COBOL program that you want to copy and change slightly. However, you want to EDIT your copy under TSO as a standard COB type data set, with statement numbers in columns 1 through 6. Your friend, unfortunately, has left columns 1 through 6 blank in the COBOL source, and has put line numbers in columns 73 to 80

instead. Solution: You copy the COBOL source using IEBGENER to
move the line numbers. Since you want six digit statement numbers and
the program you are copying has 8 digit line numbers, you copy only six
bytes of the old numbers, from columns 73-79. You then add two bytes of
blanks at the end of your output records to make up for the two bytes you
are leaving out of the line numbers. Your job looks like this:

```
//SMITH8I4 JOB  4,MSGCLASS=X
//*
//* COPIES AN FB 80 COBOL
//* SOURCE PROGRAM MOVING
//* LINE NUMBERS INTO
//* COLUMNS 1-6 ON THE
//* OUTPUT DATA SET.
//*
//GENER EXEC PGM=IEBGENER
//SYSPRINT DD SYSOUT=*
//SYSUT1  DD DISP=SHR,
//   DSN=JONES.SOURCE.CNTL(TESTPGM)
//SYSUT2  DD DISP=(,CATLG),
//   DSN=SMITH.NEW.COB(TESTPGM),
//   UNIT=TEST,
//   DCB=(LRECL=80,RECFM=FB,
//   DSORG=PS,BLKSIZE=23440),
//   SPACE=(CYL,(1,,16))
//SYSIN   DD *
GENERATE MAXFLDS=80,MAXLITS=2
RECORD  FIELD=(72,7,,7),                    C
        FIELD=(6,74),FIELD=(2,' ',,79)
```

In the above example, your input file is member TESTPGM in your
friend's data set JONES.SOURCE.CNTL, and you create a new data set
for the output. You make the output data set a library, and you give the
member the name TESTPGM. Remember that IEBGENER will treat a
single member of a library as if it were a flat file.

Now a few words about the MAXLITS parameter and the FIELD parameters shown above.

Just as MAXFLDS specifies how many FIELD parameters you will have, MAXLITS specifies how many literals you will have. In this case you will have two bytes of literals, the two blanks you are adding to your output records to make up for the two bytes you are leaving out of the line numbers.

There are 3 fields specified in FIELD parameters on the RECORD statement.

The first FIELD says that you want a field of length 72 to appear in each of your output records. It is to be copied from starting position 7 on the input record, and placed in starting position 7 on the output record.

The second FIELD is to be 6 bytes long. It is copied from position 74 of the input record. In other words, it is composed of columns 74-79 of the input record, the middle six digits of the line number. Since you do not specify an output location, the starting position on the output record defaults to column 1.

The last FIELD that you specify in the above example is the 2 byte literal field. When you specify a literal in this way, you enclose it in single quote marks, and it takes the place that would otherwise have been occupied by your specification of the starting column from the input record. 79 is the output location for this field in this example. Two bytes of blank spaces will be placed into columns 79 and 80 of your output records.

Next example: Your friend has a document you want to copy. Your friend keeps his documents in his all-purpose CNTL library, which has RECFM FB and LRECL 80. You prefer to keep your own documents as RECFM VB and LRECL 256, a common standard for TEXT files. For our example, you copy the member TEXTDATA from your friend's CNTL library into a new member of a new TEXT library which you create with this job. Looking at the data before you copy it, you notice that your friend has line numbers in columns 73-80 of his document. You decide to set up your IEBGENER in such a way that it moves the 8-digit line numbers from columns 73-80 of the input into columns 1-8 of the output, a standard for TEXT file line numbers. The job you run looks like this:

```
//SMITH8I5 JOB 5,MSGCLASS=X
//GENER EXEC PGM=IEBGENER
//*
//* COPY A MEMBER FROM AN FB DATA SET
//* INTO A NEW MEMBER OF A NEW VB DATA SET,
//* MOVING THE POSITION OF THE
//* LINE NUMBERS
//* FROM COLUMNS 73-80
//* ON THE INPUT RECORDS
//* INTO COLUMNS 1 – 8
//* ON THE OUTPUT RECORDS
//*
//SYSPRINT DD SYSOUT=*
//SYSUT1  DD DISP=SHR,
//     DSN=SUZUKI.IN.CNTL(TEXTDATA)
//SYSUT2  DD DISP=(,CATLG),
//     DSN=SMITH.NEW.TEXT(TEXTDATA),
//     UNIT=TEST,
//     DCB=(LRECL=256,RECFM=VB,
//     DSORG=PS,BLKSIZE=23476),
//     SPACE=(CYL,(5,,32),RLSE)
//SYSIN   DD *
GENERATE MAXFLDS=2
RECORD  FIELD=(72,1,,9),FIELD=(8,73)
```

In the above example:

72 = Length
1 = From-position
9 = To-position

8 = Length
73 = From-position
default To-position is 1.

Chapter 18

JES2 CONTROL STATEMENTS

MVS is a very impressive piece of software engineering. It controls the use of smallish computers with only a few megabytes of real storage and a single processor through to the extremely large computers which have thousands of megabytes of real storage and several processors.

The task of getting jobs into MVS is not done by MVS though. Most installations use a Job Entry Subsystem called JES2. You may give certain instructions to JES2 about the way a JOB is to be processed. The JES2 control statements all start with /* in positions 1 and 2 followed immediately by a keyword starting in position 3.

Let's imagine there is a company that has two MVS computer installations. There are two MVS systems in the company headquarters at San Diego, and there is one MVS system in a manufacturing location in Ireland. The company also has a European sales office in London which is connected to the computer in Ireland.

MVS will allow a job to be executed at any of the computers no matter where the job is submitted from. Of course that does depend on the way the MVS systems have been set up by the systems programmers. But for the sake of the examples, let's imagine they have set up a full network.

SIGNON AND SIGNOFF

When the London sales office wants to submit a job it must be through the MVS system in Ireland. The London sales office has a special remote terminal called RMT44. The MVS system in Ireland will receive a signal from the terminal in London and the connection will be made. Depending on the way the systems programmers set the network up, a JES2 SIGNON control statement may be required. If a SIGNON statement is required, the precise way it is coded will be provided to you. It might look something like this, the remote name of RMT44 must start in position 16.

```
/*SIGNON    RMT44
```

At the end of the day, when the London office closes, a SIGNOFF to JES2 should be sent from the London office. The JES2 system in Ireland will complete any communications that is currently active with the London office and no more will start until another signon is done. The SIGNOFF will look like this.

```
/*SIGNOFF
```

Any jobs from the London office will automatically run in the MVS system in Ireland. Naturally the jobs submitted in the computer installation in Ireland will also be run there.

RUNNING A JOB IN ANOTHER COMPUTER INSTALLATION

If a job is to be run in the San Diego computer installation, a JES2 control statement should be part of the job stream that is submitted in Ireland. JES2 will allow either of two statements to be used. One is the XEQ statement the other is the ROUTE XEQ statement.

The job that is to run in San Diego could have this coded:

```
//FARAWAY JOB .....
/*XEQ SANDIEGO
//STEP EXEC .....
```

A job submitted in San Diego to run in Ireland might have this:

```
//FACTORY1 JOB
```

```
/*ROUTE XEQ IRELAND
//STEP EXEC .....
```

Each of these jobs will be run in a computer installation far from where the job was submitted. The job will be scanned for any obvious JCL errors before being transmitted to the other system. The printed output will be sent automatically to the place where the job was submitted.

Sending Printed Output to another location

It is possible to print the output at another location. Suppose a job submitted in Ireland has to be printed in the London office. The ROUTE PRINT statement will help here. It will look like this.

```
//SALESRPT JOB ...
/*ROUTE PRINT RMT44
//STEP EXEC .....
```

JES2 will print all the output from the job SALESRPT in the London office when the remote terminal is signed on. Normally a job will be executed on the system that initially receives it and the output will print in the location that submitted it. We have seen how that can be changed using JES2 control statements.

Running the JOB on a specific Computer

The imaginary San Diego installation has two MVS systems. One is used primarily for Research and Development, and the other for Production. It is important that jobs get run on the correct system, even though the job might be submitted to either system.

JES2 will allow the system to be nominated, or more than one potential system may be nominated. JES2 will need to know the system affinity the job requires. This peculiar use of the term affinity is one that was covered in the UNIT=AFF discussion.

If the two MVS systems in San Diego are known to JES2 as PROD and

RD, then the system affinity may be assigned to either of those names. The SYSAFF parameter is part of the JES2 JOBPARM statement.

This job will run on the Research and Development system, no matter which system it was submitted to in San Diego.

```
//RESEARCH JOB ...
/*JOBPARM    SYSAFF=RD
//STEP  EXEC .....
```

If a job were submitted to the MVS system in Ireland but had to be executed on the PROD system in San Diego, then the following would be used.

```
//PRODRUN JOB ...
/*XEQ SANDIEGO
/*JOBPARM    SYSAFF=PROD
//STEP  EXEC .....
```

JES2 has the capability to allow a job to be submitted at one location and executed or printed at nearly any other location it knows about. However, these things are not always made available to everyone who is allowed to submit work to an MVS system.

SENDING MESSAGES THROUGH JES2

JES2 will also allow messages to be sent to the operator. In fact it will allow two different types of messages to be sent. Both message types are given to the operator when the job is read by JES2.

The more common of the two message types is the MESSAGE statement. One or more of these may be put into the job and will be sent to the operator when the job is read. An example is shown here

```
//PAYROLL JOB ...
/*MESSAGE CALL ACCOUNTING DEPT AT EXT 327
/*MESSAGE WHEN THE PAYROLL JOB IS DONE
//STEP EXEC ...
```

While this seems to be a very simple request, you will be surprised how many times the operators don't make the call that was requested. It has nothing to do with operators being awkward or troublesome or anything like that.

The message is sent to the operator at the time the job is read. The job might not be executed for some time. In fact it might run when the next shift is on, the operator who saw the message may have gone home, or be at lunch, etc., etc.

If there is a need to know when a particular job completes, use the NOTIFY parameter in the JOB statement. Or the JES2 equivalent which will be discussed shortly.

Some installations will be happy to have messages sent to the operators, others will not. Indeed some operators will be happy to receive them, others not. If messages are frowned on, it is most likely a very busy installation with several thousand jobs being run on a single MVS system each day.

SPECIFYING TAPE OR DISK REQUIREMENTS TO JES2

The second type of message that can be sent to the operator has to do with the use of tapes or removable disks. The message is used to advise the operator that there are certain volumes that should be SETUP before the job is executed. The volume serial numbers must start in position 11 of the SETUP statement. Several SETUP statements may be used.

```
//TAPEJOB JOB ...
/*SETUP   A58964,T31495,B75324
//STEP  EXEC.....
```

When the job is read by JES2 it is 'held' until the operator releases it. The operator will receive the SETUP message with the serial numbers for the required tapes. When all the tapes have been assembled, the operator should release the job.

If a job contains XEQ SETUP JOBPARM and MESSAGE statements,

the SETUP JOBPARM and MESSAGE statements will be processed at the system where the job is going to execute.

The SETUP and MESSAGE statements will also be processed at the system where the job is initially input if the XEQ is placed after the other statements in the job stream. The MESSAGE statements may not have any great relevance at the input system, and the SETUP statements surely won't mean anything at the input system.

The imaginary computer installation in Ireland has sent three tapes to the San Diego installation by an express courier. A job needs to be run on the PROD system in San Diego location which uses those three tapes plus several others that are already in San Diego. The job could look like this

```
//TAPEWAIT JOB .....
/*XEQ    SANDIEGO
/*JOBPARM SYSAFF=PROD
/*MESSAGE    THREE TAPES SENT BY
/*MESSAGE    COURIER SHOULD ARRIVE
/*MESSAGE    THURSDAY AT 9AM YOUR TIME
/*MESSAGE    TAPES FROM IRELAND ARE
/*MESSAGE     IRL460 IRL461 IRL462
/*MESSAGE    TIME DIFFERENCE OF 9
/*MESSAGE    HOURS BETWEEN US
/*MESSAGE    DONT PHONE
/*MESSAGE    SEND FAX IF ANY PROBLEMS
/*SETUP   IRL460,IRL461,IRL462
/*SETUP   CAL241,CAL242,CAL243,
/*SETUP   CAL244,CAL245,CAL246
/*NOTIFY  IRELAND.OPSTSO7
//STEP  EXEC .....
```

The complete job will be sent to San Diego and will eventually be run on the production system. A number of messages explaining the tapes and the time difference will be displayed to the operator at the San Diego installation. The SETUP statements will ensure the job is held until the operator releases it, hopefully the operator will not release it until all the tapes are available.

When the job has run, a notification message will be sent to the operator in Ireland with the TSO id of OPSTSO7. The JES2 NOTIFY statement should be used instead of the NOTIFY parameter on the JOB statement. The JES2 NOTIFY is more comprehensive than the JOB statement version. The JOB statement NOTIFY is an instruction to the MVS where the job happens to be executed, and in some circumstances MVS may not be able to send the messages to the terminal.

The XEQ and ROUTE XEQ are used to transmit a job which will be executed at the other system. Before the job is transmitted it is scanned for JCL errors.

SENDING A JOB TO ANOTHER TYPE OF SYSTEM (NON JES2)

If the system you want to transmit the job to has a different version of MVS, and you are using some new JCL statement or parameter that is available on the new system but is not on the system you are transmitting from, then you will get a JCL error when the job is scanned.

JES2 provides another method of sending information to a different system without doing a scan prior to transmission. It is the XMIT statement. If the first record that is transmitted is a JOB statement, then the job will be executed at the system that receives it.

A job that is transmitted from the imaginary San Diego system to the system in Ireland could look like this.

```
//FROMUSA JOB .....
/*XMIT   IRELAND DLM=7E
//NOSCAN  JOB .....
   ...
   remainder of job to be sent to Ireland
   ...
7E
```

The job 'FROMUSA' is read at the input system in San Diego, however the JOB statement 'FROMUSA' is not transmitted. The job 'NOSCAN' is not scanned for JCL errors on the input system in San Diego but is transmitted with possible JCL errors to the processing system.

Because a /* statement is included in the job stream which is being transmitted, a DLM is included on the XMIT statement. Did you notice that there is not a comma in front of the DLM parameter. This is a JES2 statement and the comma is not used here. I know what you are thinking, the use of the comma would make this parameter consistent with the DLM parameters in JCL. Ah well, just keep it in mind if you are using the XMIT.

You could also use the XMIT statement to transmit jobs to systems other than MVS JES2. You could send a job to a JES3 system, or a VSE system, or even to a guest system running under VM. You simply put the name of the target system on the XMIT statement, and let JES2 take care of it.

Chapter 19

TAPE TECHNIQUES

One of the most enduring, though not necessarily endearing, computer media types is tape. One of the first types of tape used with computers was paper tape. It's true. Very long strips of paper had holes punched through which represented the letters and numbers. There were special machines which punched the holes in the paper, and other machines which detected the holes. All very clever machines, but not very practical.

You could not use the tape a second time. Once a hole was in the paper, it was there to stay. And what if you made a mistake. Suppose you wanted the letter E, but through a simple error got the number 3. There is a 3, right in the middle of the tape, where you wanted an E. You can't fill in the holes, it is like taking a bite of a piece of bread, once it's gone, it's gone. As I said, not very practical.

The next bit of development was using magnetic tape instead of paper tape. It was so simple really. They more or less converted the paper tape technique to magnetic tape. If there was a hole, then write a one. If there was no hole then write a zero.

TAPES FROM MVS (STANDARD LABEL TAPES)

Well magnetic tape has come a long way from those first days. Modern methods have improved tape reliability and increased the capacity of storing large amounts of data.

Modern tape drives put a lot of information in one inch of tape. The amount of data that is recorded on an inch of tape depends of the recording density used by the tape drive. If the drive uses a density of 800 bits per inch, or BPI to use the jargon, your DCB might have a sub-parameter that says DEN=2. A recording density of 1600 BPI would use DEN=3, and a recording density of 6250 BPI uses DEN=4.

You would only use the density parameter if your installation has several types of tape drives. Some types of tape drive can only use one density, others provide you with a choice of two. You only need to use density if the drive you are using is a dual density drive.

The way you specify which type of tape drive you need is with the UNIT parameter. Remember that from Chapter 8? You might have to specify UNIT=3420-4 or UNIT=3420-7 or whatever the specific model tape drive is that you need.

If you need to use tape drives, ask one of the people you work with what the valid unit names are for tape drives in your installation. If no one knows for sure then ask your local friendly systems programmer.

Suppose you need to read a tape file that has been created at another computer site in the company you work for. The file is very big, in fact it is so big it can't even fit on one tape, or even two.

A box has been delivered to your desk which contains the tapes, eight tapes in all. Inside the box is a note that tells you the sequence of the tapes. Which tape contains the first part of the file, which contains the second, and so on.

The note also says the tapes have been written as one file. Which means all the tapes have the same data set name. It also means you won't have to concatenate the tapes. The DD statement for your program could be coded something like this

```
//TAPEIN DD DSN=BIG.TAPE.FROM.WINNETKA,
//   DISP=OLD,UNIT=3420,
//   VOL=SER=(W32583,W42684,
//       W26415,W04067,
//       W34956,W61782,
//       W08436,W22514)
```

As the note gave you the sequence of the tapes by their serial numbers, all you need to do is copy them in the right sequence. If you get the sequence wrong the job will abend. Lets consider the job that created those eight tapes. If you saw the JCL for the job that created that tape file it would look a little different. In the early days when programmers were not as clever as you, it was not uncommon for a program to go into a loop which might write output forever. It would not take very long for tape after tape to be written to. In order to prevent creating lots of tapes in error it was decided to put a default limit of five output tapes to a single output file. In order to get past that limit of five you need to code a positional sub-parameter in the volume parameter. If the following looks awkward, that's because it is.

```
//TAPEOUT DD DSN=BIG.TAPE.FROM.WINNETKA,
//     DISP=(,KEEP),
//     UNIT=3420,VOL=(,,,8)
```

When a single file of data spreads across more that one tape the term that is used is 'Multi Volume File.' That is to say one file which is spread over more than one volume.

Music tape cassettes are in some ways similar to what in computer terms is called a Multi File Volume. If you think of each song as a file, and think of the cassette as a volume. You can play either side of the cassette and listen to complete songs until the end of that side of the tape.

There is even a list of which songs are on the tape and the order they are in. It doesn't make much difference whether you play side A or B first. It is really you choice.

The Multi Volume File that we looked at in the previous discussion is more like a book that is on cassette tape. It would not make much sense to play the tapes in any order other than tape 1 side A followed by tape 1 side B and so on. Multi Volume Files, like books on cassette tapes, are really meant to be read in the correct sequence.

Back to the computer side of things, sometimes there is plenty of room on a tape to hold more than one file, when you do that you have what is called a 'Multi File Volume.' It is not difficult to create one, but you really need to keep track of where things are yourself. Just like the table of contents that comes with the music cassette.

Why would you want to create something like a Multi File Volume?

Suppose you have several small files that you use on disk, and you realize that if there were a major problem with the disk you would not have those files any longer. Basically you need to 'backup' the files to tape for security purposes. You know the files are small enough to fit on one tape.

The following example will show how to put several files on one tape.

Each file on the tape will occupy a different position on the tape. This is done with the LABEL parameter which will specify the label number.

The tape files will have similar file names as the disk versions of that same data.

And the tape serial number will only be coded once. This will be accomplished in the VOLUME parameter by using a backwards reference to the only step in the that makes specific mention of the serial number..

```
//GENER1 EXEC PGM=IEBGENER
//SYSPRINT DD SYSOUT=*
//SYSIN   DD DUMMY
//SYSUT1 DD DSN=MY.VITAL.FILE.A,
//    DISP=SHR
//SYSUT2 DD DSN=MY.TAPE.VITAL.FILE.A,
//    DISP=(,KEEP),UNIT=TAPE,
//    VOL=(,RETAIN,SER=H35872),
//    LABEL=1
//GENER2 EXEC PGM=IEBGENER
//SYSPRINT DD SYSOUT=*
//SYSIN   DD DUMMY
//SYSUT1 DD DSN=MY.VITAL.FILE.B,
//    DISP=SHR
//SYSUT2 DD DSN=MY.TAPE.VITAL.FILE.B,
//    DISP=(,KEEP),UNIT=TAPE,
```

```
//     VOL=REF=*.GENER1.SYSUT2,
//     LABEL=2
//GENER3 EXEC PGM=IEBGENER
//SYSPRINT DD SYSOUT=*
//SYSIN   DD DUMMY
//SYSUT1 DD DSN=MY.VITAL.FILE.C,
//     DISP=SHR
//SYSUT2 DD DSN=MY.TAPE.VITAL.FILE.C,
//     DISP=(,KEEP),UNIT=TAPE,
//     VOL=REF=*.GENER1.SYSUT2,
//     LABEL=3
//* THESE BACKUPS CAN CONTINUE
//* FOR SEVERAL MORE FILES
//* THIS JCL CAN BE SAVED
//* FOR FUTURE USE AND SIMPLY
//* BE CHANGING THE TAPE
//* SERIAL NUMBER IN THE FIRST
//* STEP THIS JCL CAN BE RUN AGAIN
```

You should be careful that you don't use more than one tape in this environment. You now know about Multi Volume Files and about Multi File Volumes. Don't try to get too tricky and mix the to methods.

TAPES FROM NON-MVS COMPUTERS

Sending tapes between computers that operate under MVS is pretty straight forward really. MVS uses Standard Label tapes, that is to say LABEL=(,SL), unless you specify something else.

If you receive a tape that was not created on an MVS computer the chances are you will have to use some other sub-parameter with LABEL.

NEARLY STANDARD LABELS (BUT NOT QUITE)

Some computers create tapes with labels that look like MVS labels. But the tape cannot be processed successfully. There is a possibility that a tapemark was recorded before the first label on the tape. If that is the case then you should code the label parameter as LABEL=(,LTM).

ASCII LABELS
(DEFINITELY NOT IBM STANDARD LABELS)

There is more type of tape label that you might come across. It is called the ASCII label or sometimes it is known as the ANSI label. No matter, it is the same label, and it is referred to on the DD statement with the parameter LABEL=(,AL).

ASCII labels are most often used on tapes that are created on non IBM computers. They can also be created on IBM computers for tapes that are to be sent to non IBM computers. ASCII tapes conform to common standard which nearly all manufactures have agreed to make available.

You might wonder why it is not used all the time for tapes, particularly as everyone seems to agree to have it available.

Well, it is not as efficient as IBM standard format tapes. You see the ASCII standard was designed to make sure a tape created on one type of computer could be read on another type of computer. As a result there is only one way to write each of the numerals, for example. MVS systems allow at least five ways to handle numbers. Other types of computers could have things that would not be readily understood by MVS systems.

The commonalty used on ASCII tapes suits those areas where the exchange of information is more important than the efficiency of the media.

One thing to remember about using ASCII tapes. The data stored on ASCII tapes is stored in ASCII code, while the MVS system and your program would prefer to work in EBCDIC code. MVS will translate any ASCII tape into EBCDIC when the records are read. If you are creating an ASCII tape MVS will translate the EBCDIC code in memory into ASCII when the records are written. As far as you are concerned the data looks the same in memory. The ASCII character set consists of the numbers, and the letters in upper and lower case, there are also some special characters. So as long as the data you are working with can be defined with that character set you can happily work with ASCII tapes.

DATA COMPACTION

The 3480 tape system operates with a feature called 'Data Compaction'. This is a way to get more information on the tape. If you are sending a 3480 tape cartridge to some other computer system that can read 3480 tapes but cannot use the data compaction feature. Then you must be able to create a tape without data compaction operating. There is a DCB sub parameter that can be specified called the TRTCH (pronounced tretch, like stretch without the ess). It is coded TRTCH=NOCOMP to turn data compaction off or TRTCH=COMP to turn data compaction on. Normally you do not need to use this parameter, you only ever use it for tapes to other types of computers. Compaction is only supported for IBM Standard Label tapes.

// UNIT=3480,DCB=TRTCH=NOCOMP

There are other values that can be coded with TRTCH but they are associated with a very old type of tape called 7 track. You would be very unlikely to ever need the other TRTCH values.

Chapter 20

GENERATION DATA GROUPS (GDG)

For some unknown reason, data has traditionally been referred to in the masculine for a very long time. I suppose this is to balance the fact that programs have been referred to in the feminine.

If one program invokes another, the relationship is known as mother-daughter. If the daughter program invokes yet another program, we have a grandmother-daughter-granddaughter relationship, as well as the two mother-daughter relationships.

For data, if a program reads an input file, makes some changes, and writes a new output file, the files have a father-son relationship. You can see that it is possible to have grandfather files and grandson files.

With all these generations of files around it is very easy to see how a population explosion of data might occur. You will need to plan the size of the data family, or in other words, you are now getting into the computer version of family planning.

When planning your data family, you will need to know how many versions (generations) of the data you want to keep. I don't want you to get too emotional about planning the demise of a member of the family.

Let's say you want to keep 15 generations of a particular type of data. If you use a manual control system for the generations, you will be expected to delete the oldest generations of the data from disk, that is to say the generations that are older than 15 generations. If the data is on tape, you will have to return the oldest tapes to the library.

You also have to devise a method for identifying one version from another. You can't give them all the very same name, each name must be unique in some way. If the file names do not have some uniqueness, they would be like the programmer who wrote on the program listing 'LATEST LISTING,' and kept several of those of the desk.

Uniqueness of file names can pose a problem for the DSN parameter of the JCL. If the names are not unique you do not have to change the DSN parameter. If they are unique changes are necessary.

Or are they???

MVS allows the use of something called Generation Data Groups, or GDG for short.

GDG depends on the use of the catalog for identifying the location of any file. And the nice thing about GDG is the fact that each file has a unique name, which you don't have to worry about.

When you use GDG you have to give the catalog some special instructions about the data. It could be considered the family planning information.

You must tell the catalog how many generations it is to keep track of. You can also tell it to delete the oldest generations if they are located on disk.

Let's look at an imaginary GDG definition. The catalog will need to know the name that the GDG is known by. It will also need to know how many generations to keep track of. And finally, it will need to know if the oldest generations of disk data are to be deleted.

So our example says something like the following:

```
GDGNAME    MY.MASTER.FILE
GENERATIONS   15
DELETE     YES
```

When the first generation is created and cataloged, the catalog will record a DSN of MY.MASTER.FILE.G0001V00.

The G0001V00 means generation 0001 version 0. Don't worry about the version number, because the catalog doesn't.

As you create more and more generations of the data, the catalog will contain higher and higher generation numbers. But it will only ever contain 15 entries. And if the data has been kept on disk, the oldest generations will be deleted automatically, as soon as the oldest generation falls off the catalog.

Suppose we have been running the system for some time. The catalog might well have entries for generations G0203V00 to G0217V00. That certainly provides the uniqueness that is necessary to identify any file, the latest always having the highest number.

How do you get that uniqueness coded in the DSN parameter of the DD statement? MVS allows you to use a numeric relative position to the latest generation. That is to say, if the latest generation is called 0 the father generation can be referred to as -1, the grandfather generation as -2, and so on.

New generations will be referred to as +1 for the son, +2 for the grandson, and so on. All very neat isn't it?

Let's look at an example. A program will read the old master file and create a new master file based on the information located on the changes file.

```
//WATCHOUT EXEC PGM=UPDATE
//UPDATE  DD DSN=MY.UPDATE.INFO,
//    DISP=OLD
//MASTIN  DD DSN=MY.MASTER.FILE(0),
//    DISP=OLD
//MASTOUT DD DSN=MY.MASTER.FILE(+1),
//    DISP=(NEW,CATLG,DELETE),
//    UNIT=SYSDA,SPACE=(CYL(5,5)),
//    DCB=MY.MODEL.DSCB
```

MVS will look for the latest generation of the file which will be used for the DD MASTIN. When the next generation is created it will be given the next generation number. At this time the oldest generation will be deleted if it is on disk and if you specified the SCRATCH option when you originally set up the GDG.

Because you are so sharp eyed at this stage, I know you have spotted the DSN reference in the DCB parameter in the MASTOUT DD statement.

MVS expects a model definition of the DCB that will be used for the GDG file. Creating the model is very easy. Basically you specify the DCB information you want the Generation Data Set, also known as the GDS, to have. This is called a model DSCB. You do not have to define the model DSCB at the same time as you set up the GDG. You just have to create the model DSCB before you create any files using your GDG. For convenience, our example will set them both up at the same time. The example that was used before will be used again, but this time using all the proper control statements.

```
//CATALOG EXEC PGM=IDCAMS
//MODLDSCB DD DSN=MY.MODEL.DSCB,
//     DISP=(NEW,CATLG),
//     UNIT=SYSDA,
//     SPACE=(TRK,(0)),
//     DCB=(RECFM=FB,
//     LRECL=147,BLKSIZE=1911)
//SYSPRINT DD SYSOUT=*
//SYSIN   DD *
   DEFINE GENERATIONDATAGROUP -
   (NAME(MY.MASTER.FILE) -
   NOEMPTY -
   SCRATCH -
   LIMIT(15))
/*
```

Looking at the example in more detail, the utility program IDCAMS does most of the work. IDCAMS is told to create a GDG in the master catalog for the DSN called MY.MASTER.FILE.

The instruction NOEMPTY is curious, but makes sense when compared to its counterpart EMPTY. With NOEMPTY used the catalog will maintain up to 15 entries for the file, any time an additional entry is added to the list the oldest is removed from the list. If EMPTY were used, everything would be fine up to 15 entries, but whenever a new entry gets

DONNA KELLY & JIM HARDING

added to the list all of the old entries will be removed. It is very like the lemmings running to the sea to make room for the new generation.

SCRATCH has nothing to do with relieving an itch. What it does is to tell MVS what to do with a file that is located on a disk when the catalog entry is removed. SCRATCH results in a file being deleted (scratched) from disk when the entry is removed from the catalog. If you don't code scratch, you might leave hundreds of unwanted files lying around the various disks. If that happens you may have to clean up the mess some day, unless such files are automatically deleted by disk space management software on your system. Just about everything has a default, the default for this is NOSCRATCH, be warned.

The instruction LIMIT specifies the number of entries that are to be maintained on the catalog. The maximum is 255, the minimum is 1.

You will also see a DD statement which creates the model DSCB, which can also be called the pattern DSCB. The DSCB, which stands for Data Set Control Block, is used on disk in much the same way as labels are used on tape. It contains DCB information.

The model DSCB won't be used to hold any data, that is why it has SPACE=(TRK,(0)) coded. The model DSCB can be used as the source of the DCB information for the file being created. I say it can be used for that, but there is nothing to prevent you from using other DCB information by overriding the information in the model DSCB – for example, by coding something like DCB=(MY.MODEL.DSCB,LRECL=93,RECFM=VBS,BLKSIZE=9304).

In the example you saw how you can create a new generation simply by saying (+1) at the end of the DSN and also saying DISP=(NEW,CATLG). If a job created two new generations, the first to be created would be called (+1) and the second would be called (+2). You can create more than one or two in the one job if you need to. But you should try to keep them down to a manageable level; remember someone may have to look at the JCL someday and you may not be there to explain it (or worse, you might be there but not remember much about it).

The way the thing works is like this. When the job starts MVS has a look at the catalog to find out what the latest generation number is. MVS will now be able to determine the next generation number easily. If the latest generation happened to be G0747V00 then when you create the relative generation (+1) you will end up with G0748V00. Aren't you impressed with that bit of mathematical wizardry?

MVS won't actually catalog any new generations until the end of the job. What can possibly go wrong?

Multiple Systems and GDG

Speaking of what can possibly go wrong ... Well., imagine you have two computers at your installation, and that you also have shared DASD and shared catalogs, which is the usual setup with two computers. Now suppose that somehow a job that creates a new generation gets started on each of the computers at more or less the same time, or anyway the second one starts before the first one finishes. The two MVS systems have a look at the shared catalog and pick up the highest generation, in this case G0747V00. Each works away quite happily creating a new generation, G0748V00.

One of the systems finishes the job and updates the catalog, which now says G0748V00 is the highest generation. The other system finishes and also updates the catalog, but in this case the second one finds a generation G0748V00 on the catalog already. MVS always tries to be helpful, and this time it will recatalog the catalog entry to point to the second copy of the generation named G0748V00. Oh well, it nearly got it right. Or, by the time you read this, who knows, IBM may have corrected that problem and introduced others; or it might all work perfectly ("You gotta ask yourself one question - do you feel lucky?")

Restarting a job with GDG

As you saw from the example of more than one MVS system, the catalog only gets updated at the end of the job. But the data sets are actually created during the job (like any data sets).

Suppose your job was active and one new generation was written to disk TEST01. But before the job ended and MVS had an opportunity to update the catalog there was a power failure. The whole system came crashing down.

If you try to start the job again, you attempt to create generation G0748V00 on disk TEST01. The job will not run because there is already a file called G0748V00 on the disk (created during the run interrupted by the power failure, but not cataloged).

One option for you is to delete the unwanted (uncataloged) files from the disk. Then rerun the job.

Another option is to catalog the files and then modify the JCL relative generation numbers. This tends to get very complicated. Personally we always go for deleting the unwanted, uncataloged files, if this approach is at all feasible.

RERUNNING A GDG JOB

Rerunning a job can also be difficult, particularly if you don't plan for it when you construct your JCL.

Suppose you ran the job and created generation G0748V00 but only afterwards did you discover that a part of the input data that is used for updating was incorrect.

Well , you get the corrected input, and you are ready to run the job again ... or are you?

The JCL says very clearly the input generation is generation (0) and the output generation is (+1). When the job ran previously it used G0747V00 as the input and created G0748V00 as the output.

If you run the job again you will use G0748V00 as input and create G0749V00 as the output. Definitely not what you want. How do you get rid of G0748V00?

Try this as a very easy and safe way to do it.

```
//DELETE EXEC PGM=IEFBR14
//GOAWAY DD DISP=(OLD,DELETE),
//     DSN=MY.MASTER.FILE.G0748V00
```

After this runs the highest generation is back to G0747V00 and you should be able to run the job again.

The catalog now points to the latest correct generation.

If possible it is much better to avoid the area of correcting the catalog entries.

However, if you are determined, then that can be accomplished sometimes by using the third sub parameter in the DISP parameter. You could add a final step to your job that will only run when conditions indicate the output is not correct.

If you know that a step must have a return code of, say, zero for the output to be reliable, you can code something like this:

```
//STEP1 EXEC PGM=UPDATE
//INPUT  DD DSN=MY.INPUT.DATA,
//     DISP=SHR
//MASTIN DD DSN=MY.MASTER.FILE(0),
//     DISP=OLD
//MASTOUT DD DSN=MY.MASTER.FILE(+1),
//     DISP=(,CATLG,DELETE),
//     UNIT=SYSDA,SPACE=(CYL,(3,2)),
//     DCB=MY.MASTER.FILE
//BADONE EXEC PGM=IEFBR14,
//     COND=(0,NE,STEP1)
//GOAWAY  DD DSN=MY.MASTER.FILE(+1),
//     DISP=(OLD,DELETE,DELETE)
```

READING ALL THE GENERATIONS

The GDG facility has another small trick that may be useful to you. You can very easily read all the generations as a single file if you want. You simply use the data set name without specifying any generation number.

Let me give you an example. You have a program that writes a small file every time it is executed. The file contains a record of the activity of the program. Kind of a log.

Your program will probably be run several times each day. At the end of the day you want to print the log.

The program that creates the log would have JCL that looks something like this.

```
//POPULAR EXEC PGM=POPULAR
//INPUT  DD DSN=BLAH.BLAH,DISP=SHR
//ACTIVITY DD DISP=(,CATLG,CATLG),
//     DSN=LOG.OF.POPULAR.ACTIVITY(+1),
//     UNIT=SYSDA,
//     SPACE=(TRK,(1,1))
```

The printing at the end of the day can read all of the generations simply by not referring to any generation number in the DSN parameter. It might look like this.

```
//PRINTLOG EXEC PGM=IEBGENER
//SYSPRINT DD SYSOUT=*
//SYSIN   DD DUMMY
//SYSUT1  DD DSN=LOG.OF.POPULAR.ACTIVITY,
//     DISP=OLD
//SYSUT2  DD SYSOUT=*
```

APPENDIX

Appendix 1

EXPLANATION OF THE EXAMPLE
PROGRAMS AT THE END OF
CHAPTER 2

Let's go through a line by line discussion of the two example programs.

In the following discussion, the lines from the examples will be identified by being indented and preceded by vertical lines.

We'll start with Example 1, in PL/I:

The first three lines of Example 1 in PL/I are JCL:

```
//SMITH1 JOB 1,CLASS=I,
//      MSGCLASS=X
//PLIXCL  EXEC PLIXCL
//SYSPRINT DD  SYSOUT=*
```

The first line of JCL is a JOB statement. It identifies this set of cards as belonging to the job named SMITH1. The bill for the job, if any, will be charged to account number 1. In reality you may need to use longer and more complicated accounting information.

The job will run in class I. Here "I" is an arbitrary letter specified by the systems programmers. Therefore it varies from one system to another. You may not need to specify a class at all on your own system.

Finally the JOB statement specifies a MSGCLASS, which determines where the output will be printed. If you said MSGCLASS=A it would in all probability be printed on a real physical printer someplace, and it might eventually find its way to you. Or it might not. This is also specified by the systems people and therefore varies from one place to another. The IBM default is that MSGCLASS=X will be available for viewing under TSO. Most places leave this default intact, but your place could be different.

In summary, everything on the JOB statement is more or less arbitrary and varies from one company to the next, so you need to find out from somebody what a job statement ought to look like for you at your current place.

The second line of JCL is an EXEC statement. It tells MVS to find a JCL procedure named PLIXCL (wherever it keeps such things) and copy all of the JCL from that procedure into the present job. It so happens that the procedure named PLIXCL is supplied by IBM and it contains the JCL necessary to run the PL/I(X) compiler followed by the Linkage editor.

The last JCL statement specifies that your PL/I listing ought to be printed in the same place as that specified by MSGCLASS on the JOB statement. You may not need this line, since there may be a line just like it within the PLIXCL procedure. On the other hand, the line within the procedure might point to someplace different. No harm to include it here.

Finally the SYSIN statement is not given. When MVS sees the non-JCL lines that follow, a manufactured SYSIN DD statement and insert it immediately preceding the non-JCL lines.

On to the program statements themselves.

Notice that PL/I program statements should start in column 2 rather than column 1, because the default margins are columns 2 and 72.

The first line of our program is a comment. Comments in PL/I are identified by being framed with the slash-asterisk on the left and the asterisk- slash on the right.

Notice that this /* ... */ arrangement is a PL/I rule and has nothing to do with the /* or the //* in JCL.

The /* and the */ are both required with PL/I comments.

Totally blank lines are ignored by the PL/I compiler, just like the comments. In our particular program, the comment at the beginning looks like this:

```
/* COPYCAT
ULTRA-SIMPLE PL/I PROGRAM
READS DATA FROM WHEREVER IT SAYS
ON THE INFILE DD STATEMENT IN
THE JCL WHEN THE PROGRAM RUNS,
AND WRITES THAT DATA OUT TO
WHEREVER IT SAYS ON THE OUTFILE
DD STATEMENT IN THE JCL */
```

Next we have the first actual line of PL/I code. It is a PROC statement. A PL/I PROC statement is an entirely different thing than a JCL PROC statement. A JCL PROC statement begins a JCL procedure. A PL/I PROC statement begins a PL/I procedure, which is to say, a PL/I program.

On the PL/I PROC statement you specify the name of the program, in this case COPYCAT. You are free to change the name if you wish, provided that the name you choose is no longer than 7 letters.

The PL/I programming language has a limitation that the names of programs written in PL/I and the ddnames of files used by PL/I programs can be only 7 characters long.

You can specify various options on the PL/I PROC statement. In our simple program the only option we specify is that this is a main program, as opposed to a subroutine. A subroutine is a program that is called from other programs. It does part of their work for them and then returns control to the calling program. Our present program is not like that. It is a main program. It will be called by being specified on an EXEC statement in the JCL towards the end of the example. The PROC statement which begins the program looks like this:

COPYCAT: PROC OPTIONS(MAIN);

After this we have more comments:

```
/***************************/
/* READ RECORDS FROM INFILE AND WRITE THE
    SAME */
```

421

/* RECORDS OUT TO THE DD STATEMENT FOR
OUTFILE. */

/*************************/

Next we have DECLARE statements.

The DECLARE (sometimes abbreviated DCL) statements tell PL/I the names of the things our program is going to use.

First we tell PL/I that we will have an input file named INFILE and an output file named OUTFILE. Our program will read its input from the input file and write its output to the output file. Notice that each statement in PL/I is terminated by a semicolon. We could have chosen other names rather than INFILE and OUTFILE, but the length limit is 7. Not 8 as you might expect, but rather 7. The declarations for our two files look like this:

DECLARE INFILE INPUT FILE;
DECLARE OUTFILE OUTPUT FILE;

We now tell PL/I that we will have a variable called LINE. Line will be 80 characters long. We want PL/I to assign it an initial value of blanks. What this means is that PL/I will set aside a little 80 byte area of memory that will be used whenever we say the word "LINE" within the program. Here is the DECLARE:

DCL LINE CHAR(80) INITIAL(' ');

What next? Another variable which we name END_OF_INPUT. Variable names in PL/I can be quite long, and can include the underscore (underline) character in addition to letters and numbers. We are setting aside a 3-byte area of memory to be named END_OF_INPUT. We are making it 3 bytes long because we intend for it to have two possible values, either 'NO' or 'YES'. We have PL/I initialize it to 'NO'. This means that it will contain the value 'NO' when our program starts.

DCL END_OF_INPUT CHAR(3) INIT('NO');

We have finished making our declarations of variables. Next we tell PL/I to do something; or rather, to stand ready to do something. What we are telling PL/I to stand ready to do for us is this: Whenever PL/I comes to the end of our input data, we want PL/I to set the value in our variable END_OF_INPUT to contain the word 'YES'.

The instruction we give to PL/I to accomplish this is:

> ON ENDFILE(INFILE)
>   END_OF_INPUT = 'YES';

Now we tell PL/I to read our first record from INFILE, putting the record into the area of memory that we named LINE:

> READ FILE(INFILE) INTO(LINE);

The following group of statements is called a DO LOOP. We are telling PL/I that we want him to do the statements within the group over and over again until some special condition is met. Doing things over and over again like this is called looping. If the special condition that tells PL/I to stop never happens, then we have an infinite loop, much dreaded. In the present case, the special condition that must be met is this: as long as our variable named END_OF_INPUT contains the word 'NO', we want PL/I to keep doing the instructions within the group. When it changes, then PL/I is to stop looping. We know that when all of our input data has been read, PL/I will set this variable equal to the word 'YES', because we told him to do that in our ON ENDFILE(INFILE) statement. So, in effect, we are telling PL/I to continue doing the instructions within the loop for as long as there is data to process.

The end of the loop is specified by the statement "END;"

Between the DO and the END there are two statements. The first one tells PL/I to write the contents of the variable LINE to the file named OUTFILE. The first time this is executed, the first line of data will be written out to OUTFILE, because we read the first line before starting the loop.

The second statement within the loop tells PL/I to read the next line of input data. This is the same as our first READ statement that was executed before going into the loop. As long as there are more lines of data available, this READ statement will work correctly and the program will loop back to the top of the loop, where it will write the line before attempting to read the next one. When there are no more input cards to read the READ statement will fail and the ON ENDFILE statement will catch the failure. It will set the value of the variable END_OF_INPUT to 'YES', which is not equal to 'NO', so the loop will terminate.

The loop looks like this:

```
READ FILE(INFILE) INTO(LINE);

DO WHILE(END_OF_INPUT = 'NO');

WRITE FILE(OUTFILE) FROM(LINE);
READ FILE(INFILE) INTO(LINE);

END; /* END OF DO-WHILE */
```

After all of the data has been processed, we call the subroutine PLIRETC to set the return code to zero. This is optional. The default is zero. But, just for fun, and to prove to yourself that you can actually do some simple programming thing, you can change this statement to set the return code to something else. CALL PLIRETC(8) to set it to 8, for example. The call to PLIRETC:

```
CALL PLIRETC(0);
/* SET RETURN CODE TO ZERO */
```

Finally we have an END statement that ends the Pl/I program:

```
END COPYCAT;
/* END OF PROGRAM */
```

Now we have some more JCL.

The LKED.SYSLMOD DD statement tells MVS where to put your load module:

```
//LKED.SYSLMOD DD DISP-SHR,
//   DSN=SMITH.LOAD(COPYCAT)
```

The EXEC statement tells MVS to execute the load module version of the PL/I program that was just processed:

```
//COPYCAT EXEC PGM=COPYCAT
```

The STEPLIB DD statement tells MVS where to find the load module. It should specify the same data set as the LKED.SYSLMOD DD statement above:

```
//STEPLIB DD DISP=SHR,
//    DSN=SMITH.LOAD
```

The SYSPRINT DD statement tells MVS where to write any PL/I error messages that might occur while the program is running:

```
//SYSPRINT DD SYSOUT=*
```

The INFILE DD statement provides the input data that the program will process. You can play around by changing this data once you get the program working on your own system. The lines following the //INFILE DD * are the input data:

```
//INFILE  DD *
THIS IS THE FIRST LINE OF DATA
THIS IS THE SECOND
THAT'S ENOUGH
```

Finally, the program has an output file, called OUTFILE. Thus the JCL has a DD statement for OUTFILE. In this case it says that the output is to be printed. You could, if you preferred, have the output placed into in a data set. If you don't know how to do that yet, read the rest of the book. By the end of Part 2 (Chapters 3-10) you will find it a pretty easy task. The OUTFILE DD statement:

```
//OUTFILE DD SYSOUT=*,
//       DCB=(LRECL=80,
//       RECFM=FB,
//       BLKSIZE=800)
```

Now for the COBOL example.

The first two lines are JCL.

The explanation of these two lines of JCL is identical to the explanation of the first two lines of JCL in the PL/I example above, except that the procedure used with COBOL, named COBUCL, is appropriate to compiling and linking a COBOL program rather than a PL/I program. Your company may use some name other than COBUCL for the procedure, in which case you should find out by asking. The two JCL lines are:

```
//SMITH2 JOB 2,CLASS=I,MSGCLASS=X
//COMPILE  EXEC COBUCL
```

Now the actual COBOL program starts.

Columns 1 to 6 of a COBOL program are reserved for line numbers.

Column 7 is reserved for use as a continuation indicator, in case a statement is continued onto more than one line.

Columns 8-11 are known to COBOL as "Area A", and columns 12-72 are called "Area B". Certain COBOL statements have to start in area A, and others should start in area B. (And you thought JCL was bad?)

A COBOL program is separated into divisions. Certain statements can occur within each division. (A place for everything, and everything in its place.)

The first two lines of the COBOL program are equivalent to the PL/

I PROC statement. They identify the name of the program, in this case COPYCAT:

> 000001 IDENTIFICATION DIVISION.
> 000002   PROGRAM-ID.   COPYCAT.

The next division in a COBOL program is the environment division. It describes the external environment in which the COBOL program will run.

> 000003 ENVIRONMENT DIVISION.

The following line has an asterisk in column 7, so it is treated as a comment, that is, it is ignored:

> 000005* INFILE AND OUTFILE ARE OUR
>   DDNAMES.

Within the environment division we have the input-output section, which describes the files the program will use. This is where we tell COBOL about INFILE and OUTFILE. The names we use here must be the same as the ddnames we will use in the JCL that executes the program. For example, if we changed the ddname INFILE to LUNCH, then we would have to change the SELECT statement below to say LUNCH in two places rather than INFILE. The COBOL statements that describe the files are these:

> 000007 INPUT-OUTPUT SECTION.
> 000008 FILE-CONTROL.
> 000009   SELECT INFILE ASSIGN TO UT-S-INFILE.
> 000010   SELECT OUTFILE ASSIGN TO UT-S-
>   OUTFILE.

The third division in a COBOL program is the data division. Here we describe variables that the program will use. We have chosen the name

INPUT-RECORD for the 80-byte area in memory that will be used to hold each one of our 80-byte input records when it is read. The FD (File Definition) statement associates the ddname INFILE with the 80-byte area named INPUT-RECORD. INPUT-RECORD is composed of one part, called INPUT-LINE. If you had changed the ddname INFILE to LUNCH as suggested above, you would need to change the word INFILE in the FD to LUNCH also. We have an FD for OUTFILE also, associating the ddname OUTFILE with the area we name OUTPUT-RECORD, which consists of one part, the 80-byte area named OUTPUT-LINE.

After the file section within the data division we have the working storage section. Actually the present program doesn't use the working storage, but we included it in the sample program just so you could see the correct order. You would use working storage if you were actually going to manipulate data. For example, you could move your input line into the working storage area and, while it was there, make some changes to it, before moving the final line over to the output area.

The data division looks like this:

```
000011 DATA DIVISION.
000012 FILE SECTION.
000013 FD  INFILE LABEL RECORDS ARE OMITTED.
000014  01  INPUT-RECORD.
000015    05  INPUT-LINE  PICTURE X(80).
000016 FD  OUTFILE LABEL RECORDS ARE OMITTED.
000017  01  OUTPUT-RECORD.
000018    05  OUTPUT-LINE  PICTURE X(80).
000019 WORKING-STORAGE SECTION.
000020  01  WORKING-RECORD.
000021    05  WORKING-LINE  PICTURE X(80).
```

After the IDENTIFICATION, ENVIRONMENT, and DATA divisions comes the PROCEDURE division, the start of which is identified by this statement:

```
000022 PROCEDURE DIVISION.
```

The procedure division contains all of the statements that actually tell COBOL to DO anything. Think of these statements as statements with transitive verbs.

The first thing the program says to do is to open the two files the program will use, named INFILE and OUTFILE. The program specifies INPUT on the OPEN statement for INFILE, meaning that it will be used for input, that is, the program will read from it but will not write to it. The opposite is true for OUTFILE, where we will write our output.

```
000023 OPEN-FILES.
000024     OPEN INPUT INFILE.
000025     OPEN OUTPUT OUTFILE.
```

Next the program says for the computer to do a group of statements over and over again. First there is a statement label, arbitrarily called READ-A-LINE. That label does nothing in and of itself, but it is used as a name for that particular place in the program. Later, in line 30, when the program says "GO TO READ-A-LINE.", the action will return to this statement label.

After the statement label come four statements.

The first one says that the computer is to read file INFILE. From the above definition of INFILE, we know that the record that is read from the INFILE DD statement will be placed in the area called INPUT-RECORD.

The next statement says to take the data that is now in the area called INPUT-RECORD, that is, that data that was just read, and move it to the area called OUTPUT-RECORD.

The next statement says to write OUTPUT-RECORD. From the file definition of OUTFILE above, we know that the record named OUTPUT-RECORD will be written to the DD statement named OUTFILE.

Finally the program says for the computer to go back up to the label READ-A-LINE, from where it will do all of the same things again until it has read all of the data from INFILE. Then it will go to the label below named END-OF-PROGRAM, because the READ INFILE statement tells it to go there AT END, meaning at the end of the input data.

```
000026 READ-A-LINE.
000027    READ INFILE AT END GO TO END-OF-PROGRAM.
000028    MOVE INPUT-RECORD TO OUTPUT-RECORD.
000029    WRITE OUTPUT-RECORD.
000030    GO TO READ-A-LINE.
```

Here we have the label END-OF-PROGRAM. After it are three more COBOL program statements. The program says to close both of the files, INFILE and OUTFILE, because it is finished using them. Then the statement STOP RUN. tells COBOL that the program is finished.

```
000031 END-OF-PROGRAM.
000032    CLOSE INFILE.
000033    CLOSE OUTFILE.
000034    STOP RUN.
```

The end of the COBOL program is followed by JCL similar to that at the end of the PL/I program above, except that it is tailored to COBOL programs rather than to PL/I. The STEPLIB data sets may have different names at your own company than the names below. Ask someone there if the example JCL here doesn't work for you.

```
//LKED.SYSLMOD DD DISP=SHR,
//   DSN=SMITH.LOAD(COPYCAT)
//COPYCAT EXEC PGM=COPYCAT,
//     COND=(8,LT)
//STEPLIB DD DISP=SHR,
//      DSN=SMITH.LOAD
//      DD DISP=SHR,
//      DSN=SYS1.VSCLLIB
//      DD DISP=SHR,
//      DSN=SYS1.VSCOLIB
//SYSPRINT DD SYSOUT=*
//SYSOUT  DD SYSOUT=*
```

```
//INFILE  DD *
THIS IS THE FIRST LINE OF DATA
THIS IS THE SECOND
THAT'S ENOUGH
//OUTFILE DD SYSOUT=*,
//      DCB–(LRECL=80,
//      RECFM=FB,
//      BLKSIZE=800)
```

Index

Symbols

A

M

Q

R

Printed in the United States
43574LVS00001B/10